Medieval Woman's Companion

Women's Lives in the European Middle Ages

Susan Signe Morrison

 OXBOW | books

Oxford & Philadelphia

Dedication

To those women in the Middle Ages – some named, many
anonymous – who continue to inspire us today

First published in the United Kingdom in 2016. Reprinted in 2017 by

OXBOW BOOKS

The Old Music Hall, 106–108 Cowley Road, Oxford OX4 1JE

and in the United States by

OXBOW BOOKS

1950 Lawrence Road, Havertown, PA 19083

© Susan Signe Morrison 2016

Paperback Edition: ISBN 978-1-78570-079-8
Digital Edition: ISBN 978-1-78570-080-4

A CIP record for this book is available from the British Library

Library of Congress Cataloging-in-Publication Data

Names: Morrison, Susan Signe, 1959- author.
Title: A medieval woman's companion : women's lives in the European Middle
    Ages / Susan Signe Morrison.
Description: Oxford ; Philadelphia : Oxbow Books, 2015. | Includes
    bibliographical references.
Identifiers: LCCN 2015040589 | ISBN 9781785700798 (pbk.)
Subjects: LCSH: Women--Europe--History--Middle Ages, 500-1500. |
    Women--Europe--Social conditions.
Classification: LCC HQ1147.E85 M67 2015 | DDC 305.4094--dc23 LC record available at
http://lccn.loc.gov/2015040589

For a complete list of Oxbow titles, please contact:

United Kingdom	United States of America
Oxbow Books	Oxbow Books
Telephone (01865) 241249	Telephone (800) 791-9354
Fax (01865) 794449	Fax (610) 853-9146
Email: oxbow@oxbowbooks.com	Email: queries@casemateacademic.com
www.oxbowbooks.com	www.casemateacademic.com/oxbow

Oxbow Books is part of the Casemate group

Front cover: *Judith with the Head of Holofernes* by Lucas Cranach the Elder, 1472–1553. © The Metropolitan Museum of Art, New York. Image source: Art Resource, NY.

Printed and bound in Great Britain by Marston Book Services Ltd, Oxfordshire

Contents

Acknowledgements

Thanks to Texas State University for support, especially to Mike Hennessy, Dan Lochman, Cynthia Opheim, Eugene Bourgeois, and Melody Edwards. Warm gratitude to Elizabeth Makowski, who has been an inspiring colleague, collaborative co-teacher, and brilliantly provocative thinker. The Interlibrary Loan Office at Alkek Library provided me with intellectual sustenance. Countless students have inspired me over the years. To you, consummate gratitude for teaching me so much.

Appreciation for help with images goes to John Twyning, University of Pittsburgh; Sigríður Sigurðardóttir, Director, Skagafjörður Heritage Museum, Iceland; Tara S. Smith, Alkek Library; Conna Clark, Philadelphia Museum of Art; Maria Singer, Yale Center for British Art. Thanks to the Master and Fellows of Corpus Christi College, Cambridge and Gill Cannell, Parker Library, Corpus Christi College; Karen Richter, Princeton University Art Museum; Gayle Richardson and Brian Moeller, Huntington Library; Tricia Buckingham, Linda Townsend, and Samantha Sherbourne, Bodleian Libraries; Gerhard Gruitrooy and Liz Kurtulik Mercuri, Art Resource; Nikki Braunton and Yiqing An, Museum of London; Chris Rawlings and Jovita Callueng, British Library; Wendy Zieger, Bridgeman Art Library; Richard Sorensen, Smithsonian American Art Museum; Julie Zeftel, Metropolitan Museum of Art; Chris Suthers, British Museum; Philippe Bretagnon, Bibliothèque nationale de France; Dr Gerhard Lutz, Dom-Museum Hildesheim, Germany; and Gerd Welin.

There have been many supporters in my life, helping to foster my love of all things medieval. To my cousin and his wife, Lars and Gerd Welin, who made a pilgrimage of their own to Saint Birgitta's convent, echoing the pilgrimage made by our Swedish forebear to North America over one hundred years ago. To the memory of an early feminist medievalist, Debby Ellis. Her dynamic daughters, Jenny and Molly Odintz, carry on Debby's legacy.

To my father Bob, who delighted in teasing me about 'the Dark Ages'. To my mother Joan, who loved Shaw's *Saint Joan*. They both took me on pilgrimage to Canterbury, England, when I was 7 years old, instilling in me a love of the Middle Ages that has resonated all my life. And to my family, who never tire of hearing about werewolf romances, Viking women, and transvestite saints.

Website and blog

This book is accompanied by a website and blog

A Medieval Woman's Companion: http://amedievalwomanscompanion.com/

Why – and How –
Do We Study Medieval Women?

"I read [history] a little as a duty, but it tells me nothing that does not either vex or weary me. The quarrels of popes and kings, with wars or pestilences, in every page; the men all so good for nothing, and hardly any women at all – it is very tiresome …"

Catherine Morland, heroine of Jane Austen's novel *Northanger Abbey* (1803)

Poor Catherine! Bored by history that in the early nineteenth century would have mainly focused on men and popes and kings and wars. If only Catherine could come back today when much medieval history focuses on gender and the everyday lives of girls and women.

Where would we be without those foremothers who trail-blazed paths for women today? Without those first brave souls who worked in fields dominated by men, women might not have the presence they currently do in professions such as education, the law, and literature. In the field of medicine, for example, many women deserve our gratitude, including those countless nameless women who, since humans evolved, assisted at the childbirths of their daughters, sisters, and friends, enabling new lives to come into the world. They passed down information about medical treatments via word of mouth, some of which was later written down. An Old English birth charm requires the speaker to utter these words as she steps over a dead man's grave: "This is my remedy for hateful slow birth, / this my remedy for heavy difficult birth, / this my remedy for hateful imperfect birth".[1] An early spell from the tenth century suggests how pregnant women tried get rid of agony during delivery. The midwife would have uttered: "A swollen woman / Sat in a swollen road; / A swollen child / She held in her lap … The pain goes out … Let mother earth receive the pain".[2] These scraps of information tell us that women attempted to control the ability to conceive a child and the pain of labor. Such charms open a window into the minds and lives of women in the past.

Duke: And what's her history?
Viola: A blank, my lord …
      William Shakespeare, *Twelfth Night* (II.iv.110–1)

Uncredited, unacknowledged, unnoticed – is this what women have been? Virginia Woolf, the ground-breaking English novelist, wrote *A Room of One's Own* in 1929. She imagined what the life of William Shakespeare's imaginary sister might have been like, conjuring up a depressing fate for her ambitious character. Woolf suggested, "I would venture to guess that [Anonymous], who wrote so many poems without signing them, was often a woman."[3] Save with a few exceptions like Jane Austen and Emily Dickinson, women writers were almost non-existent on school curricula until about 40 years ago. Unlike for Shakespeare's character, the history of women in the past, far from being a blank, has been richly carpeted with detail, wisdom, and inspiration. A massive reconsideration of women's history has taken place.

In 1405 Christine de Pizan wrote *The Book of the City of Ladies* in which she catalogued the achievements of hundreds of women. Fighting misogyny (hatred of women), Christine stands as a role model for people who want to credit those who have added to the culture of the world. Designed for students in high school and university and those just coming to the history of medieval women for the first time, *A Medieval Woman's Companion* balances standard histories of the past to include virtuous virgins, marvelous maidens, and daring dames of the Middle Ages.

Woolf asserted that a woman needs a room of her own in order to write. Some of the women you will encounter in this book did have rooms of their own – including secluded cells for religious contemplation as in the case of Teresa de Cartagena, a deaf nun who welcomed her solitary life as a stable refuge where she could be self-sufficient. Others created lives of daring, wit, and courage in the face of oppression, danger, and challenge. These women are now considered vital for understanding the Middle Ages in a full and nuanced way.

What are the 'Middle Ages'?

What do you think of when you hear the words 'Middle Ages' or 'medieval'? Perhaps princesses in towers, dragons, dwarves and ogres, *Monty Python and the Holy Grail*, Vikings with horned helmets, or the video games *World of Warcraft* and *Skyrim*. Chivalry and the cult of knighthood attract the popular

Christine de Pizan and Reason clearing the Field of Letters of misogynist (anti-woman) opinion in preparation for building the City of Ladies (Bruges, Belgium, c. 1475. © The British Library Board, ADD.20698 f17)

imagination, though the flipside of heroic and noble derring-dos includes the slaughter of Jews and Muslims by Christian Crusaders. Writers inspired by medieval literature include Sir Walter Scott, whose nineteenth-century novel *Ivanhoe* pictures honest Anglo-Saxons oppressed by rich and snooty Normans; Mark Twain, whose hero in *A Connecticut Yankee in King Arthur's Court* introduces mechanical innovations to the Arthurian Round Table; and J. R. R. Tolkien, the great Anglo-Saxon scholar, whose *Lord of the Rings* series brilliantly re-imagines Old English, Old Norse, and Germanic mythology and literature.

What are the Middle Ages? When were they? And where did they occur? People in 1200 did not walk around saying, "I'm in the Middle Ages". It was the present to them, just as 2016 or 2025 (depending on when you're reading this) is *now* to you. Perhaps it was a woman who founded the Middle Ages, as was suggested in 395 by Ambrose, the archbishop of Milan. He credited Helena, mother of the emperor Constantine, at her funeral with finding the cross and nails with which Christ was crucified, suggesting that this discovery ushered in the Christian Empire.

When do the Middle Ages end? When does any age 'end'? Think of the 1960s. When most people imagine the 1960s, they may think of hippies, peace signs, rock and roll, the *Beatles*, Vietnam, protests, the Civil Rights movement, and miniskirts. Do all those go away once the clock told us it was the 1970s? Did they 'end' on January 1, 1970? No, and so it is with any era designated by historians as a distinct 'period'.

Different ages have understood the Middle Ages in varying ways. In the sixteenth century, religious tumult accompanied a rejection of the past, including the wholesale destruction of irreplaceable manuscripts, artworks, and architectural masterpieces by King Henry VIII's thugs. The eighteenth-century English historian Edward Gibbon dismissed the Middle Ages as a barbaric and superstitious backwater. Some late eighteenth- and early nineteenth-century writers romanticized the period as a rural idyll. And Victorian Pre-Raphaelites re-envisioned medieval aesthetic with their own architecture, art, and literature that extolled tragic honor and lofty ideals.

The Middle Ages in this book refer to the years 500–1500 CE in Western Europe, its civilization and culture. While the focus is on Christian Western Europe, other faiths that existed within its borders will be referenced.

When writing about a particular time period, it is difficult – and unwise – to make generalizations. But there were certain continuities in Western Europe between the acceptance of Christianity by the Roman Empire in the fourth century and the start of the Protestant Reformation. The timing and naming the

---

Middle Ages and Medieval

Middle Ages and *medieval* are post-medieval words. *Medieval* derives from the Latin language, meaning 'middle' and 'age' or 'era.' The 'Middle Ages' are an idea of the *Renaissance*, a time ranging from about 1300 to 1600. *Renaissance*, meaning *rebirth*, suggests that the period before it – the Middle Ages – was dead or dormant. Nothing could be further from the truth.

Middle Ages is a useful designation in many ways. It can help us focus on an historical period that has recurring elements in Western Europe. These include: the spread of Christianity and general suppression of other religions such as Judaism, Islam, paganism, and heretics. But many exceptions exist. While most western Europeans would be categorized as Christians (or heretical Christians, in some cases), there were substantial populations of Jews and Muslims within these geographical boundaries. The Iberian peninsula of Spain and Portugal provides a particularly lively example of three major monotheistic religions occupying one region. This is not to say it was always peaceful, but there was certainly an awareness of a multi-ethnic population that did not share the same belief systems or traditions. Recent work on Jewish, Muslim, and Christian women suggests interfaith interaction in various ways that included cosmetics, childbirth and midwifery, wet-nursing, business such as money-lending, caring for the dead, and slavery (as slaves and owners).

Religion remained a fundamental basis for society – not only in matters of faith, but also law, politics, architecture, art, and literature. Architects constructed monumental structures such as cathedrals, churches, towers, bridges, and castles. Urban culture expanded. Disease was combated through the medical knowledge of the time, though epidemics – such as the Black Plague of the 1340s – devastated Europe. The use of Latin in the church and law had its roots in the ancient world. Other key elements, such as the Roman Catholic Church, are still present today.

The Middle Ages was a time of great technological innovation (Gothic cathedrals), scientific advances (from optics to medicine), cultural fruition (from Gregorian chants to philosophical refinement), political and religious development (from the Magna Carta to affective piety), linguistic and literary richness (from stirring verse in the vernacular to courtly love poems), and artistic achievement (from stained glass to illuminated manuscripts). Medieval women were fundamental to many of these developments.

While this book focuses on medieval Christian European women, they do not fully represent what was happening worldwide. Women of action existed on virtually every continent (see *Learn More* at the end of the Introduction). Here the focus is on women of (mainly) European descent in order to show the wide range of women's lives possible within a unified area with many similar cultural elements. This geographical contiguity allows us to see how women from related territories have a wealth of diverse experiences.

There is no such thing as a single 'Middle Ages' – rather *multiple* 'Middle

Ages' with widely assorted lives, activities, achievements, and legacies. A twelfth-century woman doctor like Trota had more in common with her Muslim female counterpart – a healer – than she would with an English estate manager like Margaret Paston almost 300 years later. The 'Middle Ages' of a princess living in France in 1370 would be very different than that of a Norwegian peasant in 1050. They were different from one another, just as they are different from us. It might be best to imagine many Middle Ages – the rich and complexly woven tapestry of an era.

How do we find out what the Middle Ages 'really' were like?

Our knowledge is determined by our sources. Scholars use *primary sources*, documents actually produced during the period we study. There are many examples of medieval sources from which we try to piece together a picture of the past. A source can be a written text – like a poem or a legal document. Chronicles written at the time of, or in the few hundred years after, an historical event are very useful, but need to be treated with caution. Though it may have been recorded by a medieval person either when an incident occurred or in the years following, that does not mean everything transcribed was true or without prejudice. After all, no historian is totally unbiased. Legal records give us direct information, such as laws explicitly discussing women (inheritance provisions or marital rights) and indirect information (perhaps from legal testimony, which in many cases was restricted to men). For example, in one court case concerning bigamy, a witness, Amabilia Pynder, remembers a key date – it was when she had been sent a written charm to use while in labor with her son.

The subtleties of women's rights are impossible to generalize about since they vary over time and geographic location. Their rights were certainly noted, particularly within the domestic sphere, as wives, and in terms of taking care of children. Women's legal responsibility depended on when and where they lived. They might be more mildly punished than men for the same crime or more severely, such as in cases of infanticide. Some law codes assessed women as being worth more than men in terms of *wergild* ('manprice' – the payment for injury or death in Germanic realms), perhaps because of their capacity to bear children. Often the ecclesiastical courts (church law) might be more egalitarian or equal than secular or state law, such as in marital rights and expectations. Marital age varied, with women in the Mediterranean region typically wed at an earlier age than their counterparts in northern Europe. A woman could be married and still exercise a fair amount of power or individual agency – power over her own destiny.

A source can also be a structure, like a building, cathedral, or monument. Feminist architectural historians point out that monasteries or cities spatially organize people according to gender. For example, we can enter a medieval convent to see how a religious woman might have understood her place in the world. Archeologists discover burial sites, tombs, and buildings, literally uncovering greater knowledge about the past. A source may be an object, like an astrolabe that sailors used to navigate. It could be clothing, like a shoe or jacket that somehow survived. It could be fashioned from glass, as in a stained glass window or a drinking chalice. Or it could be an actual body within a tomb or mass burial ground, created out of desperation due to fatalities from plague. It could be embroidery or needlework crafted by women. Feminist demographers explore women's mortality (their length of life), fertility (how many children they bore), and migration patterns (where women might have traveled). All of these are 'sources'.

Innovations in research can help us learn more about the past. Paleopathology looks into the remains of humans to determine disease patterns and how male and female bodies differently responded to illness and the environment. As one scholar writes, "The historian must become a detective, sifting and rearranging fragments of information, like pieces of a jigsaw, to attempt to reconstruct a personality".[4] In the case of trying to figure out a queen's spiritual learning, for example, we might look at her "book-purchase, commissions of translations, choice of chapel decoration, destinations of pilgrimages, recipients of charity, and even the names of her children".[5] Clues come from written texts as well as material culture, objects that might have been given to, ordered by, or created by or for the woman in question.

Queens are one relatively well-documented group of women. Early on, from 300 to 700 CE, queenship was not yet well structured. A queen need not have been born into nobility. The father of Empress Theodora (497–d. 548) was a bear-keeper. She became an actress at his death and may have even sold her body just to get by. Justinian, who ruled as emperor of the Byzantine Empire in 527–565, was influenced by his wife in revising the law code to better women's lives, such as making divorce proceedings fairer. Balthild, queen to the Frankish King Clovis II (d. 657), was said to have been either a slave or a hostage of higher rank. She worked to end infanticide, the enslavement of Christians, and the slave trade. Many early queens, who might have ruled along with the king and run the treasury, became recognized as saints, in part due to their patronage of churches and monasteries. Not infrequently they converted their pagan husbands.

Counsel, advice, and influence constituted three ways women achieved dominance at court. The queen's maternal role remained key to her identity. Gradually the queen, though less likely to inherit the throne than a man, became legitimized as the bearer of the king's son and heir. The mothers of kings often could wield power, achieving royal influence. The years between 1100 and 1350 further emphasized the queen's sole right (as opposed to a concubine or unofficial wife) to bear a dynastic heir. In mid-thirteenth-century Norway, for example, King Hákon Hákonarson determined that only his legitimate children could take the throne. Sometimes a woman became queen regent who gained power when her husband died and her male child was still too young to rule. The queen might have had a key function as mediator or intercessor, often enabling diplomatic solutions to take place during strife. And from 1350 to 1500, we see some queens ruling in the place of their husbands who had become mentally ill or were absent at war. Some areas were even ruled by a queen-regnant, who ruled in her own right, not on behalf of another, such as Margaret of Denmark (1353–1412). She married King Hákon VI of Norway and Sweden and, through this alliance, wielded huge power after his death. Queens inherited dynastic control in kingdoms as wide-ranging as those in Spain and Italy to Eastern Europe.

Reconstructing the past

The late twentieth- and early twenty-first centuries have been a heyday of uncovering women's history from past times. What remains to be discovered in an archive or archeological site? There is an art to interpreting this evidence. A famous medieval historian, Elizabeth Makowski astutely observes, "It's the questions that make us scholars."[6] Take, for example, Elizabeth de Burgh, lady of Clare, born in 1295. An extremely rich and powerful woman in the first half of the fourteenth century until her death in 1360, Elizabeth is well-documented due to her high status in society. As a patroness of "embroidery, goldsmiths' works, illuminated manuscripts, carvings in ivory and jewelry",[7]

Elizabeth was an active connoisseur of such treasures. She founded Clare College at the University of Cambridge, as well as two friaries and a number of other religious institutions. She hired illuminators to decorate manuscripts; she donated and gifted books to recipients as widely varying as her own daughter and King Edward III of England (ruled 1327–1377). She was also highly committed to pilgrimage, establishing a Franciscan priory in 1347. We have records of her payments to artisans who crafted artifacts for devotional veneration. From this information, scholars attempt to reconstruct Elizabeth's worldview and her spiritual outlook.

Elizabeth was a well-known woman of her time. Yet much information about average people has been lost or remains undiscovered. How else can we find out about the past? How did people in the Middle Ages imagine their worlds? How can we re-imagine what it was like to be a woman in the medieval period? Some sources can never be recovered, the key one being people's thoughts. Even a diary cannot include every thought. And the percentage of people who could read or write (which were taught and mastered as separate skills in the medieval period) was tiny. Much information was passed on orally. Orally produced poetry was beautifully sophisticated; we have examples of such literature eventually written down, such as *Beowulf*. But what have we lost? The vast majority of people we can only access through chance remarks or sources such as wills, inquisition records, and miracle accounts. How can we document the undocumented?

Literature has been used to tease out information about lives from the past and can provide many clues. A magical romance may not reflect 'reality' directly, yet through it we can learn about how a culture imagined itself. Fiction can give us a sideways glimpse of history. For example, we can figure out that women sang lullabies to their children. How do we know? Many songs exist in which the Virgin Mary sings such calming music to her child, Jesus.

> This yonder night I saw a sight,
> A star as bright as any day,
> And ever among a maiden sang
> "By, by, lully, lullay".
> This maiden was Mary, she was full mild,
> She kneeled before her own dear child ...
> She soothed him, she blessed him,
> She sang "dear son, lullay".[8]

Nursery rhymes, references to games, and carols suggest a lively presence of children in the historical and literary record.

Noble girls would have gained an education from a tutor at home or at a convent where they might be sent before marriage. Most girls, if they were taught to read, learned the vernacular or everyday language spoken at home. Did girls learn at school? They were not allowed to attend university, though many women founded colleges and universities. In Muslim countries, women were also generous and powerful, establishing religious foundations, mosques, and Sufi convents.

A peasant working in the fields before the fourteenth and fifteenth centuries would be illiterate. A 1406 statute from Parliament in England proclaimed the right "of every man or woman, of whatever estate or condition he be, to set their son or daughter to take learning at any manner of school that pleaseth them".[9] Reading would be encouraged so that girls and women could access holy and devotional writings contributing to their religious education. Reading was considered a necessity for merchants and noble people to conduct business and political negotiations. Records from the fourteenth and fifteenth centuries offer tantalizing details, such as mention of an 8-year-old girl named Elizabeth Garrard attending a school run by a priest. Here

she learned the *Paternoster*, the *Ave*, and *Credo*, "with further learning" [see 'Vernacular' in the Glossary]. There were schoolmistresses, such as 'Agnes, *doctrix puellarum*'[10] (teacher of girls) from before 1440. And a will from a London grocer in 1406 bequeaths 20 shillings to be left to a schoolmistress.

'The Visitation' shows the Virgin Mary, pregnant with Jesus, greeting her relative Elizabeth, pregnant with John the Baptist (attributed to Master Heinrich of Constance, German, active in Constance, c. 1300. The Metropolitan Museum of Art, Gift of J. Pierpont Morgan, 1917 (17.190.724). © The Metropolitan Museum of Art. ARTstor: MMA_IAP_1039651278)

What would children have read and been taught? We have evidence about boys' education from the male enclaves of grammar schools where youths were taught Latin. Courtesy books from the later Middle Ages, aimed more at boys, attempted to instill good behavior during social situations. A knight in the 1240s wrote a book in verse to help Denise de Montchesney teach her children how to learn French. Juliana Berners is said to have written a guide for youths on how to identify animals and hunting terms. Since it was in rhyme, it would be easy to learn by heart. She even explained why the hare excretes poop pellets while standing up:

> All beasts that bear suet, and stand upright, you must see,
> Let their scat fall when they stand, you may be sure of that,
> And other beasts – the squatting kind – get rid of it when they squat.[11]

Children's natural interest in toilet matters was present in the Middle Ages and is, in fact, of great importance in the field of natural history and hunting – even today.

ABC books also existed, such as one by Geoffrey Chaucer, the great English poet of the late fourteenth century. Not unlike our 'A is for apple, B is for ball' books teaching reading, the ABC poems typically included religious sentiments. In this poem, each stanza begins with a letter of the alphabet and praises the Virgin Mary and child. Here is the stanza beginning with 'G':

> Gracious Maid and Mother! Who was never
> bitter, neither on earth nor in sea,
> But full of sweetness and of mercy ever,
> Help, that my Father be not angry with me![12]

Another verse, *The Good Wife Taught Her Daughter* (mid-fourteenth-century) depicted the scene of a mother advising her daughter on how to conduct her life. Each four-line stanza ends with a memorable and sensible proverb.

> And if thy need be great and help is short,
> Go thyself and do a housewife's work:
> [The servants] will do better if their mistress by them stands;
> Work is done sooner by many hands.
> *Many hands make light work.*[13]

Women's literacy is much researched. Ample evidence suggests numerous women owning books; we know of this from wills, such as one from Joan Buckland, a fishmonger's daughter, who died in 1462. She bequeathed religious books to Syon Abbey. In return, she asked for the nuns to pray for her soul. Beatrice Milreth, the widow of a London merchant, left a number of holy texts as well as a French primer in 1448. Not all books were strictly devotional in nature. The allegorical poem *Piers Plowman* was left to Agnes Eggesfield by one William Palmer in 1400. Eleanor Purdelay left Marie de France's *Saint Patrick's Purgatory* to her servant, Johanna, in 1443. Many more wills and church court material need to be discovered and analyzed for evidence of women. Perhaps you can do this research one day and add to the knowledge we are gaining about women of action in the Middle Ages.

How to read the Middle Ages

Christian scholars in the Middle Ages would interpret the Bible in various ways. A standard method was to see a moment in the Jewish Bible as prefiguring a moment in Christian Scripture. For example, Jonah trapped in the belly of the whale (*Jonah* 1–2) prefigures Christ's descent into Hell for three days after his crucifixion (*Ephesians* 4:8–10). Making these links trained Christians to read the world allegorically or symbolically. Medieval literary texts expect us to read that way too.

In the Old English saint's life of St Agatha, a cruel pagan governor named Quintianus desires the virgin Agatha as his lover. He sends the devout Christian girl to a depraved woman named Aphrodisia to pervert her. Yet Agatha remains steadfast in her faith. The writer tells us:

> When Aphrodisia saw she could not bend the mind of the maiden with her shameful temptations, she went to Quintianus and said to him, "Stones may soften and stiff iron become like molten lead, before the faith in Agatha's breast can be ever extinguished."[14]

Aphrodisia speaks metaphorically. Agatha's faith is not *physically* in her breast, but *spiritually* in her heart. Quintianus, though, is ignorant and faithless. He cannot read allegorically and has Agatha's breasts torn off. Not only does God restore her breasts, but, as Agatha defiantly tells her torturer, "I have my breast sound in my soul".[15] This is a standard scene in a legend praising virgin martyrs, girls who, though young – sometimes as young as eight, more typically in their early teens – fearlessly stand up to male authority, including their own fathers when necessary. The heroines of these legends acted as role models for young women to remain firm in their devotion.

Are these girls and women feminists?

Can we apply a modern term to an earlier age? If we adhere to this definition of a feminist – 'a woman who valued other women as women'[16] – we will see that, yes, some of our women were feminists. A feminist acts to fulfill her inner calling, as Margery Kempe does. A feminist helps others to achieve fulfillment, like Hildegard von Bingen who sets up a convent for her fellow women. A feminist takes on a 'man's role', like Joan of Arc, Margaret of Beverley, and the explorer Gudrid Thorbjarnardottir. A feminist champions the idea that women should be recognized as human beings, like Christine de Pizan. There are many types of feminists and feminisms.

Some stories may seem strange or odd. How could someone really believe that visiting a saint's bone would help heal her? Why would someone scream and cry at the thought of Christ's crucifixion? Why would anyone put up with the oppression caused by husbands or fathers? If we 'think medievally', women and their actions can be understood *in the time they lived in*, not judged by us *now*. It is not necessary to agree with every view expressed by writers and thinkers. Rather, consider how a tenth-century Saxon girl would have read Hrotsvit's plays. Or how a twelfth-century Frenchwoman would have understood Heloise's love story. A number of prominent medieval women were visionaries – seeing heavenly beings or hearing voices. While many people today reject the idea of visions, many medieval people *did* believe it.

Self-determination for a medieval woman might, at times, differ from the agency of a post-medieval woman. That is, it may not *seem* like 'freedom' to permit oneself to be walled up into a cell next to a church as an anchorite (religious hermit), but for medieval people such a spiritual guide *would* be considered a woman of action and power, worthy of great respect. Her action of praying was perceived as achieving something valuable, perhaps even more so than conventional, physical forms of movement.

These women are significant because, first of all, we have evidence of them in documents. Their stories show how they survived and thrived even when circumstances might have crushed their spirits. They show how they made their way in a world in which they were told they were lesser than the dominant group – men. Many of us can relate to this, whether it is in terms of gender, age, class, race, sexual orientation, or religious faith. Lastly, these women teach how never to lose hope despite trying circumstances.

The women in this book both defended women from misogyny (hatred of women) and showed the many possible paths for women in the Middle Ages. Some were saints; some definitely were not. These daring dames show something true in the Middle Ages and today: women should be allowed to be what everyone should be given – the right to be human.

The Light Ages

Petrarch, an Italian poet living 1304–1374, was credited with "putting the darkness in the 'Dark Ages'",[17] though the term itself does not appear in English until 300 years after the Middle Ages. 'Dark Ages' suggests a time of dissolution, deprivation, destruction, and death. But the medieval period was not a time of darkness. Light filtered through the stained glass of the jeweled box that is the thirteenth-century church Sainte Chappelle in Paris. Brightness glittered from the sparkly illuminated manuscripts toiled over by monks, nuns, and scribes for the greater glory of God. Hildegard von Bingen imagined flames of fire as she had visions of God, whom she called the 'Living Light', whose "splendid Light pours forth all that shining fire",[18] illuminating her. These women, the Lovely Ladies of the Light Ages, shed a luminous glow.

Learn More
Sources about women's history from around the world can be found at: http://www.fordham.edu/Halsall/women/womensbook.asp.

How to use this book
A Medieval Woman's Companion introduces readers to medieval history, medieval women's lives, Catholic beliefs, and the art and literature of the Middle Ages. This volume is intended for a general audience and to help students in high school and college to become familiar with a vast array of aspects affecting medieval women's lives. Most chapters focus on a particular medieval woman, while a few look at general issues, such as language, medieval understandings of the body, and the importance of clothing in the Middle Ages. The final chapter suggests ways in which recent feminist and

gender theories both can enhance our understanding of medieval women's lives and be shaped by the experiences of medieval women.

BCE and CE refer to 'Before the Common Era' (formerly 'BC') and 'Common Era' (formerly 'AD'). If you see something like this – 'b. 1245' or 'd. 1413' – it means the person was *born* or *died* in that particular year. If you see '*c.* 1413', it means something happened about (*circa*) that year. Birth and death dates are notoriously uncertain from the medieval period, so sometimes just the century the person was active in is indicated. When in doubt, I opt for the date one scholar convincingly suggests, fully admitting another scholar may have a slightly different date. If you see a date like this – 1155/56 – it means the activity took place in one of those years, we just are not exactly sure which one.

Every quote you read in the portraits of our women was written *in* the Middle Ages. If there is a difficult word or concept, check the Glossary for handy reference.

Several sections in the back of the book contain more information about medieval women. The Bibliography lists the sources used for this book. The Primary Sources are modern editions of works written *in* the Middle Ages. The Secondary Sources are work written recently *about* the Middle Ages. The section called Websites lists some reliable and fascinating virtual pages to explore. The end of each chapter suggests ways to Learn More about the woman under discussion, whether by reading a book written *in* the Middle Ages or exploring material *about* the Middle Ages, such as seeing a film, hearing some music, or reading recent fiction inspired by the Middle Ages. The website and blog at http://amedievalwomanscompanion.com/ accompany this book.

About the images: We have tried to contact all copyright-holders of the images in this book. If, through accident, credit has been missed, please contact the author and publisher so that arrangements can be made.

Notes

1. L. M. C. Weston, 'Women's Medicine, Women's Magic: The Old English Metrical Charms', *Modern Philology* 92 (1995), 288.
2. William D. Paden and Frances Freeman Paden, *Troubadour Poems From the South of France* (Woodbridge, Suffolk: D. S. Brewer, 2007), 16.
3. Virginia Woolf, *A Room of One's Own* (Boston, MA: A Harvest Book/Houghton Mifflin Harcourt, 1989), 51.
4. Rachel Gibbons, 'The Piety of Isabeau of Bavaria, Queen of France, 1385–1422', in

Courts, Counties and the Capital in the Later Middle Ages, edited by Diana E. S. Dunn (Stroud: Sutton Publishing, 1996), 206.

5. *Ibid.*, 206.
6. Elizabeth M. Makowski, personal communication.
7. Frances Underhill, 'Elizabeth de Burgh: Connoisseur and Patron', in *The Cultural Patronage of Medieval Women*, edited by June Hall McCash (Athens, GA: University of Georgia Press, 1996), 267.
8. Nicholas Orme, *Fleas, Flies, and Friars: Children's Poetry from the Middle Ages* (Ithaca, NY: Cornell University Press, 2011), 10.
9. M. Caroline Barron, 'The Education and Training of Girls in Fifteenth-Century London', in Dunn, 139.
10. *Ibid.*, 147.
11. Dorothy Gilbert, 'Juliana Berners: From the Book of St Albans', in *The Norton Anthology of Women's Literature: The Traditions in English*, 2nd edition, edited by Sandra M. Gilbert and Susan Gubar (New York: Norton, 1996), 27.
12. Geoffrey Chaucer, *The Riverside Chaucer*, edited by Larry D. Benson, 3rd edition (Boston: Houghton Mifflin Company, 1987), 638; my translation.
13. Orme 2011, 52.
14. Leslie A. Donovan, *Women Saints' Lives in Old English Prose* (Woodbridge, Suffolk: Boydell and Brewer, 1999), 38.
15. *Ibid.*, 41.
16. Barbara Hill, 'Actions Speak Louder Than Words: Anna Komnene's Attempted Usurpation', in *Anna Komnene and Her Times*, edited by Thalia Gouma-Peterson (NY: Garland Publishing, 2000), 45–6.
17. Marcus Bull, *Thinking Medieval: An Introduction to the Study of the Middle Ages* (Basingstoke: Palgrave Macmillan, 2005), 45.
18. Elizabeth Alvilda Petroff, *Medieval Women's Visionary Literature* (NY: Oxford University Press, 1986), 153.

PART I

IONEERS

Frederick Stuart Church's 'The Viking's Daughter' (1887). The nineteenth century saw a revival of interest in all things medieval (gift of John Gellatly 1929.6.19. Smithsonian American Art Museum, Washington, DC/Art Resource, NY)

CHAPTER 1

Gudrun Osvifsdottir
(c. 970–1050)

VIKING VIXEN

Can a bad girl become a good girl? This Icelandic woman, of Viking stock, took men's hearts by storm. Jealous, murderous, demanding, she ultimately became the first Icelandic nun.

Who were the Vikings? They were Scandinavians who wandered by ship to attack, plunder, colonize, settle, capture humans for the slave trade, and assimilate in areas as far-reaching as Russia, France, Norway, Sweden, Denmark, Greenland, Iceland, Canada, and even Constantinople (now called Istanbul). They settled in Ireland, England, Orkney in northern Scotland, the Faroe Islands between Ireland and Iceland, and the Isle of Man. The Vikings were popularly thought of as men, but women travelled with them too, as wives, slaves, and adventurers. The Viking Age lasted roughly 800–1100 CE; thereafter, Iceland was settled and Christianized. During this period Iceland transformed from being the Wild West of the North Atlantic to conforming to many habits and beliefs of medieval Christian Europe.

Written in prose with occasional poetic interludes and telling of the stories of the settlers of Iceland, the sagas depicted adventures with tough, forthright, and sometimes violent women. These lively narratives took place between the late ninth century with the arrival of the first pagan colonists and 1262 when Icelanders were forced to accept the ruler of Norway as their master. How much we can trust the sagas about historical truth has been long debated. The sagas played out in an imaginative space conjured up by Icelanders several hundred years after the action is set. While some things were unlikely (ghosts and trolls), other aspects, such as genealogy, legal disputes, and familial strife, were based on fact. Thus most historians turn to the sagas for understanding medieval Iceland. While sagas had their roots in oral stories passed down over the centuries, the details of political rule and mayhem make them useful for understanding who was in power and how men and women interacted with one another.

Richly textured with bold women who seem familiar to us in the twenty-first century, the sagas argued how females were crucial to the founding of Iceland, a newly settled country. Several sources, including the *Laxdaela Saga*, tells of the 13 female land claimants numbered among the 400 original settlers. Ninety other women accompanied their husbands. Unn the Deep-Minded founded a farm with her vast wealth. Close to death, she cleverly hosted a party where all the attendants had to bear witness to her intention to leave her property to her grandson. These observers were bound to uphold the desires of this "exceptional woman".[1] Worthy of the most dignified of funerals, she "was placed in a ship in the mound, along with a great deal of riches, and the mound closed."[2] Archeologists have located such ship burials, like that of Oseberg in Norway in which the skeletons of two women were discovered. People were typically buried with grave goods, items important to the deceased in life and beyond. Physical evidence from a Viking settlement on Orkney includes a pit with a young woman and her newborn child, buried with wool combs and other domestic items needed in the world to come. Jewels and brooches festoon the grave, decorated with glass, beads, silver, gold, and amber. Some elaborate burial sites suggest that women could be major leaders in their communities. While women typically were buried with women's items, having to do with spinning for example, there are cases where they were buried with male-identified items like weapons.

Gudrun Osvifsdottir, the dominant figure of the *Laxdaela Saga*, enacted vengeance with a bloody outcome. Gudrun "was the most beautiful woman ever to have grown up in Iceland, and no less clever than she was good-looking".[3] She married four times starting at the age of 15. Her first husband, not to her liking, slapped her, to which Gudrun responded, "Fine rosy colour in her cheeks is just what every woman needs, if she is to look her best".[4] This understated response carried a sharpness fulfilled when later she plotted for a divorce. A key year was 1000 when the Althing (Parliament) decided that pagan Iceland should convert to Christianity. This new religion highlighted two forms of marriage: the Germanic model, by which the marriage was a bridge to secure property and alliance, and the Christian model of man and woman consenting to unite. Married partners were encouraged to stay in their same social class. Often unions were intended to help patch up troubles between warring families by joining the son and daughter of feuding parties. A father could not force a girl to marry who wanted to be a nun – though with only two nunneries in Iceland, she might not have had many options. Though they

---

Another Gudrun

The *Poetic Edda* tells the foundational mythology of Scandinavian and Germanic cultures. Beloved by the hero Sigurd, the mythological Gudrun remarried after her husband's murder. After her new husband, Atli the Hun, slaughtered Gudrun's brothers, she secretly killed her sons in retaliation. Once Atli had feasted, she told him, "You are digesting, proud one, slaughtered human meat ...[Y]ou will not see again ... the bounteous princes ... cantering their horses."[5]

---

were still disadvantaged politically as women, older widows had the most power among women in Icelandic society. Thorgerd, widowed but still young enough to have more children, "was free to decide for herself"[6] concerning a second marriage. Christianity attempted to control looser pagan ways concerning relationships. Sometimes secret marriages were valid if consent were proven.

Divorce was relatively easy to get – if you were too poor to care for your children, if a husband planned to take his wife's property out of the country, or if one spouse committed violence towards the other. Women kept economic independence in marriage, yet their power and influence varied. A woman named Vigdis was furious at her husband who had double-crossed her fugitive kinsman. Angry, she took the money pouch filled with his treacherous payoff and "swung the purse up into his face, striking him on the nose which bled so that drops of blood fell to the ground".[7] Her husband managed to swindle her out of her rightful claim to half the property. She took with her "nothing but her own belongings".[8]

Gudrun met her soul mate, the dreamy Kjartan, at the hot-springs. Taken with her "as she was both clever and good with words",[9] he nonetheless had to go off for the coming-of-age trip all young Icelandic men made: to Norway to meet the king. Occupied by Norwegians who fled the dominance of King Harald Fairhair (ruled late ninth–tenth centuries), Icelanders wanted to have their own land and freedom, though at a cost. The typical male Icelander would return to Norway in his youth to curry favor with royalty, make connections, and – if he were lucky – make money in trade and goods. When Kjartan told Gudrun he had to make this trip, she gave this shocking response: "I want to go with you this summer, and by taking me you can make up for deciding this so hastily, for it's not Iceland that I love".[10] He pointed out that she could not. No woman had ever done that – certainly no woman who was unmarried (though once divorced and once widowed). Kjartan asked her to wait three years for him. She refused. Kjartan and his best friend, Bolli, went to Norway. When Christianity comes to pagan Iceland, Kjartan does not. His delay in returning allowed his rival to vie for Gudrun. Men competed over the scarce women who, in turn, could demand more rights than they had had in Norway. While in Norway early law permitted the infanticide of deformed babies or females, Icelandic daughters were more valued. Children were typically named according to their father. Boys had 'son' after their father's name as in Bardi Gudmundarson (son of Gudmundar). Girls had 'dottir' (daughter) after their father's name, as in Jorunn Thorbergsdottir (daughter of Thorberg). If the father died while the child was still an infant, she or he could take the mother's name.

Bolli, who secretly loved Gudrun, suggested that Kjartan and the Norwegian princess were romantically involved, whereupon Gudrun lost her sparkle and married Bolli. Yet "Gudrun showed little affection for Bolli".[11] When Kjartan returned still a bachelor, he opted for the lovely Hrefna who tried on a gold studded head-dress originally intended for Gudrun. Kjartan said, "To my mind the head-dress suits you very well, Hrefna. I expect the best thing for me would be to own both the head-dress and the comely head it rests upon".[12] While the sagas did not present love in a fanciful glow, they suggested deep emotional ties between men and women. Sometimes romance provoked poetic verse. In another saga, the lovely Helga floated to Greenland on a fragment of frozen ice and fell in love with Skeggi. The affair ended at her father's insistence and she mourned. "Strife eats my soul ... I gape open with grief. / I speak sorrow to myself".[13]

In *Laxdaela Saga*, Gudrun and Hrefna compete for who could possess the seat of highest honor at the dining table. The golden head-dress disappeared, with suspicion falling on Gudrun. Tensions rose until Gudrun gave her husband Bolli an ultimatum over her proposed vengence: "[I]f you refuse to go along it will be the end of our life together".[14] A scene of violence and mayhem ends pathetically when Kjartan throws down his weapons so that his best friend can give him the death blow. "I'd rather receive my death at your hands than cause yours".[15] Bolli then "took up his body and held him in his arms when [Kjartan] died". Upon hearing what has occurred at her prompting, Gudrun could only say, "[M]ost important, to my mind, is the thought that Hrefna won't go to bed with a smile on her face this evening." To her husband Bolli, Gudrun commented, "Now I know that you won't go against my will".[16]

While Gudrun comes across as cold, her ruthlessness stemmed from despair at losing her beloved Kjartan. If only she had been permitted by society's traditions at the time to have accompanied him to Norway. She may have *seemed* indifferent to Bolli. Yet after he, in turn, was murdered, she waited over 12 years to exact revenge for *his* death. If a kinsman were killed or wounded, the victim's kinsmen were expected to pay back the culprits with violence. The law system in Iceland encouraged financial compensation for crimes in an effort to stem the tide of savagery. Icelanders met annually at the *Thing* or *Althing* – the national assembly – to pronounce legal suits and achieve resolution. According to these dynamic sagas, even if a financial settlement were made to appease the victim's family, someone inevitably wanted to draw blood. Not only could women possess land, they could also become involved in legal disputes, trade, and undertake business, including piracy. If a family had no son, a woman could inherit or avenge a death. Women typically needed a man to represent them in legal disputes, though the rare woman was known to have acted as an arbitrator in disputes and initiated lawsuits. With these rights came responsibilities. A woman disobeying the law was subject to exile, capital punishment, and being outlawed just like men. While her sorcerer son Odd was hanged, the witch Katla was stoned to death. Saga women appeared as the descendants of legendary Valkyries in their roles as encouragers of battle, vengeance, and retaliation. To urge her sons (one is only 12 years old) to avenge their father's death, Gudrun spread "out garments of linen, a shirt and breeches much stained with blood. She then spoke: 'These very clothes which you see here reproach you for not avenging your father.'"[17]

Valkyrie

Icelandic women had strong role models for their stern speech and actions. The Norse gods and goddesses got up to all sorts of intrigue, battling giant-maidens and frost ogres. Valkyries ('corpse-choosers'), armed maidens in Germanic and Norse mythology, were empowered to select male warriors on the battlefield and guide them to Valhall, where dead warriors were welcomed with a cup of mead and feasting. Saxo Grammaticus, writing around 1200, described Viking women warriors in this way. They "aimed at conflict instead of kisses, tasted blood, not lips, sought the clash of arms rather than the arm's embrace, fitted to weapons hands which should have been weaving."[18]

Gudrun, "the most determined of women",[17] married happily one last time, though this husband eventually drowned. A ghost told her of the tragedy, saying "'News of great moment, Gudrun', to which Gudrun replied, 'Then keep silent about it, you wretch.'"[18] Even a specter from the other side of the grave could not stop her from uttering a snappy comeback.

In her old age, Gudrun turned to God, becoming "very religious". In fact, she came to be "the first Icelandic woman to learn the Psalter, and spent long periods in the church praying at night",[19] erecting a church near her home at Helgafell. Ever the initiator, Gudrun became "a nun and anchoress",[20] again the first in Iceland. Though she lived a full life of intense and even dubious actions, her conversion at the end of the saga signals a similar change in Iceland itself through its Christianization. It may also suggest how the pagan society that limited women to certain set roles where they were defined by men – daughter, wife, encourager of vengeance – failed its female members. Removing herself from that male-centered world allowed her a kind of freedom where she could truly mourn. As we shall see, Christianity allowed women access to power and authority.

Before Gudrun dies, her son wants to know: "Which man did you love the most?"[21] Except for her first husband, all the other three had admirable qualities, she admits. At last Gudrun confesses, "Though I treated him worst, I loved him best."[22] Was that Bolli, her third husband? Or Kjartan, whom she

never even married? We'll never know. Yet her life, immortalized in this saga, has drawn readers for hundreds of years, fascinated by her passion, ruthlessness, and, ultimately, her piety.

This silver-gilt pendant from the sixth century depicts a Valkyrie offering a mead horn (from Oland, Sweden. Statens Historiska Museet, Stockholm, Sweden. Photo credit: Werner Forman/ Art Resource, NY).

Learn more

- Donna Jo Napoli's *Hush: An Irish Princess' Tale* (NY: Atheneum Books for Young Readers, 2007) tells the story of the teenager Melkorka, daughter of the Irish king, when she was kidnapped and enslaved by Vikings. Melkorka's father ultimately offers the throne to her son. While the *Laxdaela Saga* dealt with Melkorka's later life, this Young Adult book explores her teenage years in a gripping and poignant adventure.
- To find out more about the tantalizing and legendary Gudrun, check out the J. R. R. Tolkien website dedicated to the author of *The Lord of the Rings* and *The Hobbit*. http://www.tolkienestate.com/sigurd-and-gudrun/.
- Watch and listen to the famous operatic 'Ride of the Valkyrie' by Richard Wagner: http://youtu.be/xeRwBiu4wfQ.

Notes

1. Keneva Kunz, trans., *The Saga of the People of Laxardal and Bolli Bollason's Tale*, edited by Bergljót S. Kristjánsdóttir (London: Penguin Books, 2008), 6.
2. Kunz *Laxardal*, 10.
3. Kunz *Laxardal*, 63.
4. Kunz *Laxardal*, 69.
5. Judith Jesch, *Women in the Viking Age* (Woodbridge, Suffolk: Boydell Press, 1991), 147.
6. Kunz *Laxardal*, 11.
7. Kunz *Laxardal*, 26.
8. Kunz *Laxardal*, 27.
9. Kunz *Laxardal*, 83.
10. Kunz *Laxardal*, 85.
11. Kunz *Laxardal*, 97.
12. Kunz *Laxardal*, 99.
13. Sandra Ballif Straubhaar, trans. and ed., *Old Norse Women's Poetry: The Voice of Female Skalds* (Cambridge: D. S. Brewer, 2011), 35.
14. Kunz *Laxardal*, 113.
15. Kunz *Laxardal*, 115.
16. Kunz *Laxardal*, 116.
17. Kunz *Laxardal*, 135.
18. Jesch, 176.
19. Kunz *Laxardal*, 153.
20. Kunz *Laxardal*, 170.
21. Kunz *Laxardal*, 171.
22. Kunz *Laxardal*, 172.
23. Kunz *Laxardal*, 171.
24. Kunz *Laxardal*, 174.

This sculpture (1939) made by Asmundur Sveinsson depicts Gudrid Thorbjarnardottir and her son Snorri, the first European born in what became North America (Skagafjörður Heritage Museum, Iceland)

CHAPTER 2

Ⓖudrid Thorbjarnardottir
(born c. 980)

FEARLESS EXPLORER

Ⓞne of the most compelling Icelandic women was Gudrid Thorbjornssdottir in the *Vinland Sagas*, said to have been "the most attractive of women and one to be reckoned with".[1] Her foster-father told a would-be suitor, who failed in his effort to marry her, that Gudrid was "choosy about her husband".[2] Though born in Iceland, she and others traveled to Greenland, only sparsely settled a few years earlier. After marrying Thorfinn Karlsefni, she was among the first women to travel with some Greenlanders to a country as yet undiscovered by Europeans. Where they ended up exactly is still debated – but they certainly travelled to parts of Canada, including Baffin Island, Labrador, Newfoundland, and 'Vinland', in the Gulf of St Lawrence. It was called Vinland or Wineland because of grapes grown there. The travellers wondered at wheat that sowed itself. The Greenlanders traded with the native population, though fighting periodically broke out.

Gudrid's travels from Iceland to Greenland to Vinland suggest how women often traveled for marriage. At last, in their second year, "Gudrid, Karlsefni's wife, gave birth to a boy, who was named Snorri".[3] He was the first European child born in the New World, 500 years before those offspring born to native women and Spanish explorers after Christopher Columbus's arrival in 1492. Archeological evidence at L'Anse aux Meadows in Newfoundland confirms Viking presence hundreds of years before Columbus sailed to the 'New World'.

One way that Gudrid and women like her gained power and respect was through language, such as words of peace. In *Laxdaela Saga*, Hoskuld listened to his wife Jorunn's counsel. He intended to cheat his half-brother out of a rightful inheritance. Jorunn advised, "I think you'd better do right by your brother ... [H]e is no fool. He must see that it would do honour to both of you."[4] Hoskuld wisely obeyed her. Wise women like Jorunn could help prevent bloodshed with their forthright and honest speech. A speaking poet was called a *skald* (Icelandic *skáld*), a word related to our English word *scold* – someone who speaks harshly and to the point. Such poetic passages pop up, particularly at moments of great emotional turmoil. For example, in *Njal's Saga*, Thorhild, angry at her husband for making goo-goo eyes at a 14-year-old girl, said, "Your manners are missing / Mister Bug-Eyes".[5] Displeased, he divorced her and married the teenager.

Insults and *whetting* were modes of speech that include women humiliating men for their lack of action. Through verbal aggression, a woman encouraged a man to avenge a murder or wrong committed against her family. In *Eyrbyggja Saga*, Geirrid scorned her husband, saying, "It's true what they say about you …You're more like a woman than a man."[6] He in turn went and split the bad guy's head in two with an axe, whereupon his wife commented, "My words gave you an edge".[7] It could be a woman's duty to instigate retaliation. When Thorgerd tried to get someone to take vengeance for the death of her husband Vigfus, she pulled out his decaying head and said to her uncle Arnkel, "Here's a head that would never have shirked action if you'd been killed and its help had been needed."[8] The tongue became a kind of sword – as brutal and violent as the metal weapon itself. Women were known to speak in order to goad men into action. In one saga, Thurdid provoked her sons to attack the killers of their brother. "Rain blood with your blade / on these brother-slayers! / Pay heed to this poem, for / people will scorn you".[9]

Another kind of important language controlled by women was that of prophecy. A key figure in *Eirik the Red's Saga*, the Greenlander Thorbjorg, called the 'Little Prophetess', would travel around various farms in the wintertime and tell people's fortunes. Adorned in black and white clothes made from lamb, calf, and catskin, she carried charms "needed for her predictions".[11] Thorbjorg

Violent Language

Just like their Icelandic literary counterparts, whose tongues were like swords, women writers in the Middle Ages took up arms via the pen. Christine de Pizan in *The Book of the City of Ladies* depicted her namesake, St Christine, as tortured brutally by her father. She defied him, only to be imprisoned. An evil judge had her tongue cut out, which miraculously caused her to speak "even better and more clearly than before". Not only that, St Christine spit "this cut-off piece of her tongue into the tyrant's face, putting out one of his eyes".[10] That was one sharp-tongued woman.

wanted women who "knew all the chants required for carrying out magic rites, which are called warlock songs". Gudrid, a devout Christian, said, "I have neither magical powers nor the gift of prophecy, but in Iceland my foster-mother, Halldis, taught me chants she called warlock songs". Gudrid then sang as the other women formed a ring around Thorbjorg. "Gudrid spoke the chant so well and so beautifully that people there said they had never heard anyone recite in a fairer voice."[12] Thorbjorn thanked Gudrid, assuring her that her family's future would be prosperous. "Over all the branches of that family a bright ray will shine".[13] While such a prophetess was believed to be able to see the fate of an individual, she would be unable to alter it.

Gudrid's opposite, the Greenlander Freydis Eiriksdottir, remains emblazoned on the reader's imagination. Unlike Gudrid, whose very name *Gud* suggests a Christian God, Freydis was named for the heathen Freyja, the fertility goddess. The real distinction in Icelandic society was not between male and female, but between who was powerful and who was powerless, who could or could not enact his or her will. In *The Saga of the Greenlanders*, we hear how Freydis was a "domineering woman".[14] That's putting it mildly. She made a deal with two brothers to equally share in the profits from their journey to Vinland. Each "was to have thirty fighting men aboard his ship and women in addition".[15] Freydis hid five extra men. She did not let the brothers stay in her house, forcing them to build shelter right away.

One night, Freydis snuck away from the house wearing her "husband's cape" and visited one of her partners. He agreed to her demand to take the larger ship, if only to stop the bad blood between them – ill-will always instigated by Freydis. When she returned home and popped into bed with her husband, her cold feet awakened him. She lied, saying the brothers hit her and refused to trade ships. Then she proceeded to scold her husband. "[Y]ou're such a coward that you will repay neither dishonour done to me nor to yourself ... [U]nless you avenge this, I will divorce you!" Unable to "ignore her upbraiding any longer", he arranged for all the men to be killed.

Freydis's men refused to kill women. "Freydis then spoke: 'Hand me an axe.' This was done, and she attacked the five women there and killed them all ... Freydis was highly pleased with what she had accomplished."[16] Her brother Leif was appalled when the truth came out and predicted that Freydis's descendants "will not get on well in this world".[17] She was one tough broad.

Pregnancy did not limit women's lives. Often they would work in the fields until labor started. One woman strapped her baby to her back as she continued to rake the hay cut by her husband. Another woman had twin boys while shepherding sheep. Freydis frightened away the natives of Vinland. Pregnant, she smacked a sword on her bared breast, terrifying the inhabitants. Her violent, pagan ways were rejected for the Christian ones of Gudrid.

Despite the realistic seeming nature of the sagas, strange things happened. After Gudrid's earlier husband, the very handsome Thorstein, died, he sat back up to tell her what fate she had for the future. He reassured her that she would marry an Icelander and "have many descendants, promising, bright and fine, sweet and well-scented". He requested a Christian burial at a church. Finally, he assured her that before her death, she would "travel abroad, go south on a pilgrimage and return to Iceland to your farm, where a church will be built. There you will remain and take holy orders and there you will die".[18] That is, of course, exactly what happened. Her descendants included a number of bishops, attesting to her pious nature and worthy character. Like Gudrun Osvifsdottir, Gudrid likewise became an anchoress.

These sagas alter the national narrative of the United States in which the Americas were 'undiscovered' until the late fifteenth century. In fact, northern Europeans encountered the native peoples of today's Canada. Some may have been Algonquin and others possibly Inuit or First Nations. The Greenland colony did not prosper after the late fourteenth century, when a little ice age first began, making the settlements in Greenland unsuited to supporting these adventurers. The Inuit wiped out the Greenlanders further north and attacked those in the south, until the last ship left in about 1410.

Gudrid's husband captured two boys in Markland (Labrador) who eventually came to learn their language and were baptized. Such kidnappings commonly happened in human history, as scientific evidence reveals concerning women's migration patterns. The tooth enamel of a woman buried on the Isle of Lewis, Scotland, about 900 CE indicates her area of origin as southern England. Undoubtedly she ended up at this Norse settlement after being enslaved by Viking raiders. Recent DNA evidence has shown that some Icelanders today descend from a Native American woman from about the year 1000 CE. Captured, she was forced to travel with – and bear children for – the adventurers from Greenland and Iceland at some point in these early trips as recorded in the sagas. Slavery lies at the heart of European colonization of the 'New World' starting in the late tenth and then again in the late fifteenth centuries with the arrival of Spanish explorers.

What DNA Evidence can teach us about women's history

DNA analysis can enhance our understanding of gendered migration patterns. In an Icelandic study, patrilineal ancestry stemmed 75–80% from Scandinavia and 20–25% from Scotland and Ireland, while matrilineal ancestry could be traced 37% to Scandinavia and 63% from Scotland and Ireland. This suggests a large number of women were enslaved to bear children for Viking men.

Learn more

- The beautiful and classic *D'Aulaires' Book of Norse Myths* (NY: The New York Review of Books, 1967) by Ingri and Edgar Parin d'Aulaire captures the thrill of Norse mythology.

Notes

1. Keneva Kunz, trans., *The Vinland Sagas* (London: Penguin, 2008), 28.
2. Kunz *Vinland*, 29.
3. Kunz *Vinland*, 16.
4. Kunz *Vinland*, 34.
5. Sandra Ballif Straubhaar, trans. and ed., *Old Norse Women's Poetry: The Voice of Female Skalds* (Cambridge: D. S. Brewer, 2011), 17.
6. Hermann Pálsson and Paul Edwards, trans., *Eyrbyggja Saga* (London: Penguin Books, 1989), 51.
7. Pálsson and Edwards *Eyrbyggja*, 54.
8. Pálsson and Edwards *Eyrbyggja*, 75.
9. Straubhaar 20.
10. Christine de Pizan, *The Book of the City of Ladies*, translated by Earl Jeffrey Richards (NY: Persea Books, 1982), 239.
11. Kunz *Vinland*, 31.
12. Kunz *Vinland*, 32.
13. Kunz *Vinland*, 33.
14. Kunz *Vinland*, 4.
15. Kunz *Vinland*, 18.
16. Kunz *Vinland*, 19.
17. Kunz *Vinland*, 20.
18. Kunz *Vinland*, 14.

This reliquary bust of Saint Juliana, a virgin martyr, dating from c. 1376, would have held her relics or sacred body parts, typically bones. Like the girls in Hrotsvit's plays, Juliana had to stand up to a pagan governor who desired her. Although her own father threatened her with torture, she stood firm, saying, "Never shall you intimidate me with your threats." (Metropolitan Museum of Art, The Cloisters Collection, 1961 (61.266), © The Metropolitan Museum of Art. ARTstor: MMA_IAP>10313503485)

Hrotsvit of Gandersheim
(c. 935–c. 1000)

FIRST WOMAN PLAYWRIGHT

Hrotsvit von Gandersheim had many firsts to her credit: first medieval playwright; first Western female playwright; first female German poet; first dramatist of Germany – indeed, the first known dramatist in Europe since the classical period; and first female German historian. How did she get to be first?

Most likely the daughter of a noble Saxon family, she was educated by women at the wealthy abbey of Gandersheim, a religious foundation in the Harz Mountains in Germany. It functioned as a religious center, school for girls with a valuable library, and hospital. The nuns had to obey parts of the Benedictine Rule – obedience and chastity – but they did not have to follow the rule of poverty. They could keep their own wealth – an extraordinary privilege and appealing perk for families with money. As disadvantaged members in a warrior society, noblewomen would gain power through the church. A canoness could have her own servants, buy her own books, entertain guests, travel freely, and even leave to marry without consequence. Hrotsvit was highly educated and was familiar with the key writings of dozens of Christian and pagan authors, of literary and religious texts. She was also well versed in grammar, mathematics, and music as we can see in her writings, dedicated to various members of Emperor Otto's family. Her teacher Rikkardis gave Hrotsvit a foundation in the liberal arts, particularly the *quadrivium* (music, arithmetic, geometry, and astronomy), while Abbess Gerberga II focused on the *trivium* – grammar, rhetoric, and dialectic. In addition to the writings of the Church Fathers, those professional Christian thinkers of the medieval Catholic Church, Gerberga also taught Hrotsvit the Roman pagan authors who would be so important for her future writing.

Most impressive are Hrotsvit's six plays, written in rhymed prose sometime after 962 CE. These works may have been performed at court or read aloud as spoken theatre while nuns ate in the area of the abbey called the refectory (cafeteria). Hrotsvit had been introduced to the comedies written by the playwright Terence. This Roman writer was highly praised by St Jerome, making the pagan wordsmith a proper object of attention. But Terence wrote immoral comedies with low plots lines featuring love affairs and women of less than perfect reputation. His women embodied the worst of misogynist beliefs. Hrotsvit took these well-plotted, but immoral, plays and turned them into morally admirable dramas featuring worthy women and weak men. Girls stood up to those who did not let them lead the lives they chose. What could have been happier for a devout medieval Christian than to end up in heaven?

Medieval women wisely used the pretense of weakness to gain respect and power. Hrotsvit used a common convention utilized by many women writers called the *modesty topos*. She would say how unworthy she was, only to deliver her zinger: my work will be the best. "Therefore I / the strong voice of Gandersheim, have not refused to imitate [Terence] in writing / whom others laud in reading". She said how, rather than writing about shameless women, she wrote about sacred and chaste maidens, "within the limits of my little talent".[2] Hrotsvit had to put herself down, as was conventional for female writers, to get male scholars to accept her creations. She referred to her "own worthlessness" and "inelegant style", describing herself as being of "little learning and worth" and a "worthless woman".[3] God should be praised, not her. All this putting down of herself enabled her to find a position of strength. It would be wrong for her to deny God's gift that she could write.

Hrotsvit's plays reflected the freedom of her privileged position when she wrote about characters who were not very nun-like, such as prostitutes and sinful men. The settings of her works ranged from the high and lofty – such as the room of a holy hermit – to the lowest – such as a brothel or a religious cell stinking with excrement. Action swiftly passes; no play took longer than half an hour to perform. In addition to lively battle scenes, she described the torture and martyrdom of saintly girls, slapstick comedy, and the conversion of pagans. Hrotsvit's plays about prostitute saints reassured women and girls that, no matter what, it was never too late to find God's forgiveness. She wove into the dynamic plots lessons about mathematics, music, and theology, providing girls in the abbey a memorable way to recollect the material they had to memorize. Hrotsvit's dialogue could be funny, quick-witted, solemn, and sharp.

Triumphant female weakness conquered male strength. In *Dulcitius*, three holy virgins named Agape, Chionia, and Hirena (Love, Purity, and Peace) refused to give up their faith and confronted the Emperor Diocletian, famous for killing Christians in the early fourth century. Agape boldly proclaimed that God was more important than the earthly power of the emperor. Consequently, the emperor thought they were mad. Yet we know the true madman was his own Governor Dulcitius who was in charge of their captivity and eager to love these nubile maidens. He locked up the girls in a pantry. At night, secretly, he made his way to the kitchen in order to kiss and cuddle with them. God intervened to confuse the nasty man into thinking that cooking pots were really lovely young girls. In a scene of naughty humor, Dulcitius went into the kitchen and, while he embraced the dirty pans, our young heroines spied on him through a crack in the wall and mocked him. Their prayers to God came true. When he came out of the kitchen, he was covered in soot. His own soldiers fled, thinking he was the devil. Once Dulcitius came to his senses, he demanded that the girls "be publicly stripped of all their clothes".[4] But the soldiers could not – the clothes clung to the girls miraculously.

The two older girls were to be burnt alive. They prayed and, once dead, their bodies were utterly untouched by fire. The youngest, Hirena, was threatened with being taken to a brothel. She proclaimed that if her soul was against something, she was innocent no matter what her body may be forced to do. Mysteriously, she was not brought to the brothel but guided by angels to a mountain. Shot by an arrow, she was triumphant as a saint and

---

Perpetua and Felicitas

In her early 20s, the historical Perpetua wrote down her visions in a prison notebook up to the time of her martyrdom in 203 CE. A wife and mother, Perpetua defied her pagan father by insisting on retaining her identity: "Father, do you see this vessel for instance lying here, waterpot or whatever it may be? Can it be called by any other name than what it is? So also I cannot call myself anything than what I am, a Christian."[5] Her comrade, Felicitas, gave birth just before death, dripping milk from her breasts as she was killed. A witness described how Perpetua modestly covered her thigh with her "torn tunic"[6] when she was attacked by a mad cow. Perpetua even helped the frightened Roman soldier commanded to kill her pull the sword to her own throat.

mocked her torturer in her final words: "Wretched [man], blush for shame, and proclaim your miserable defeat because without the help of weapons, you cannot overcome a tender little virgin as your foe."[7] These little girls were the true heroes, while the superficially strong males were revealed to be foolish, misguided, and weak.

The Martyrdom of the Holy Virgins Fides, Spes, and Karitas [Faith, Hope and Charity], began with the warning to Emperor Hadrian that three little girls threatened the security of the state. So bad was the influence of the girls' faith, that pagan men's wives "despise us so that they refuse to eat with us". The emperor admitted, "I admit that poses a danger".[8] The girls, ages 8, 10, and 12, instructed Hadrian in complicated mathematical calculations. Seen as rebels and threatened with torture, their mother Sapientia [Wisdom] declared, "You may lacerate my body with the weapons you wield, / but you will never succeed in compelling my soul to yield".[9] Fides, age 12, had her breasts wounded, but, instead of blood, milk poured out. Ten-year-old Spes felt no pain at being beaten, but only smelt a "fragrant heavenly scent".[10] The youngest, 8-year-old Karitas, was thrown into a fiery hot furnace. Rather than burning her up, it exploded and killed 5000 men. As the little girl defiantly told the Emperor, "I may be young in years, yet I am expert enough to confound you in argument".[11] Though they were ultimately executed, leaving their mother to care for their corpses, their speech triumphed over male immorality. As in all of these saints' legends, martyrdom proved the power of faithful virtue over paganism and misguided violence.

Living after the period of Christian persecution, the Christian maidens reading or hearing such works did not need to fear being killed for their faith.

> ### St Mary of Egypt
>
> In the desert, a monk met a woman with long wooly white hair who seemed to hover in the air before him while she prayed. She told how she had lived a wicked life for many years. Distraught at miraculously not being allowed to enter a church, she saw a vision of the Virgin Mary, prayed, and was allowed access. Thereafter, Mary of Egypt lived alone in the desert for 47 years, surviving on only three loaves of bread and plants she could scavenge. The monk came to realize that the holy harlot Mary of Egypt was more pious than he was and, when she died, buried her devoutly.

Hrotsvit's plays contributed to the vitality of women's stories that provided inspiration. Girls in the Middle Ages read such stories of virgin martyrs, themselves between the ages of eight and their mid-teens as in Hrotsvit's plays, and found them to be strong role models. Such stories would have been heartening – strong, vital females refusing to cave into threats or physical violence. Choosing to obey her heavenly father rather than her earthly father, a young woman stood fast in her faith. Such tales also gave hope for women at

a time when many well-respected male scholars and priests criticized women for being weak and sinful, accusations that we see many medieval women like Hrotsvit defied.

Like her young character Hirena, Hrotsvit was "rebellious and utterly resistant".[12] The nuns listening to the play may have giggled when the holy virgin Fides says of the violent emperor, "I have called him a fool, / I now call him a fool / and I shall call him a fool / as long as I live".[13] And, like the 8-year-old Karitas after her torture fails, the nuns and girls at Gandersheim would have sung "hymns of praise to [their] God".[14]

St Mary of Egypt carrying the three loaves of bread she survived on in the desert for decades (fifteenth-century miniature from the South English Legendary: Lives of Saints, and Temporale (Passion of Christ). MS. Tanner 17, f. 085r., with permission of the Bodleian Library, Oxford University)

Learn more

- Visit http://www.fordham.edu/halsall/sbook3.asp to read saints' lives from the Middle Ages, including those of male and female martyrs, transvestite saints, and the life of St Mary of Egypt. The story of Perpetua can be found here: http://www.fordham.edu/halsall/source/perpetua.asp.

Notes

1. S. A. J. Bradley, trans. and ed., *Anglo-Saxon Poetry* (London: J. M. Dent and Sons, 1982), 306.
2. Katharina Wilson, trans., *The Plays of Hrotsvit of Gandersheim* (NY: Garland Publishers, 1989), 3.
3. Wilson 1989, 4.
4. Wilson 1989, 43.
5. Adapted from Elizabeth Alvilda Petroff, *Medieval Women's Visionary Literature* (NY: Oxford University Press, 1986), 70.
6. Petroff 76.
7. Wilson 1989, 49.
8. Wilson 1989, 126.
9. Wilson 1989, 132.
10. Wilson 1989, 141.
11. Wilson 1989, 144.
12. Peter Dronke, *Women Writers of the Middle Ages* (Cambridge: Cambridge University Press, 1984), 78.
13. Wilson 1989, 136.
14. Wilson 1989, 145.

CHAPTER 4

Anglo-Saxon and Norman Women

POLITICAL POWER, DYNASTIES AND STEADFAST SOVEREIGNS

Emma of Normandy (c. 985–1052)

We all know of political families: the Kennedys, the Bushes, the Clintons. John F. Kennedy was the 35th President of the United States. His daughter Caroline began her Ambassadorship to Japan in 2013. The wife of Bob Dole, Senator from Kansas (1969–1996) and presidential nominee, was Elizabeth, herself a Senator, who served in a number of presidential administrations. Bill Clinton was Governor of Arkansas and then the 42nd President of the United States; his wife, Hillary Rodham Clinton became Senator from New York State and Secretary of State. Political dynasties are not unique to democracies. They have existed for a long time.

Related kin in Anglo-Saxon England married, fought, and struggled for dominance. Relations between the Danish Vikings and English were violent. The Danes had been invading England for centuries, starting as early as the late eighth century in 793 when the monastery on the holy island of Lindisfarne in Northumbria was destroyed. Attacks continued until a treaty was signed allowing the Vikings to live in part of England as long as they converted to Christianity. Despite their assimilation into English ways, the Danes wanted to rule England. The tenth century witnessed heightened confrontations. The Anglo-Saxon King Aethelred II even massacred numerous Vikings in 1002 on St Brice's Day; these remains have recently been found.[1] In retaliation, Richard I, a Norman from the northern part of France just across the Channel from England, offered the Vikings support.

Richard was married to Gunnor, herself of Danish descent. Even though her son was almost of age to rule, Gunnor acted as a regent after her husband's death. Someone bidding a request is said to have cried at her feet. Their daughter Emma was born during this time of political turmoil. A speaker of Norman French, Emma was promised as a bride and married the murderous Aethelred in 1002 in order to help create peace. As *The Anglo-Saxon Chronicle* puts it, "[T]he Lady, Richard's daughter, came hither to this country".[2] While Aethelred had

39

Emma's eleventh-century Encomium (a work that praises) shows Emma with the monk author of the book kneeling and her sons, Harthacnut and Edward the Confessor, beside her (© The British Library Board, Add. 33241, f.1v)

been married before and had numerous children, Emma gave birth to three children: two sons – Edward (who would later become King of England as 'Edward the Confessor') and Alfred – and a daughter Godgifu. Their names alone suggest a mingled heritage of English, Danish, and Norman French.

The Vikings could not be stopped, with Swein winning the throne of England in 1013. Things were topsy-turvy for some time. Emma and her children fled to her native Normandy, returning only after Swein's death, whereupon her husband Aethelred regained the kingship. Widowed in 1016, Emma bore witness to her stepson's rule. Yet Edmund Ironside was king for only a few months until he was savagely murdered while on the toilet.

One poem imagined a woman watching as Swein's son Cnut captured London:

> The pure widow living in
> the stone house will look out and see ...
> the victory-eager Danish
> chief with energy attack the
> town's defenders, blood-icicle [sword]
> crashes on British mail-coats.[3]

That woman could have been Emma, whose sons fled back to Normandy as Cnut began his long rule in 1016.

The following year in 1017, Cnut sent for Emma, wanting her to be his bride. Cnut "commanded the widow of the late king Aethelred, Richard's daughter, to be brought to him so that she might become his wife".[4] As widow of the Anglo-Saxon king and new bride of the Danish king, Emma exemplified the role of woman as peace-weaver. By uniting warring factions, she literally embodied a union of rival parties. Seeking her hand was self-

---

Torn between two loyalties

A woman married to a man in another country as part of political negotiations could be caught between an allegiance to her extended birth family and the family of the man she married and gave birth into. *Beowulf* tells the poignant story of the Danish Hildeburh who married the Frisian King Finn in a peace-weaving marriage. When the Danes attacked, she lost her son and brother. The feud continued until Hildeburh's husband was murdered. She returned to her birth family. "The woman wailed and sang keens".[5]

serving and practical on the part of Cnut. One chronicler wrote that in compensation for her hand in marriage, Cnut "handed over her weight in gold and silver to the army".[6] But the role of unifier was not an easy one.

While Cnut had had a number of illegitimate sons from a previous relationship, he and Emma produced two children – a boy Harthacnut and a girl Gunnhild. To make sure her legitimate children got what they were owed, Emma forced Cnut to promise to let *her* children rule. In fact, she would only become his queen if "he would never set up the son of any wife other than herself to rule after him, if it happened that God should give her a son by him".[7] She secured her legacy.

Yet when Cnut died in 1035, his illegitimate son, Harold Harefoot, struggled with Emma's son, Harthacnut, for power. Blood and gore flowed. There was no love lost between Emma and her stepson, whose buddy captured Emma's son Alfred. After suffering horribly from torture, "[H]is eyes were put out on board ship",[8] before he was murdered. The archbishop refused to crown Harold, saying, "Cnut committed *them* [Cnut's and Emma's sons] to my faith, I owe this faith to *them*, and I will keep it to *them* faithfully."[9] We told that in 1037 Emma "was driven from the country without any mercy to face the raging winter".[10] Exiled to Flanders on the continent, Emma remained there until Harold's death in 1040.

Emma returned to England with her son Harthacnut who named his half-brother Edward to be his successor. Edward was the offspring of her first marriage to Aethelred, while Harthacnut was a son from her second marriage to Cnut. Edward remained in exile in Normandy after Cnut came on the

---

Aethelflaed (c. 870s – ruled 911–918)

Called 'Lady of the Mercians',[11] Aethelflaed was the daughter of Alfred the Great and sister of Edward the Elder who ruled in Wessex. Her role was to bring about peace to a troubled area. Her familial links bolstered support of her powerful claims to rulership as regnant widow of Aethelred of Mercia. Building numerous forts to defend her people, she battled the Vikings with her brother. She brilliantly captured Derby, a city taken by the Danes, in 917. Aethelflaed was described two hundred years later in glowing terms: "Some call her not only lady, or queen, but even king ... worthy of a man's name... more illustrious than Caesar."[12]

throne. Surprisingly, Harthacnut died in a short time, ruling only from 1040–1042, with, some say, Emma co-ruling.

Once Edward came on the throne, he seized his own mother's lands. Angered by his mother's support of her son by Cnut rather than supporting his own claim, Edward sought his revenge. He allowed her return to court only in 1044.

We know Emma's story in part from a biography she commissioned about her own life. The *Encomium Emmae Reginae* cannot be taken as utterly factual. "That your excellence transcends the skill of anyone speaking about you is apparent

> ## Edith
>
> Edith (*c.* 1025–1075) was the daughter of the most powerful man in England: Earl Godwin of Wessex and Gytha of Danish royalty. Though she was raised at the nunnery at Wilton where she was highly trained in subjects of both the trivium and quadrivium, her father pushed her to marry the older King Edward the Confessor in 1045 in order to increase his own power. After six years of marriage and no children, Edward sent her to a nunnery for a year. Her lack of children made her position vulnerable. Leading a pious life secured her legacy.

to all to whom you are known, more clearly than the very radiance of the sun."[13] This work did not result from disinterested generosity, but as propaganda, explaining her actions to give her side of the story. Emma donated beautifully crafted textiles like altar cloths, books, and even relics to churches. Patronage helped to solidify the giver's reputation among those recipients of her largesse. In her final years, she retired into a nunnery in the city of Winchester where she died and was buried next to Cnut.

In the greatest of Old English poems *Beowulf* – which was orally sung for centuries before it was written down in the eleventh century – Emma may have been immortalized in the figure of Wealhtheow, the idealized queen, ruling at the hall Heorot. She was "[a]dorned in her gold … queenly and dignified, decked out in rings." The name Wealhtheow literally meant foreign captive or slave. Nevertheless, she spoke boldly to the warrior Beowulf, reminding him to help her young sons out when they come of age. "Treat my sons / with tender care, be strong and kind".[14] Since the poem undoubtedly was known at court, it could have sent the message that Emma was respected in her role as queen.

St Margaret of Scotland (c. 1046–1093)

descendent of King Alfred the Great, Margaret had a tumultuous childhood. After the murder of her grandfather Edmund Ironside (see above), who ruled England for a short time in 1016, his frightened family fled to Hungary. There, Margaret was born to Agatha, married to Edward Aetheling, son of Edmund Ironside.[15] Invited back to England in 1057 by his uncle, the King Edward the Confessor, Margaret's father had claim to the English throne. But Margaret, by then ten years old, and her younger siblings, Christina and Edgar, suffered the death of their father within a year of their arrival. Little Edgar was too weak and lacked the power to take the throne when Edward the Confessor died in January 1066. Their mother sought refuge for her family at the Scottish court shortly after the Norman Conquest in 1066.

Margaret was fluent in French since she had spent her teenage years at the Norman-influenced court in England. She learned the Scriptures in Latin, and knew the writings of St Augustine. The *Anglo-Saxon Chronicle*, a history recorded by monks, wrote that King Malcolm III of Scotland "was very anxious to marry Edgar's sister".[16] She passionately wished to devote her life to the church and her early life was devoted to God. "She swore she would be no man's bride".[17] Nevertheless, Margaret finally did agree to marry Malcolm, although he was about 16 years her elder in 1170. Her piety helped turn Malcolm to God. Frequently in Anglo-Saxon history, we see Christian wives converting their husbands to a more righteous path. Margaret's marriage fell into this pattern. Margaret and Malcolm had six sons (Edward, Edmund, Ethelred, Edgar, Alexander, and David); the three youngest became kings of Scotland.

Just as Emma had given finely woven materials to the Abbey Church of Ely, Margaret – trained in needlework along with her court ladies – made cloths for use on altars, as well as finely sewn vestments for priests. She adorned holy books with jewels and gold. She founded hospices with shelter and food for pilgrims on their way to the shrine dedicated to the Patron Saint of Scotland, St Andrew. She made donations to hermits and established a Benedictine church in Dunfermline. Most famously she established a free ferry for pilgrims across the Forth, a large body of water near Edinburgh, that to this day is called Queensferry.

Margaret made Malcolm's palace gleam with gold and fine decorations. Much like Queen Wealhtheow in *Beowulf*, Margaret served the king and his courtiers with "gold or silver plated"[18] vessels. Deeply troubled by her husband's tradition of plundering into the north of England and kidnapping slaves, an early biographer assured the reader that Margaret "hastened to their assistance, paid their ransom, and restored them to freedom".[19] She was said to have fed nine little orphans daily, sitting them on her lap and personally feeding them. And she inspired the king to serve 300 poor people food and drink on a regular basis.

Sadly, her husband and son Edward were killed in battle a few days before she died. She learned of their deaths, uttered the words "Deliver me",[20] and passed away. Canonized as a saint by 1250, her relics were thought to be holy and some now reside in the palace of Escorial near Madrid, Spain. Her undershirt was seen as a helpful garment for women in childbirth to wear, including later queens of Scotland.

You can make a pilgrimage to the Chapel of St. Margaret on the grounds of Edinburgh Castle. About a thousand years old, it was once used to house gunpowder. Today it has reverted to being a tiny, simple, and holy spot with a stained glass image of St Margaret to commemorate her virtue.

St Margaret's Daughter: Matilda of Scotland (1080–1118)

In addition to their sons, Margaret and Malcolm had two daughters: Matilda (b. 1080)[21] and Mary (b. 1082). At the age of six, Matilda went to a nunnery with St. Margaret's sister, Christina. Matilda stayed there to be educated until she was 13 years old. One chronicler told of the harshness of Christina's teachings. Matilda described her education in this way: "I … went in fear of the rod of my aunt Christina … and … she would often make me smart with a good slapping and the most horrible scolding, as well as treating me as being in disgrace."[22] While it was rumored that Matilda took the veil (became a nun), she hotly denied this and was determined to marry King Henry I of England. "I did indeed wear [the veil] in [Aunt Christina's] presence, but as soon as I was able to escape out of her sight, I tore it off and threw it on the ground and trampled on it and in that way … I used to vent my rage and the hatred of it which boiled up in me."[23] She had to defend herself before a church court. Upon being told she was free to marry, she had a "happy expression"[24] on her face.

Matilda married King Henry I of England and Duke of Normandy in 1100, uniting the ruling Norman and Saxon royal families. She commissioned a translation of the *Voyage of Saint Brendan*, as well as the life of her mother in Margaret's honor. This work praised her mother's life, but also established Matilda's own lineage and solidified her own power. Luxurious needlework, embroidery, and metalwork constituted a vital part of her identity. She was known as a generous gift-giver, as the monk William of Malmesbury attested to: "Her generosity becoming universally known, crowds of scholars, equally famed for verse and singing, came over; and happy was he who could soothe the queen's ears with the novelty of his song."[25] As the Anglo-Saxon *Maxims I* suggested, a queen, along with her king, "must be pre-eminently liberal with gifts ... the woman must excel as one cherished among her people".[26] Matilda's letter exchange with the Archbishop of Canterbury showed how she tried to patch up problems between him and her husband. She wrote, "I embrace the little parchment sent to me by you, as I would my father himself ... [The king's] mind is better disposed towards you than many men think".[27] She commissioned buildings, including a priory in London and a shiny new leper hospital. Bridges were constructed under her sponsorship. She even had a bathhouse with running water and the first known public toilets since Roman times built in the wharf area of London called Queenhithe.

She and Henry had one son, William, who drowned in 1120. Their daughter, likewise named Matilda (b. 1102), married Henry V, Holy Roman Emperor, in 1114. She had gone to be educated at his court at the age of 8 in 1110. Widowed in 1125, this younger Matilda returned to England as her father's heir and married Geoffrey of Anjou. Though Henry I tried to secure the place of his daughter on the throne of England, powerful barons resisted the thought of a woman on the throne. Matilda and her cousin Stephen of Blois[28] ruled in opposition to one another, each minting coins and collecting taxes. She was described as giving "the best and most valuable advice. In the whole army there was not a baron as astute and experienced in war as she was, and there was much talk about her throughout England."[29]

She had the last, albeit posthumous, laugh. Stephen died in 1154, whereupon the throne of England passed to Matilda's son, Henry II, great-grandson to St Margaret, grandson to Matilda of Scotland.

He, in turn, married Eleanor of Aquitaine.

4. Anglo-Saxon and Norman Women

Learn more

- A letter to St Margaret from Lanfranc, Archbishop of Canterbury, can be found here: http://epistolae.ccnmtl.columbia.edu/woman/9.html.
- For numerous letters to and from Matilda of Scotland, look here: http://epistolae.ccnmtl.columbia.edu/woman/64.html.
- Listen to a section of the Old English *Beowulf* where the hero fights the monster Grendel as performed by the world's leading *Beowulf* performer, accompanying himself on an Anglo-Saxon harp. http://www.bagbybeowulf.com/video/index.html.
- For good Young Adult novels about the Anglo-Saxon period, see Rosemary Sutcliffe's *Beowulf: Dragonslayer* and Rebecca Tingle's books about Aethelflaed as a teenager, *The Edge on the Sword* and *Far Traveler*.
- For *Beowulf*, the translation by Nobel laureate Seamus Heaney makes for a riveting read (New York: W. W. Norton, 2001). For more contemporary takes on the *Beowulf* characters, John Gardner's classic *Grendel* (NY: Vintage, 1971/1989) examines the material from the point of view of the 'monster', while Susan Signe Morrison's *Grendel's Mother: The Saga of the Wyrd Wife* (Top Hat Books 2015) gives it a feminist twist.
- Patricia Bracewell's trilogy set in eleventh-century England depicting Emma of Normandy's tumultuous life begins with *Shadow on the Crown* (Viking 2013) and Emma's marriage to King Aethelred II.

Notes

1. http://www.bbc.co.uk/news/science-environment-14476039.
2. G. N. Garmonsway, trans. and ed., *The Anglo-Saxon Chronicle* (London: J. M. Dent and Sons, 1990), 134.
3. Judith Jesch, *Women in the Viking Age* (Woodbridge, Suffolk: Boydell Press, 1991), 154.
4. Garmonsway, 154.
5. Seamus Heaney, trans., *Beowulf: A New Verse Translation* (NY: W. W. Norton, 2000), 77.
6. Theresa Earenfight, *Queenship in Medieval Europe* (NY: Palgrave Macmillan, 2013), 108.
7. Helen Damico, 'Beowulf's Foreign Queen and the Politics of Eleventh-Century England', in *Intertexts: Studies in Anglo-Saxon Culture Presented to Paul E. Szarmach*, edited by Virginia Blanton and Helene Scheck (Tempe, Arizona: ACMRS/Brepols, 2008), 227; Earenfight. 109.
8. Garmonsway. 160.
9. Joan M. Ferrante, 'Women's Role in Latin Letters from the Fourth to the Early Twelfth Century', in *The Cultural Patronage of Medieval Women*, edited by June Hall McCash (Athens, GA: University of Georgia Press, 1996), 92.
10. Garmonsway, 160.
11. Earenfight, 106.
12. Earenfight, 106.

13. Alistair Campbell, ed. and trans., *Encomium Emmae Reginae* (Cambridge: Cambridge University Press, 1949/1998), 5. Heaney, 41, 43.
14. Heaney, 41–43, 87; see Earenfight, 112; Damico 2008, 220–223.
15. Edward Atheling with his wife Agatha. Margaret was kin to the Holy Roman Emperor Henry II.
16. Garmonsway, 201.
17. Garmonsway, 201.
18. Wilson, Alan J., *St Margaret Queen of Scotland* (Edinburgh: John Donald, 1993), 87.
19. Wilson, 90.
20. Wilson, 100.
21. Her name was Edith, but, like some other medieval women, her name would change depending on whom she was married to. She was also sometimes called Maud or Mary.
22. Wilson, 115.
23. Derek Baker, ed., *Medieval Women* (Oxford: Basil Blackford, 1978), 123–124.
24. Lois L. Huneycutt, '*Alianora Regina Anglorum*: Eleanor of Aquitaine and Her Anglo-Norman Predecessors as Queens of England', in *Eleanor of Aquitaine: Lord and Lady*, edited by Bonnie Wheeler and John C. Parsons (NY: Palgrave Macmillan, 2002), 120.
25. Lois L. Huneycutt, '"Proclaiming her dignity abroad": The Literary and Artistic Network of Matilda of Scotland, Queen of England 1100–1118', in McCash, 156.
26. S. A. J. Bradley, trans. and ed., *Anglo-Saxon Poetry* (London: J. M. Dent and Sons, 1982), 348.
27. Anne Crawford, ed. *Letters of the Queens of England, 1100–1547* (Stroud, Gloucester: Sutton, 1997), 22–23.
28. Margaret's other granddaughter (Mary's daughter), Maud or Matilda (there are a lot of Matildas!), became Queen of England, married King Stephen, who was grandson to William the Conqueror.
29. Helen Nicholson, 'Women on the Third Crusade', *Journal of Medieval History* 23.4 (1997), 345.

CHAPTER 5

The Importance of Language

English

Emma of Normandy's greatest legacy was how we speak the English language today. She united Anglo-Saxon, Anglo-Dane, and Anglo-Norman cultures. As queen of one of the last Anglo-Saxon kings and step-mother and mother to the last ones, she would have spoken Old English – the form of English that existed in this Anglo-Saxon period. As queen of a Danish king, she would have been conversant in Danish, the language of the Vikings. As a Norman-born French speaker, her first language ultimately enriched the English language with a fertile and abundant wordstock of thousands of French words.

Perhaps the most relevant and familiar medieval source is one you are using right this minute – the English language. The language you are reading and speaking is a remnant of the Middle Ages. A dead language, like Latin, does not change; but a living language, like

Viking chess piece. Discovered in the sands of the Isle of Lewis, Scotland, this piece was part of a chess set originally crafted from walrus ivory and whales' teeth in Norway between 1150 and 1200 CE. The queen sits in a position modeled on that of the Virgin Mary contemplating the crucified Christ. You may recognize her as the model for the chess game played in the dining hall in the film Harry Potter and the Philosopher's Stone *(© The Trustees of the British Museum)*

Anglo-Saxon women

An eighth-century Anglo-Saxon missionary to Germany and saint, Leoba was a pious nun. "God had performed many miracles through Leoba."[1] Of Queen Aethelthryth (d. 679) was it said: "Although she lived with [her husband] for twelve years, she preserved the glory of perpetual virginity."[2] Founder of a double monastery, she became an abbess and, ultimately, a saint. Hild, a seventh-century abbess, was patron of the first known poet in the English language (Cædmon), an advisor to kings, and host of the Synod of Whitby, a key gathering in church history. "Kings and princes used to come and ask her advice in their difficulties and take it."[3]

English, is constantly undergoing alteration. New words are being created every year, even every day.

There are three main time periods for English; two of them were in the Middle Ages. Old English was used from about 450–1150, mainly during the Anglo-Saxon period of rule in Britain. It is a Germanic language, one of the many related languages called the Indo-European languages. The heroic epic *Beowulf* was written in Old English.

Upon the death of Edward the Confessor in January 1066, several men strove to attain the English throne: the Anglo-Saxon (English) Harold Godwinsson; the Viking Harald Hardrada; and the Norman William. Within months of the Anglo-Saxon Harold's coronation, the Danish Harald invaded northern England. After the English waged a decisive victory ending in Harald's death, William sailed to the southern coast of England. Harold had to hurry his troops south hundreds of miles. Meeting in Hastings, the battle ended with an arrow in Harold's eye and William's success. This invasion was decisive for the development of the English language, which subsequently absorbed thousands of French and Latin words, altering it irrevocably.

After the Norman Conquest in 1066, when French speakers invaded Britain, the language gradually changed. This newly developed language was called Middle English and its heyday was from 1150–1500. The Normans invaded in 1066 speaking Norman French, but a language cannot change overnight. It took 100 years for the Norman dialect to infiltrate the Old English still spoken by the vast majority of people. Only the upper classes spoke French or Anglo-Norman.

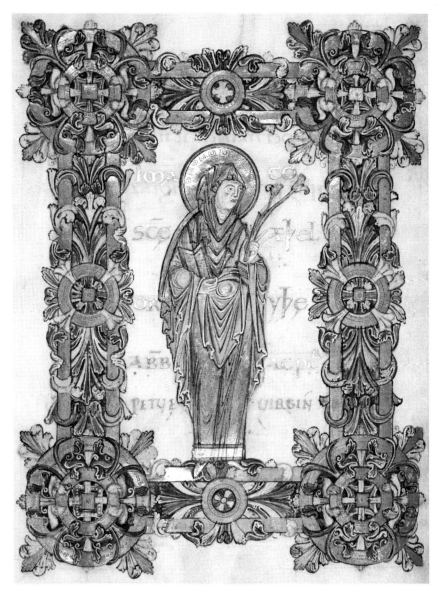

Æthelthryth, sometimes called Etheldreda (from the Benedictional of St Æthelwold, © The British Library Board, Add. 49598 f.90v)

Eventually the language changed substantially, so that after about 1500 the language becomes Modern English – what we speak today. Shakespeare wrote in Modern English. His poetry may be difficult to understand sometimes, but it was basically the same language that we communicate with –with a few tweaks here and there in terms of grammar and many changes in terms of vocabulary. English was 'made in the Middle Ages'.[4]

Latin

Medieval Christianity was rooted in Latin. Latin, the language of the ancient Romans, was used as the language of scholars in the Middle Ages. The main translation of the Bible from Hebrew and Greek was that of the fourth-century Church Father Saint Jerome into Latin, an elite language appropriate to scholars and those in the Church. It was the standard version of the Bible until the Protestant Reformation in the sixteenth century. Laws were typically written in Latin, which was seen as a permanent or eternal language. Theological, legal, medical, and poetic works were written in Latin. Even untutored peasants would repeat standard prayers in Latin while in church. This was true all over the world until Vatican II, a summit of Catholic leaders in the 1960s, which decided that people could start participating in the mass in their own tongue, not Latin. Monks and nuns were trained in Latin – the grammar, the holy words, and musical chants.

The vernacular, on the other hand, was the language of everyday speech. There were dozens of vernaculars: English, French, German, Spanish, Italian, and so on. But the mastery of Latin gave the speaker cultural authority and, with that, power. Language also had gender implications. Though numerous women learned Latin, over time it became a language identified with powerful, educated people – typically men. That means it was associated with the authority men wielded in what was a patriarchal society. It was only in the later Middle Ages that the vernaculars weakened the dominance that Latin maintained during the Middle Ages. Translations helped reduce the exclusive stranglehold Latin texts had on culture. Translations could be controversial since they allowed a new audience – including women and lower classes – to have access to knowledge formerly restricted to educated males.

The division and tension between oral and written medical information remained central to issues concerning gender and medicine throughout the

Middle Ages. For example, midwives only conversant in their native tongue and not Latin would have to wait until the fifteenth century for writings they could read or, if they were illiterate, have read to them. One literate woman could share a piece of writing with many others, thus sharing vital information. An early fifteenth-century Middle English translation of a text attributed to the female doctor Trota, called *Knowing of Woman's Kind in Childing*, addressed women helping women. This rare book explicitly stated it was written in English so that women could better understand it. The book warned men not to abuse women with private information about their gynecology. The manuscript stated, "[T]o assist women, I intend to write of how to help their secret maladies so that one woman may aid another in her illness and not divulge her secrets to such discourteous men".[5] Secrecy – while allowing women privacy – could disempower them if medical knowledge were not made available in the languages they were literate in.

A Latin medical work was intended for an exclusive, mainly male, audience, while a vernacular translation was designed for a more general audience including women. Male doctors seemed to have wanted to control women's access to such information. A medical work translated into a vernacular such as English would enable women to gain that knowledge for themselves, understand their own bodies, sicknesses, and cures, and give them power over their own bodies. The vernacular became a channel for authority for those who were denied access to the cultural power of Latin.

Learn more

- For letters to and from Leoba, look here: http://epistolae.ccnmtl.columbia.edu/woman/55.html.
- To examine the Benedictional of St Æthelwold, look here. Be sure to 'turn' the pages and see many lovely images. http://www.bl.uk/manuscripts/Viewer.aspx?ref=add_ms_49598_fs001r.
- Nicola Griffith's novel *Hild* (NY: Farrar, Straus and Giroux 2013) traces Hild's life from her girlhood and explores her impact on the Anglo-Saxon world.

Notes

1. Elizabeth Alvilda Petroff, *Medieval Women's Visionary Literature* (NY: Oxford University Press, 1986), 111.
2. Leo Sherley-Price, trans., *Bede: Ecclesiastical History of the English People*, revised by R. E. Latham; Introduction by D. H. Farmer (London: Penguin Books, 1990), 236.

3. *Ibid.*, 244.
4. Marcus Bull, *Thinking Medieval: An Introduction to the Study of the Middle Ages* (Basingstoke: Palgrave Macmillan, 2005), 4.
5. Monica H. Green, 'Women's Medical Practice and Health Care in Medieval Europe', *Signs* 14.2 (1989), 463; Beryl Rowland, ed. and trans., *Medieval Woman's Guide to Health: The First English Gynecological Handbook* (Kent, OH: Kent State University Press, 1981), 59.

PART II

FEARLESS FEMALES

Christina became an anchorite, a recluse voluntarily confined in a cell to contemplate God. Here is an image of a woman being enclosed by a bishop (early fifteenth century. Corpus Christi College, Cambridge, Parker Library MS CCC79, f. 96r (detail). Thanks to the Master and Fellows of Corpus Christi College, Cambridge)

CHAPTER 6

St Christina of Markyate (1096/98–1155/56)

RESOLUTE VIRGIN

Like Dorothy in *The Wizard of Oz*, many children and teenagers dream of running away from home. But while many think about it, few do so. And those that do often end up facing incredible challenges, even death. Christina of Markyate was a teen runaway who escaped her cruel parents, especially her abusive mother, only to suffer physical ordeals and emotional trials. Christina would be the ideal patron saint of runaways, watching over those so desperate they felt they had to leave their home. She would also be a perfect patron saint for those who are bullied, for she was physically and emotionally abused by none other than her own parents. Homeless, she fled to the only place of safety she could think of: a holy woman's sanctuary.

Wouldn't you think Christian parents would have been delighted to have had their daughter become a member of the church, the institution medieval society deemed most worthy spiritually here on earth and after death? Not Christina of Markyate's parents, Auti and Beatrix. They would have preferred to have her marry for money and position – and to make the connections they so desperately needed. Born after the Norman Conquest, Christina came into the world to an Anglo-Saxon family, whose position under their new overlords, the French-speaking Normans, was shaky. What better way to secure their position than have her marry illustriously? Who cares what Christina herself might have to say on the matter?

Born about 30 years after the Norman Conquest in the town of Huntington near Cambridge, Christina's real name was Theodora meaning 'Gift of God'. But early on she changed her name to match that of her favorite saint who fought for her virginity and defied oppressors – just like this Christina herself had to do. As was true in many virtuous women's lives, Christina's mother had a vision while pregnant. Beatrix saw a dove who nestled "in her lap, now in her bosom"[1] for seven days. This miraculous encounter showed that the infant would be graced by the Holy Spirit, often depicted as a dove in artwork.

As a child, Christina talked to God when she was in bed, "as if he were a man whom she could see. She did this in a high, piping voice".[2] When others heard her talking to God, they teased her mercilessly, causing Christina to stop. People weak and fearful enough to resort to cowardly teasing oppressed innocent faith. Christina was helped on her path to God by numerous supporters, just as all of us rely on special people who help us in times of need. Her first helper was Sueno, a monk. He pointed out how her path to remain a virgin was difficult. When others insulted him, Christina leapt to his defense: "If you have anything good to say, speak, and I will listen; if not, I am going."[3] Snap! If only all of us had her courage.

As a young teenager, she made a pilgrimage to the monastery dedicated to St Alban who had been killed for his faith. Many children like Christina were recorded as having made pilgrimages out of devotion to God or in hopes of a healing cure. Moved, Christina carved graffiti with her fingernail on the door – making the sign of the cross. Then she vowed to remain a virgin.

But the devil was determined to destroy her plan.

Christina's aunt, Ælfgifu, was the concubine or unoffical wife of the bishop of Durham, Ranulf. Although Ranulf and Ælfgifu had several children, Ranulf took one look at Christina and Satan "put into his heart an evil desire for her".[4] Ranulf brought the innocent girl to his chamber and made his wishes known. She carefully checked. The door was not yet bolted. She asked to be able to lock the door so no one could find them. He agreed. Whereupon Christina scurried to the door, opened it, and fled. Now imagine, for a moment, that you were a girl in the twelfth century listening or reading this story. What would you think? Ranulf was clearly the bad guy. Perhaps this story would make you want to devote your life to God too.

Unfortunately, this was "the beginning of all the calamitous troubles which followed". Christina scorned Ranulf's silken gifts. Furious at being made a fool, he persuaded a young man Beorhtred to become her betrothed, knowing this was against Christina's will. Her parents tried in vain to get her to agree. "I wish to remain chaste, for so I have vowed".[5] Her parents attempted everything: presents, cajoling, threats. Finally, they browbeat her into agreeing to become engaged (betrothed).

They never let up. She was put under guard. Her parents only allowed silly and frivolous company to accompany the maiden. They would not even let her visit a monastery dedicated to the Virgin. Christina stood firm: "Even though you can block my way to the monastery of my Lady, for certain you will never erase its memory in my heart."[6] They deliberately tried to make her drunk at a party, so that she would succumb to the charms of Beorhtred. They even allowed him into her bedroom. She greeted him "as if he had been her brother".[7]

Christina talked to Beorhtred about St Cecilia, a third-century martyr under the cruel rule of the pagan Roman Empire when Christianity was a renegade religion. On their wedding night, Cecilia told her new husband, Valerian, that she had a lover. Valerian quickened with anger, threatening to kill this other man, only to learn his rival was none other than Christ Himself. Cecilia persuaded her husband Valerian to remain chaste and dedicate his life to God. Valerian and his brother converted, were martyred, and became saints. Cecilia spoke defiantly with a cruel pagan governor. She merrily survived her torture and was executed, but not before converting people.

After telling this dramatic tale, Christina consoled Beorhtred: "Do not feel shame that I have spurned you". Beorhtred seemed open to her suggestions, but, when he was mocked by his friends as a "spineless and useless fellow", he returned. Christina hid before he could find her. She clung "trembling"[8] to a nail on the wall behind her bed curtains. Through God's help, she was not discovered.

St Cecilia, patron saint of music. (By Sir Edward Burne-Jones, stained and painted glass, c. 1900. Museum purchase, Surdna Fund (1974–84). Image © Princeton University Art Museum)

The torment never let up. Auti and Beatrix planned the wedding day, and, miraculously, the festival preparations burned up in a conflagration. Even her friend, the monk Sueno, abandoned Christina to her fate. "[W]hile the young woman stood firm, the man had faltered; unexpectedly, she was now abandoned and on her own in the midst of her enemies".[9] Auti, Christina's father, went to churchmen arguing, "[If Christina] resists our authority and rejects it, we shall be made the laughing-stock of our neighbors".[10] They only cared about their reputation, not Christina's feelings. A prior chastised Christina for being obstinate. When the prior insinuated that Christina wanted to break her engagement with Beorhtred because she had a richer bridegroom in mind, Christina retorted, "A more wealthy one certainly, for who is richer than Christ?"[11] She even agreed to be tested by ordeal with hot irons to prove that she had made an oath to virginity.

All seemed hopeless. Easily bribed, the bishop supported the parents who "did not know how to see beyond earthly possessions". But Christina "subverted her parents' expectations".[12] When Beorhtred agreed to Christina's demands, the parents, in a fury, stripped "her of all her clothes except her undershirt"[13] and prepared to send her out of the house, stopped only by the presence of a guest.

The official position of the church argued against forced marriages. In fact, a penitential – a church legal guidebook – dating from shortly before Christina's time explicitly stated: "Parents may not give a betrothed girl to another man unless she flatly refuses [to marry the original suitor]; but she may go to a monastery if she wishes. [A] girl of seventeen years has the power of her own body."[14]

Despite this, her mother Beatrix was unstoppable, even hiring "old crones who tried, using love potions and charms, to drive Christina out of her mind with lewd desires".[15] Needless to say, such schemes had no effect on this virtuous girl. The mother resorted to child abuse, grasping Christina by the hair and beating her. "The scars on her back never faded as long as she lived".[16] Only a vision of the Virgin Mary gave Christina hope for the future.

A scheme developed between Christina and a helpful hermit. He would aid her escape to hide in the cell of a holy woman, Ælfwynn. Christina hid male clothing for a disguise in the sleeve of her cloak, only to have her sister spot it. Pretending to visit the monastery, Christina made her way to the horses a helper had brought. "She seized one of them, but then hesitated, overcome with embarrassment. Why delay, oh fugitive? Why respect your

---

Anchorite

Being an anchorite was not for everyone. The process of being enclosed in a cell was ritually undertaken with a religious ceremony. 'Buried' from the cares of the world to pray, meditate, and dedicate themselves to God, anchorites had a window to see the altar of the church and participate in the mass. Another window allowed charitable visitors to give women food and drink and take away their waste. Anchorites could achieve renown and respect as holy women. Daily activities included reading the psalter, playing and listening to music, and studying religious works.

---

femininity? Put on manly courage and mount the horse like a man".[17] Which was exactly what she did. She hid in a tiny, uncomfortable cell for two years, hidden from her parents who vainly tried to seek her out.

People in Christina's day thought that the devil, angry at her successful escape, punished her in a bizarre way. As Christina sat and read a holy book in her confined space, ugly toads sat on the book, staring at her with frightening eyes. When she remained undaunted, singing holy songs, the toads gave up.

After two years with this holy woman, Christina moved to hide in the narrow closet of a kindly old hermit named Roger. For four years she stayed concealed in this secure but grueling spot. She barely had enough air to breathe and was only let out at night "to satisfy the demands of nature"[18] (go to the toilet). Thirsty and hungry, she endured these physical trials for the sake of spiritual triumph. At last she was rewarded when her fiancé, Beorhtred, inspired by his own vision of the Virgin Mary, released Christina of her vows.

Have you ever daydreamed? Have you ever been called for dinner, but were so intent on fanaticizing, you didn't even hear the voices summoning you? That's the state Christina was in – only she contemplated religious matters. She was said to be rapt, that is, in a state of rapture or other worldliness. Her visions occured when she suffered hardships, anguish, and grief in the trials forced on her by her scheming parents. Christina gained power through her visions as her devout nature became widely known. A woman with epilepsy was cured by drinking water the holy young woman had blessed. When

Christina herself suffered paralysis, "underneath [her] eye you could see the skin flickering without stopping, as if there were a little bird lurking inside striking it with its wings."[19] She was saved by "celestial medicine"[20] from the Virgin Mary. Now, the actual cause for these cures we can never know. What is important to consider is what medieval people believed.

Many men wanted her to join their religious institutions in order to enhance their own power, due to her reputation. She turned them down for Markyate where her beloved hermit and father figure Roger was buried. Christina took vows and became the superior over a number of other virgins in a religious community recognized as a priory in 1145. Christina's sister, Margaret, joined her in living a holy life.

Many holy men relied on holy women to teach or inspire them. By defending and protecting virgins, men increased their own spirituality. A number of men there became monks due to Christina's influence. Her authority was confirmed in a vision in which angels placed a crown from Christ Himself on her head. Many religious men and women had friendships devoted to God during the Middle Ages. Following in this tradition, Christina's dearest friend towards the end of her life was Abbot Geoffrey of St Albans. Like a nurturing father, he supported her and her community financially and politically, while she helped him in his spiritual journey to God. One of the last things we know about her was that King Henry II ordered 50 shillings to support Christina in 1155-6.

An elaborately illustrated book dating from the early twelfth-century, the Saint Albans Psalter, has been associated with Christina. While not the

> ### Christine Carpenter
>
> In 1329 Christine Carpenter wished to be granted permission to be "shut up in a narrow place in the churchyard adjoining the parish church" to "vow herself solemnly to continence and perpetual chastity". Within 3½ years, she requested to be reenclosed since she had "left her cell inconstantly and returned to the world". Although she could be excommunicated for having transgressed her vow, the letter bid that she be allowed to return, "lest by wandering any longer about the world she would be exposed to the bites of the rapacious wolf". This request was granted so that she might not be "torn to pieces by attacks of the Tempter [Satan]".[21] Her fate is unknown.

commissioner of the psalter, she was its first owner. It was even adapted to Christine and her story, including mention of the deaths of Roger, her parents, and her brothers. The psalter includes *The Life of Saint Alexis*, who, like Christina, broke a marriage vow to live a chaste life. An image of Christina was pasted in, suggesting how the Psalter was specifically adapted for Christina. Psalm 105 shows Christina on the left hand side of the image with a group of monks behind her; Christ stands in greeting on the right hand side of the page. Fantastically rich in illuminations, you can 'turn' pages of this manuscript online.

Christina was a woman of action, from keeping her vow of virginity to valiantly living in trying circumstances to withstanding public and familial resistance to her life's path. Long after Christina's death, women at Markyate rebelled against a papal decree (called the *Periculoso*) in 1298 ordering almost all nuns to be strictly enclosed – with virtually no ability to visit family without special license. When the Bishop of Lincoln visited the nuns in 1300 to explain this papal decree, "certain of the nuns, disobedient to these injunctions, hurled the said statute at his back and over his head and ... following the bishop to the outer gate of the house [declared] unanimously that they were not content in any way to observe such a statute".[22] Even after Christina's death, her vital presence and refusal to back down were a legacy to the women at Markyate.

Learn more
- You can digitally flip through an actual religious book owned by Christina of Markyate: http://www.abdn.ac.uk/stalbanspsalter/english/index.shtml. Be sure to check out page 285, under Psalm 105, where you can discover an image of Christina herself. http://www.abdn.ac.uk/stalbanspsalter/english/commentary/page285.shtml
- You can contemplate the advice given to such women in the thirteenth-century *Rule for Anchoresses*, including prohibitions on keeping any beast but a cat. See [http://www.bsswebsite.me.uk/History/AncreneRiwle/AncreneRiwle2.htm] to contemplate what would be expected of you.
- The film *Anchoress* (1993), based on the life of Christina Carpenter, imagines in stunning black and white photography the visions and everyday realities of this holy woman.

Notes

1. C. H. Talbot, trans., *The Life of Christina of Markyate: A Twelfth-Century Holy Woman*, edited by Samuel Fanous and Henrietta Leyser (Oxford: Oxford University Press, 2008), 3.
2. Talbot, 4.
3. Talbot, 5.
4. Talbot, 7.
5. Talbot, 8.
6. Talbot, 10.
7. Talbot, 11.
8. Talbot, 12.
9. Talbot, 14.
10. Talbot, 16.
11. Talbot, 18.
12. Talbot, 21.
13. Talbot, 23.
14. See Anglo-Saxon Penitentials. http://www.anglo-saxon.net/penance/.
15. Talbot, 24.
16. Talbot, 25.
17. Talbot, 34.
18. Talbot, 40.
19. Talbot, 50.
20. Talbot, 52.
21. *Christine Carpenter*. Brochure from St James' Church, Shere, England.
22. Elizabeth M. Makowski, *Canon Law and Cloistered Women:* Periculoso *and its commentators, 1298–1545* (Washington, DC: Catholic University of America Press, 1999), 115.

CHAPTER 7

Eleanor of Aquitaine
(c. 1124–1204)

QUEEN AND COUGAR

Politically powerful women are under constant scrutiny. Even today, stories can be made up about them to limit their influence. Eleanor of Aquitaine was one such woman, who, even after her death, was not left to rest in peace. Chroniclers and poets conjured up images of Eleanor that still taint her. The early thirteenth-century writer Helinand de Froidmont wrote she "behaved not like a queen but more like a [whore]".[1] And Matthew Paris in the mid-thirteenth century suggested that Eleanor was "engendered by the devil".[2] These examples were fictions dreamed up in a world determined to break the spirit of a strong-willed woman. Fact is even more intriguing than slurs and rumors.

William IX of Aquitaine, often called the first troubadour, was one of the most powerful and wealthy men in Europe. William's son died in 1137 while on pilgrimage to the immensely important pilgrimage site of Santiago de Compostela in northwestern Spain. This left his daughter, born about 1124, to inherit extensive lands and property. Overnight, she became the most eligible heiress in Europe. Her life became worthy, not just of a short troubadour lyric, but an opera filled with romance, tragedy, and adventure. Her name was Eleanor of Aquitaine.

Said by contemporaries to be *perpulchra* [more than beautiful], she was soon snapped up by Louis VI, the king of France, nicknamed Louis the Fat. Clad in scarlet, Eleanor married his son. Within a week, Louis was dead. The 13- or 14-year-old Eleanor and her 17-year-old husband were crowned king and queen of France. Her husband was now Louis VII and Duke of Aquitaine.

The Second Crusade drew Louis VII and his wife Eleanor, by now 24 years old, to the Holy Land in 1147. Their first daughter Marie had been born two years previously. It could be that Eleanor went with him in hopes of conceiving a male heir. Women were allowed to attend crusades, though canon law stipulated a woman should be accompanied by a male family

Left: Marriage of Eleanor of Aquitaine and Louis VII of France (1137); right: embarkation for Second Crusade 1147–1149 (from Chronique de St Denis, Musée Condé, Chantilly; with permission Universal History Archive/UIG/ Bridgeman Art Library)

member or, if married, be given her husband's consent. Other females known to accompany men were cooks, washerwomen, and prostitutes.

The expedition proved to be disastrous, both politically and personally. They arrived in Antioch, near the border of present day Turkey and Syria, in 1148, where her uncle, Raymond of Poitiers, ruled. However, gossips rumored that Eleanor was too close to the uncle, suggesting illicit behavior or at least indiscretion. Writing 1170–1184, William of Tyre transformed these suspicions into definite adultery. "[Raymond resolved to deprive Louis] of his wife, either by force or by secret intrigue. The queen readily assented to this design, for she was a foolish woman".[3] Rather than help Raymond in battles against the besieging Turks, Louis insisted on finishing his pilgrimage to Jerusalem. After their departure from the Holy Land, Raymond was killed in battle.

Travelling back to Europe in 1149 in separate ships, Eleanor met up with Louis in Sicily. Their marriage under stress, they visited with Pope Eugenius III. He wanted them to reconcile. Louis was delighted, as "he vehemently loved the queen, in an almost boyish fashion".[4] But Eleanor complained that "she had married a monk".[5] The Pope supposedly "provided a royally decorated bed upon which he urged them to resume marital relations".[6] Despite the subsequent birth of another daughter, Alice, the marriage was a failure.

Once they returned to France, Eleanor suddenly – conveniently? – remembered that they were closer relatives than married couples should be. On the shaky grounds of consanguinity or closeness of blood tie, she sought out an annulment – the dissolving of her marital bond by the church. She also had not provided Louis with any male heirs, 'only' daughters. Unlike for the women we have seen in Iceland, divorce in Europe was tricky to obtain. At last the annulment was granted in 1152. Her husband got custody of the girls, but Eleanor kept her lands and territories.

Still a hot commodity, other men sought Eleanor's hand in marriage. "[A]n incomparable woman; beautiful yet gracious, strong-willed yet kind, unassuming yet sagacious (which is a rare combination in a woman)."[7] Her wealth and prestige would enable her eventual husband to extend his own power. She was even kidnapped in an attempt to force her to marry. Eleanor knew what she wanted. Without asking permission of the proper authorities, she remarried only two months after being made a single woman – to a man nine years younger. Eleanor and Henry of Anjou had met the previous year at the French court in 1151. Once she and Louis were no longer legally wed, she approached Henry, informing him that she was now available. Some time later, the writer and satirist Andreas Capellanus dared to write that

---

The Crusades

A crusade was a war called by the Pope, rather than by a secular king. Crusaders took religious vows much like pilgrims to fight for what the participants felt was a just cause.[8] Yet the crusades did not always live up to these lofty goals. Jews were killed by Christian crusaders demanding Jerusalem, due to the city's association with Jesus Christ. Under Muslim control, the city was also seen as sacred to Islam. Several women ruled as queens in the Holy Land. For 30 years, Queen Melisende (d. 1161) ruled as both queen-regnant and then queen-regent of Jerusalem for her son. Our next medieval woman was a victim in this war-torn region – a geographical area plagued by religious strife.

Eleanor prefered the "embraces and solaces of young men"[9] to those of older men. She was the original cougar.

Two years after their marriage, her husband became King Henry II of England and Duke of Normandy in France. Since Eleanor had lands in Aquitaine, he also controlled her French lands, territories Eleanor had kept from the central French crown and which extended almost to the border of present-day France and Spain in the Pyrenees mountains. To the north, Henry's realm reached up to the Scottish border. His family, the Plantagenets, ended up ruling until the Tudor dynasty prevailed in the late fifteenth century. Now Eleanor had no trouble bearing male offspring. Between the years 1153 and 1166, they had together eight children, of whom six survived to adulthood. Five (*possibly* a sixth who died young or was stillborn) sons were born (William in 1153 who died at age three; Henry in 1155, Richard in 1157, Geoffrey in 1158; John in 1166), along with three daughters (Matilda in 1156, Eleanor in 1161, and Jeanne or Joanna/Joan in 1165). At one point Eleanor was pregnant and had three children under the age of three, yet nonetheless traveled between England and the continent. A queen's duties were manifold and included legal duties, arranging strategically appropriate marriages for her children, and negotiating political situations to favor her interests. She also served as regent (like a substitute king) when Henry was overseas, and in his stead in Aquitaine from 1168 to 1174.

Eleanor was dynamic, attractive, educated, passionate, and confident. She was a superstar. A German student wrote this poem in praise of her: "Were the world all mine / From the sea to the Rhine, / I'd give it all / If so be the Queen of England / Lay in my arms".[10] She had artistic leanings. Eleanor and her daughter by Louis, Marie de Champagne, eventually held sway over a lavish court where some believe troubadours, poets, and composers thrived. Among their protégés, we can number Bernart de Ventadorn, the eminient troubadour. As he wrote about an unnamed lady, "I've lost all right / To rule my life; my life's her prize / Since first she showed me true delight / In those bright mirrors, her two eyes".[11] Could those two mirrors have belonged to Eleanor? Other members of her literary salon were Chrétien de Troyes and Thomas of England, whose Arthurian poems and tale of Tristan and Isolde lie at the heart of our image of King Arthur and his circle of knights. Chrétien dedicated his story *The Knight of the Cart* about Lancelot's tribulations in love to Eleanor's daughter. Marie de France, who merits her own chapter in this book, may have been likewise supported in this atmosphere.

Adela of Normandy (c. 1067–1137)

What did wives do when their husbands went on Crusade? Born about 1067, Adela of Normandy was highly educated, well-versed in Latin, and educated in the nunnery in Caen, northern France, founded by her parents. Her father was William of Normandy who conquered Anglo-Saxon England in 1066. Betrothed at age 13, she married Stephen of Blois, an important count from northern France, 2 years later. He went on Crusade, laying siege to Antioch in October 1097. While today we may see this as dreadful interference in an autonomous land, the Christian Crusaders' perspective was that it was righteous battle.

Adela ruled Blois while her husband was off at war and took care of their eight children, making education a key element of their lives. In a letter home, Stephen bid Adela to continue her good job: "I instruct you to do well and govern your lands excellently and deal with your children and your people honorably, as befits you, because you will certainly see me as soon as I can."[12] After his death in 1102, she continued to be a powerful negotiator, ruling as countess. She actively supported the church, religious communities, and charitable organizations, including a leper hospital. In her early 50s, Adela retired to a nunnery in 1120, which she ultimately ruled as prioress until her death in 1137 at the age of 70. Her son, Stephen of Blois, became King of England 1135–1154.

The satisfaction brought by this rich cultural atmosphere was balanced by the demands made by Eleanor's husband, Henry II. Ultimately his grown sons swarmed in revolt against their father, a rebellion the father ultimately succeeded in putting down. Eleanor aided and abetted her offspring in their endeavors as her marriage to Henry cooled. Peter of Blois wrote her a letter at the request of the church, in which he encouraged her to return to her husband:

> [T]he woman is at fault who leaves her husband and fails to keep the trust of this social bond … She is created from him, she is united to him, and she is subject to his power …[Y]ou will be the cause of widespread disaster. While you alone are now the delinquent one, your actions will result in ruin for everyone in the kingdom.[13]

'Fair Rosamund and Queen Eleanor'. This painting imagines Eleanor threatening her rival – Henry II's mistress, Rosamund (Edward Burne-Jones (1861); Yale Center for British Art, Paul Mellon Fund)

Henry went so far as to imprison her – his own wife – in 1174. She stayed locked up in house arrest until Henry's death and her son Richard's takeover of the crown – 16 years later.

Eleanor was not the only one in the family to have been involved in the Crusades. Her eldest son Richard I 'the Lionheart' participated in the Third Crusade in 1189–1192. In 1192, shipwrecked on his way home from the Holy Land, Richard continued on land, stopping in Austria, an area rife with enemies. While there, rumored to have been in the disguise of a servant cooking a chicken, he was captured. Imprisoned, he was ransomed by his enemies. Eleanor, 70 years of age, raised money for his release by using her lands in southern France and wielding power in England to put enough money together. She chastised the Pope, Saint Peter's representative on earth, for not doing more to stand up to Emperor Henry VI who was holding Richard hostage. Eleanor did not mince words: "Why then have you, so negligent, so cruel, done nothing for so long about the release of my son or is it rather that you do not dare?"[14] She was relentless in the defense of her child, refusing to soften her language.

During Richard's absence, Eleanor was in charge. She worked to control another son, John,[15] who threatened to take over the crown in his brother's absence. After Richard's return in 1194, Eleanor lived through his assassination by arrow. Actively involved in her sons' politics at court, first under Richard (d. 1199), she assured John's attainment of the throne. She strengthened the defensive fortresses along the coast of England – the threat of a French invasion haunted English strategic plans. Eleanor undertook financial and territorial transactions with regard to her property in France. Dozens of charters over her lifetime attest to her distinctly formidable rulership. Eleanor negotiated with the Papacy. Her husband Henry had essentially ordered the murder of the Archbishop of Canterbury, Thomas Becket in 1170. So it made sense to stay on the good side of the Church. A letter from Hildegard von Bingen consoled Eleanor:

> Your mind is like a wall battered by a storm. You look all around, and you find no rest. Stay calm, and stand firm, relying on God and your fellow creatures, and God will aid you in all your tribulations. May God give you His blessing and His help in all your works.[16]

Stand firm – like Hrotsvit's virgin martyrs.

As was true for many women, widowhood proved to be the most powerful time of her life. While married, a woman's legal identity was united with her husband's. Once widowed, she became legally recognized and attained the power to control lands and estates. Eleanor even made a trip when she was almost 80 years old to Paris to witness the marriage between her 12-year-old granddaughter, Blanche of Castile, and the future Louis VIII. This granddaughter inherited Eleanor's political savvy, ruling for 8 years after her husband's death until her son became old enough to rule himself. Two of Blanche's children became saints. Eleanor's bloodline spawned other women of strength, determination, and wisdom.

As many noblewomen did, Eleanor ended her life in a monastery, that of Fontevrault in her native France.

Founded on land granted by her grandparents, one of its abbesses was Henry II's aunt, so it was a family industry. In a double abbey that an abbess ruled, contemplative women were supported by holy men. Robert d'Abrissel, who founded the abbey, made sure a worldly woman would be in charge on his death. The complex included communities for noble women, for reformed prostitutes and poor women, for lepers, and for men. The main female community dominated the area. Eleanor must have appreciated the power maintained by this female-dominated religious institution. Henry II and Eleanor were entombed there, along with their son Richard I. Depicted lying down, she was shown in the active stance of reading. A book nestles open in her hands. What was she reading? A Book of Hours? A Psalter? Or was she reading about women like herself – undaunted and dynamic medieval women?

Effigy of Eleanor of Aquitaine (Fontevrault Abbey, France, with permission Bridgeman Art Library)

Learn more

- Excellent films help recreate this time period. The Oscar-winning *The Lion in Winter* (1968) dramatically imagines the marriage of Eleanor and Henry II when they were older. *Becket* (1964) focuses on the fraught and ultimately tragic friendship between Henry II and the Archbishop of Canterbury, Thomas Becket [http://youtu.be/XM6nWIcevOE]. A classic novel about the young Eleanor is Kristiana Gregory's *Eleanor: Crown Jewel of Aquitaine, France, 1136* (2002), in the Royal Diaries series. Many novels about her life continue to be written, including *Captive Queen* by Alison Weir (Ballantine 2010) and *The Summer Queen* by Elizabeth Chadwick (Sourcebooks 2014).
- For actual letters written to and from Eleanor, check this resource: http://epistolae.ccnmtl.columbia.edu/woman/24.html#letterslist.
- Enjoy wonderful Arthurian romances by Chrétien de Troyes that may have been read at Eleanor's court. http://www.gutenberg.org/files/831/831-h/831-h.htm#link2H_4_0005. Start with *Yvain, the Knight of the Lion* where the hero, torn between his duty to his beloved and his knightly prowess, goes mad.

Notes

1. Peggy McCracken, 'Scandalizing Desire: Eleanor of Aquitaine and the Chroniclers', in *Eleanor of Aquitaine: Lord and Lady*, edited by Bonnie Wheeler and John C. Parsons (NY: Palgrave Macmillan, 2002), 250.
2. Fiona Tolhurst, 'What Ever Happened to Eleanor? Reflections of Eleanor of Aquitaine in Wace's *Roman de Brut* and Lawman's *Brut*', in Wheeler and Parsons, 324.
3. McCracken, 248.
4. Elizabeth A. R. Brown, 'Eleanor of Aquitaine Reconsidered: The Woman and her Seasons', in Wheeler and Parsons, 7.

5. Margaret Aziza Pappano, 'Marie de France, Aliénor d'Aquitaine, and the Alien Queen', in Wheeler and Parsons, 347.

6. Lois L. Huneycutt, '*Alianora Regina Anglorum*: Eleanor of Aquitaine and Her Anglo-Norman Predecessors as Queens of England', in *Women and Gender in Medieval Europe: An Encyclopedia*, edited by Margaret Schaus (NY: Routledge, 2006), 244.

7. Anne Crawford, ed., *Letters of the Queens of England, 1100–1547* (Stroud: Sutton, 1997), 34.

8. Marcus Bull, *Thinking Medieval: An Introduction to the Study of the Middle Ages* (Basingstoke: Palgrave Macmillan, 2005), 121.

9. Carolyne Larrington, *Women and Writing in Medieval Europe: A Sourcebook* (London: Routledge, 1995), 47.

10. Margaret Wade Labarge, *A Small Sound of the Trumpet: Women in Medieval Life* (Boston: Beacon Press, 1986), 50.

11. Robert Kehew, *Lark in the Morning: The Verses of the Troubadours A Bilingual Edition* (Chicago: University of Chicago Press, 2005), 75, translated by W. D. Snodgrass.

12. Helen Nicholson, *The Crusades* (Westport, CT: Greenwood Press, 2004), 133.

13. Peter of Blois, Letter 154 to Queen Eleanor, 1173 from http://www.fordham.edu/halsall/source/eleanor.asp.

14. Crawford, 41.

15. The king in the Robin Hood films, who allows the sheriff of Nottingham to squeeze money from the poor until the heroic Richard the Lionheart returns to save the day.

16. Joseph L. Baird, ed., *The Personal Correspondence of Hildegard of Bingen* (Oxford: Oxford University Press, 2006), 78–9.

CHAPTER 8

Margaret of Beverley (c.1150–c.1214/15)

FIGHTING CRUSADER

document from 1366 tells the incredible story of Isolda Parewastel who survived horrors, only to ask permission to build a chapel in thanks for not dying:

> For three years [Isolda] has daily visited the Lord's Sepulchre and other holy places of the Holy Land, and has there been stripped and placed head downwards on a rack [a torture instrument], and beaten; then, half dead, she miraculously escaped from the Saracens.[1]

Isolda survived this torture, triumphing to return home to Bridgwater, England and establish a chapel devoted to the veneration of the Virgin Mary. She was not the only woman to survive hardship and imprisonment while far from home. Margaret of Beverley's dramatic life was recorded by her brother Thomas, who realized the importance of detailing his bold sister's adventures.

Margaret was born in Jerusalem to English parents, Sibilla and Hulno, who

---

Egeria (fourth century)

"You know how inquisitive I am".[2] Women travelled on pilgrimage to see sights sacred to both the Hebrew Bible and Christian Scripture in the early centuries after Christ's death. One of these early travellers was Egeria, who recounted her journey taken between 381 and 383 CE. Travelling from Gaul (present-day France), she visited both Christian and Jewish holy places in Palestine and Egypt. Appropriate Bible passages, read aloud at sacred places, allowed Egeria to relive Christ's life. Her descriptions of local customs and religious practices make her account an incredibly valuable resource for historians and scholars of religious women today.

The Flight into Egypt (from The Hours of Jeanne d'Évreux, Queen of France. By Jean Pucelle (French, active in Paris, 1319–1334, manuscript from c. 1324–1328; Metropolitan Museum of Art, The Cloisters Collection, 1954 (54.1.2) © The Metropolitan Museum of Art. ARTstor: MMA_IAP_10313503406)

went there on pilgrimage. Margaret's parents must have been very devout to have undertaken such a grueling journey, travelling the long distance across Europe to the Mediterranean, during Sibilla's pregnancy. Like the original Holy Family – the Virgin Mary, Joseph, and the infant Jesus – they explored the geographical area Christians, Jews, and Muslims find sacred.

While in Palestine, Margaret experienced a miraculous event as a baby. Sibilla had recently given birth. Baby Margaret was seated on a donkey. As they crossed fertile land, a wolf approached eating some bloody meat. None of them was strong enough to repel the beast. To protect them, Margaret's father ripped off a branch from a tree and dragged it behind him playfully. Every time the wolf approached the small group, her father shook the branch, frightening away the wolf, who finally abandoned them. They then journeyed back to England safely.

A number of years later, Margaret's brother Thomas was born. Their parents died, leaving Margaret, 11 years older than Thomas, to care for and raise her baby brother. She brought him to school, an endeavor that paid off. He ultimately became a member of the entourage of the Archbishop of Canterbury – the most important churchman in England. This Archbishop was none other than Thomas Becket, whose later murder and martyrdom led to pilgrims flocking to Canterbury Cathedral in his honor. Margaret's brother entered the Cistercian monastery at Froidmont in France. His career safely launched, she decided to return to the land of her birth. Unfortunately, she returned in 1187 just as the great Muslim leader, Saladin, decided to reclaim Jerusalem from Christians and bring it under Muslim control. Muslims, after all, controlled the land surrounding the city, a metropolis of holy devotion for the three great monotheistic religions of the time: Christianity, Islam, and Judaism.

Margaret lived in Jerusalem as the city came under siege by Saladin's troops on September 18, 1187. They had recently attacked and overtook many other cities in the region, including Acre, Beirut, and Jaffa. Jerusalem was mobbed with refugees from these other defeated cities. During the siege, enemy soldiers surrounded the city, not allowing food or water to enter and attacking it with weapons. Everyone living in this urban nightmare had to participate in its defense.

Forced to stay, Margaret willingly set to work. "[L]ike a fierce virago, I tried to play the role of a man".[3] She told how:

> During this siege, which lasted fifteen days, I carried out all of the functions of a soldier that I could. I wore a breastplate like a man; I came and went on the ramparts, with a cauldron on my head for a helmet. Though a woman, I seemed a warrior, I threw the weapon; though filled with fear, I learned to conceal my weakness.[4]

Sometimes women had to improvise using what implements they had to protect themselves. Margaret cleverly used something identified with women and women's work – a cauldron for cooking – to protect her head from heavy objects catapulted by the enemy. She was able to use a symbol of female indoor domestic use, transforming it into a public sign of her ingenuity.

The heat was blistering. The soldiers inside the city had to battle continually to prevent their enemies from entering. Women helped by using weapons and machines such as catapults when not enough men were available, filling in ditches, and providing food and drink. Once, when Margaret gave water to the men to drink, a catapult sent a millstone over the walls. It burst apart. A small piece of stone flew off and struck her, causing blood to gush out. Tended to immediately, Margaret carried the scar throughout her life. By October 2, about two weeks after the tumult had begun, the siege was over. After being taken prisoner, Margaret was ransomed by paying some money and set free.

Saladin won. He went down in history as a magnanimous and chivalric victor. Even his Christian enemies admitted his generosity. One legend told how a little baby girl was stolen from a Christian woman. When she protested, Saladin recovered the child, returning her to the grieving mother. Controlling Jerusalem, Saladin permitted Christian pilgrimage and access to the Church of the Holy Sepulchre, a church built on the site where Christ was believed to have been crucified and buried. Nevertheless, leaders in Europe were determined to claim Jerusalem for Christians. Masses of armies from Europe – England, France, and the Holy Roman Empire – converged on the eastern Mediterranean. One of those leaders was none other than Richard I of England, 'the Lionheart', son of Eleanor of Aquitaine, who lived her own extraordinary adventure. Margaret's trials coincided with the lead-up to the Third Crusade.

European women came on the Crusades in many capacities. Noblewomen joined their husbands or brothers, while women further down the social ladder undertook chores of all kinds. Sources documented washerwomen

---

Muslim and Christian encounters

Love matches between Christians and Muslims were not infrequently alluded to in the Middle Ages. One biased account described Eleanor of Aquitaine falling in love with the great Muslim leader, Saladin – though in reality he would have only been 12 at their supposed meeting. In the violent *Romance of Richard the Lion-Heart*, Eleanor, renamed Cassodorien, married her Christian husband. Swooning and falling "like a ghost"[7] during church, she ultimately escaped by flying "out of the roof".[8] In Chaucer's *Man of Law's Tale*, the Christian princess Constance married a worthy Muslim, the sultan of Syria, who converted for her sake. The marriage does not last long, as the sultan's mother kills all the converts and puts Constance on a rudderless boat.

accompanying male crusaders, even picking lice from the warriors' bodies and hair. While multiple Muslim sources showed Muslim women prepared to fight emotionally, only Christian women were referenced as actually joining in military campaigns, some even wearing armor. One account described a female archer wearing a green cloak: "There was a woman on one of the points of the defense holding a bow of wood, firing well and drawing blood; she did not stop fighting until she was killed."[5] Dead women were found on the battlefield, attesting to their presence among the fighters.

Margaret's adventures were far from over. She and others freed from the siege began to walk toward Lachish, possibly Laodicea in today's Turkey. Suddenly, they found themselves surrounded by the enemy. For 15 months, from October 1187 until February 1189, she was a prisoner, forced to "carry out humiliating tasks; I gathered stones, I chopped wood. If I refused to obey, I was beaten with rods."[6] She never protested, enduring it all: the extreme weather, the beatings, and the threats. "My chains rusted from my tears". She was fed very little and the bruises took their toll. Refusing to give up, Margaret told how she kept sane despite the brutal torture and humiliation. "I did not give in to the torment. My inviolate faith always won the victory." At last, a generous Christian merchant from the city of Tyre (Sūr, Lebanon today) freed her and 24 of her fellow slaves after a 15-month captivity.

Dressed only in a sack from her days of captivity, Margaret commented that "[I]t scarcely covered my nudity". Her only possession was her holy book, a Psalter. For five days all she had to eat was one loaf of bread and the roots of plants she managed to scavenge. "Alone, troubled, lost, I saw nothing except solitude". One day she even woke up covered in snow. Fearful of crossing a river, she eventually plucked up the courage to cross all 12 streams she had to ford to make her way to safety. To support herself, she worked as a washerwoman.

Upon arrival in Antioch, home to the shrine of St Margaret, she gave thanks to her namesake and patron saint. Just as St Margaret was freed from the belly of a dragon, Margaret of Beverley was likewise liberated: from within the city of Jerusalem, from her slavery, and from her pitiful pilgrimage in penury.

While she was in Antioch in July 1188, Saladin's troops arrived and a skirmish ensued between the Muslim and Christian armies. Margaret was again endangered, particularly when she was accused of stealing a knife. Arrested, her execution was planned. Could St Margaret help? Imprisoned, alone, unable to speak the local language, and terrified, Margaret uttered

The patron saint of Margaret of Beverley was St Margaret, who burst forth from inside a dragon after being swallowed. She is the patron saint of childbirth (Saint Margaret with a Lady Donor is attributed to the Luçon Master (c. 1405); museum purchase, John Maclean Magie, Class of 1892, and Gertrude Magie Fund, (1992–163); photo: Bruce M. White. Image © Princeton University Art Museum)

"the name of St Mary. At this name the chief of the Infidels [was] amazed, this faithless man [became] benevolent and pious". Moved, he freed her.

In gratitude for her miraculous welfare, Margaret continued her pilgrimage of thanksgiving. By the summer of 1191, she arrived in Acre. With the Third Crusade ending in a peace treaty between Richard I and Saladin in 1192, Margaret could return to Europe. She visited numerous pilgrimage shrines, including Rome and Santiago de Compostela in Spain. After all these adventures, Margaret yearned to return to her brother, Thomas, and found him at his monastery in France. Remember, Thomas had not seen her for years. Margaret had to prove who she was.

> My father had three children. You see in me the only daughter he had ... Why do you hesitate any longer. It was Sibilla who gave us to the light of the day; she was our mother. Hulno was our father.

Medieval women of color

Women of color were known to medieval European people. The wealth of the Queen of Sheba (Ethiopia or Yeman) tantalized King Solomon in the Bible (*First Kings* 10:1–3 and *2 Chronicles* 9:1–12) and she appears in the Qur'an, where Suleiman (Solomon) persuades her to become monotheistic and follow Allah. Christine de Pizan wrote of this queen: "She herself instituted laws of far-reaching justice for governing her people ... [S]he had so lofty a heart that she did not deign to marry, nor did she desire that any man be at her side."[9] A later queen of medieval Islam, Sayyida Hurra (1048–1138, her full name is Arwa al-Sayyida al-Hurra Al-Sulayhi), ruled powerfully in Yemen. In Wolfram von Eschenbach's *Parvizal*, the knight Gahmuret married the black queen Belacane, a Muslim. "It seemed to Gahmuret that ... a more affectionate spirit of womanliness had never stolen over a woman's heart ... With thoughts of the dusky Moorish Queen he fell from swoon to swoon."[10] While he ultimately abandoned her, their black and white magpie-colored son became a companion and friend to the Arthurian hero Parzival (Perceval in the French) years later. In fifteenth-century Valencia, Spain, freed and enslaved Africans provided medical services for their fellow patriots, such as Ursola who had been beaten by her master. They even might have negotiated for the release of some held in captivity.

Hearing his parents' names, Thomas realized who she was and burst into tears along with his older sister. Thereafter, she told her life story which he wrote down. After such a tumultuous life, Margaret took her brother's advice and entered the nunnery of Montreuil-sous-Laon not far from her brother's monastery. A Cistercian lay-sister, she stayed there until she died about 1214 or 1215.

Just before her death, Pope Innocent III called on everyone to go on crusade – not literally, but by funding the armed knights who would fight in the Holy Land. In earlier days, pious women had gone with their husbands; others even went alone. Starting in the thirteenth century, women were discouraged from attending a crusade. It became an activity approved of exclusively for men. For those women who stayed behind, particularly those in Cistercian convents, tending to the poor and sick became a kind of substitute for crusading. Margaret was a crusader, whether sporting a cooking pot as a helmet during warfare or aiding a sickly patient at her convent.

Learn more

- Read Margaret of Beverley's story: http://www.umilta.net/jerusalem.html.
- You can read about the peace treaty between Richard I and Saladin here: http://www.fordham.edu/halsall/source/1192peace.asp.
- A fabulous Egyptian film tells about the Crusades from the Islamic point of view: *El Naser Salah el Dine* (1963), in Arabic with English subtitles, about Saladin, Richard III, and Louise, a woman warrior.
- To see images of people of color in European art history, including in the Middle Ages, check out this website: http://www.imageoftheblack.com/. The second volume, parts 1 and 2, of this book series edited by David Bindman and Henry Louis Gates, Jr., focuses on medieval arts.

Notes

1. W. H. Bliss, ed., *Papal Petitions to the Pope 1342–1419*, Vol. I (London: Eyre and Spottiswoode, 1896), 512–513 and Susan Signe Morrison, *Women Pilgrims in Late Medieval England: Private Piety as Public Performance* (London: Routledge, 2000), 59.
2. John Wilkinson, *Egeria's Travels to the Holy Land* (Jerusalem: Ariel, 1981), 111–112.
3. Helen Nicholson, *The Crusades* (Westport, CT: Greenwood Press, 2004), 119.
4. Nicholson 2004, 119.
5. Helen Nicholson, 'Women on the Third Crusade', *Journal of Medieval History* 23.4 (1997), 338.
6. This and all subsequent quotes from Margaret's life from http://www.umilta.net/jerusalem.html.

7. Bradford B, Broughton, ed. and trans., *'Richard the Lion-Hearted' and Other Medieval English Romances* (NY: E. P. Dutton, 1966), 154.
8. Broughton, 155.
9. Christine calls her Empress Nicaula, after the Roman historian Josephus. From Christine de Pizan, *The Book of the City of Ladies*, translated by Earl Jeffrey Richards (NY: Persea Books, 1982), 33; also 105.
10. Wolfram von Eschenbach, *Parzival*, translated by A. T. Hutto (Harmondsworth, England: Penguin, 1982), 27, 30.

PART III
WOMEN OF WISDOM

St Anne, Anna's namesake, is shown here teaching her daughter the Virgin Mary to read (The Education of the Virgin). Anna was likewise very studious (attributed to the Master of Saint Benedict. Philadelphia Museum of Art: purchased with funds contributed by Elizabeth Malcolm Bowman in memory of Wendell Phillips Bowman from the Edmond Foulc Collection, 1930)

CHAPTER 9

Anna Komnene (1083–1153)

DUTIFUL DAUGHTER

How obedient a child are you? Would you delay your own birth at your mother's request? Born to the Byzantine emperor Alexios I Komnenos and his wife, Irene, Anna dutifully waited to enter the world for two days until her father came home. Her mother asked Anna in her womb to "wait a while, little one, till your father's arrival".[1] This obedience signaled how Anna continued to support her parents through their lives and even after their deaths by writing *The Alexiad*, an epic history of her father's reign. He ruled during the time of the First Crusade. Anna shared many lively details of this violent and disruptive time when European leaders began their forays into what we now call the Middle East – countries like Syria, Palestine, Israel, and Lebanon. Well over 100,000 Europeans poured into this area through Byzantium. While the stated intent of the crusade was to 'take back' the Holy Land and place it under Christian control, Anna suggested that the true motivation was to take over her father's empire and its main city, the palatial Constantinople (today's Istanbul).

St Anne teaching the Virgin Mary

Anna's name hearkens to that of St Anne, who was often depicted in art teaching her daughter, the Virgin Mary, how to read. Images endorsing the education of young females may have reflected the actual practice of mothers teaching daughters to read so that they could be better Christians. Depictions of the Annunciation, when the angel Gabriel announces to Mary that she, a virgin, will bear God's child, Jesus, typically show her reading the Psalms. These visual representations of a woman reading with an open book suggest that women's literacy existed or was to be aspired to.

Anna had been well educated as a princess should be. Grounded in the standard education of the time, she tells of learning Greek, Aristotle's and Plato's writings, and the "*Quadrivium* of sciences".[2] Not "boasting", she describes her training to inform us of "what God has apportioned to me from above and what has been contributed by circumstance".[3] She loved learning. "[S]he made dates with her beloved grammar, just as young girls secretly gaze at their betrothed through some opening."[4]

Women were powerful in Anna's land. They could inherit property, making them more than mere pawns in male political exchange through marriage. Anna had long-held ambitions to rule after her father's death. Loyally staying beside her father while he was on his deathbed, she witnessed the illness and pain her father suffered. "God knows I took great trouble over the preparation of his food."[5] Meanwhile, her brother, John II, gained support of key military and government leaders, even snatching the imperial ring from his dying father's body. Later, Anna tried – and failed – to usurp the throne from her own brother by raising her own army. "My own lot has been far from fortunate … I have not enjoyed good luck … full of troubles, full of revolution … I have been conversant with dangers ever since my birth."[6] John banished her to the convent of Kecharitomene where she wrote her masterpiece, modeled on Homer's *Iliad* and *Odyssey*, the ancient Greek epics about the Trojan War, the warriors Achilles and Hector, the wily Odysseus, and the alluring Helen of Troy.

Sometimes called the only secular woman historian of the Middle Ages, Anna put this story down for posterity once she was in her 60s and living in a monastery at the end of the life, a common lifestyle choice for aging nobility. History attracted her since it prevented the restless stream of time from carrying things away irrevocably. Charmingly, she referenced the very act of writing while nodding over her intense labor. "As I write these words, it is nearly time to light the lamps; my pen moves slowly over the paper and I feel myself almost too drowsy to write as the words escape me."[7] Even a great historian can feel the fatigue and weariness of hard work. As one writer praised her after she died, Anna "exchanged the spindle and thread for the reed pen and the book".[8] Rather than using implements associated with typical woman-identified activities like spinning and sewing, Anna opts for the manly instruments of writing and reading.

Learn more

- Anna appears as the character Anna Comnenus, a Byzantine princess and diplomat, in the video game (rated T for Teen) *Medieval II: Total Warfare.*

Notes

1. Anna Komnene, *The Alexiad*, translated by E. R. A. Sewter; Rev. Peter Frankopan (London: Penguin Books, 2009), 167.
2. Thalia Gouma-Peterson, ed., *Anna Komnene and Her Times* (NY: Garland Publishing, 2000), 4.
3. Komnene/Sewter, 3.
4. Gouma-Peterson, 4.
5. Komnene/Sewter, 468.
6. Komnene/Sewter, 6.
7. Komnene/Sewter, 373.
8. Gouma-Peterson, 125.

The Bible tells how Adam and Eve were kicked out of Eden by an angel after eating the apple. Views about Eve affected understandings of the female body in the Middle Ages. Note the female-headed serpent between the couple (The Expulsion of Adam and Eve by a follower of Van der Weyden in present-day Belgium (mid-fifteenth century); Metropolitan Museum of Art, The Cloisters Collection, 1949 (49.109) © The Metropolitan Museum of Art. ARTstor: MMA_IAP_10311978032)

CHAPTER 10

Understanding the Female Body

Some things about the Middle Ages are certainly upsetting to read about. Yet, if we want to appreciate the past, we need to try to understand how people viewed the world at that time. One element in the world is the human body. Ancient Greek philosophy beginning with Plato established a distinction between body and soul, with the soul seen as the desirable element in a being and the body seen as the matter that negatively affects the soul's desire for virtue. In Western philosophy, the soul or mind has hierarchically dominated over the body or flesh. In the fourth century BCE, the Greek philosopher Aristotle wrote about theatre, ethics, politics, poetry, metaphysics – you name it. He was also interested in natural philosophy – what we call science. Aristotle established certain ideas that many Christian thinkers accepted. Aristotle's works had been translated into Arabic in the early Middle Ages; from the twelfth to the thirteenth centuries the mass of this material was 'rediscovered' for Christian scholars from Latin translations out of the Arabic.

Medieval women's bodies were understood in the context of both Greek and Roman medical traditions. The most important was the assertion that men provide the *form* or ability to create movement in the creation of a baby, while women provided the *matter* or *flesh*. Given Aristotle's distinction between men and women, men – who provided the higher principle – must inherently be superior to women – who were associated with the body. "[T]he female is as it were a deformed male."[1]

Grounded in this philosophical source, one dominant strand of Christianity confirmed the rejection of the body for the soul or spirit. Generally speaking, misogynist or anti-woman attitudes and laws existed. Men typically – though not always as we have seen – held the dominant positions of power. Women could be put down, even by respected churchmen. Church Fathers reading the Jewish Torah saw Eve as the epitome of flesh or matter deceiving the spirit as embodied by Adam. Only a virgin woman, untainted by the filth of sexuality, could bring forth the Son of God. Eve and the fall from the Garden of Eden opened the way for Isidore of Seville (*c.* 570–636) to argue that Eve was the "origin of ... disaster and woe".[2] St. Tertullian suggested that women were "the gateway of the devil",[3] encouraging them to "paint [their] eyes with modesty".[4] A twelfth-century abbot warned men that a woman's anger makes females "poisonous animals ... [T]he poison of asps and dragons is more curable and less dangerous to men than the familiarity of women."[5]

Not all women were vilified. The theory put forth by the second-century scientist Galen, acknowledging that the man and woman each provided a 'seed' to engender a child, repressed the anti-woman nature of some Christian thought. Positive female role models included many women from the Bible. Jewish heroines like Deborah, Ether, and Judith were strong and virtuous actors. Even Eve was considered "our first mother". Christian women were encouraged to be like men spiritually and, by doing so, "rise above her sex".[6] This religious virago would, in a sense, no longer be a mere woman. By triumphing over her weakness – which many people in the Middle Ages equated with femininity – she would be praised as strong and virtuous. Writings advised women not to marry since they would thereby lose their freedom to a controlling husband. Virginity was seen as a kind of women's liberation, a way to fulfill one's womanhood without being oppressed by a husband and threatened by the dangers and pain of childbirth.

Celibacy and chastity would allow women – and men – to escape the gender expectations society tried to place on them. As St Jerome wrote, as:

> long as woman is for birth and children, she is different from men as body is from the soul. But when she wishes to serve Christ more than the world, then she will cease to be a woman and will be called a man.[7]

As one male wrote to a nun, "Conquer the woman; conquer the flesh; conquer desire".[8] These virile women became as worthy as men. Men remained the default gender to admire.

The most important female figure in the Middle Ages was the Virgin Mary. She inspired countless artistic images, poems, plays, and church dedications. This ideal woman and mother was a figure for women to emulate. Her status as virgin mother helped make virginity a desired state for women, a status of power, not denial. In fact, Hildegard von Bingen wrote a song in praise of the Virgin. Hildegard reclaimed women's bodies as containing the possibility of virtue and goodness. "[A] bright Maiden overcame [death], / and so the highest blessing / in all of creation / lies in the form of a woman".[9] The status of virginity exemplified by Mary influenced many people in the Middle Ages. In 384 CE, Saint Jerome wrote to a young girl on her thirteenth birthday.

In the Virgin of the Apocalypse Mary cradles baby Jesus in her arms (by the Master of the Amsterdam Cabinet, Germany, c. 1480–1488; Metropolitan Museum of Art, The Cloisters Collection, 1982 (1982.47.1) © The Metropolitan Museum of Art. AR'Istor: MMA_ IAP_10311575011)

His writing, meant as a birthday gift, might surprise a teenager in the twenty-first century. The girl Eustochium received a letter praising virginity. Jerome wished:

> to recount the drawbacks of marriage, such as pregnancy, the crying of infants, the torture caused by a rival, the cares of household management, and all those fancied blessings which death at last cuts short.[10]

Eustochium, wrote Jerome, should avoid married women who might dissuade her from a life of virginity. Why should Eustochium "hasten to visit the wife of a mere man?" Rather than an earthly bridegroom, she should seek out the heavenly bridegroom: Christ Himself. "Set before you the blessed Mary, whose surpassing purity made her meet to be the mother of the Lord."

The key to her salvation – her freedom – was education. "Read often, learn all that you can. Let sleep overcome you, the roll[11] still in your hands; when your head falls, let it be on the sacred page." Only through learning could she improve herself and her lot. Today we often say education can lift you out of economic poverty; for St Jerome, education lifted women out of spiritual poverty. Eustochium eventually visited the desert fathers (hermits in Egypt). She and her mother set up a monastery, three convents, and a hospice in Bethlehem. Yes, the virgin martyrs in early history and later legend who vocally withstood male power were empowering figures for girls. The Virgin Mary was singular. Yet the vast majority of women married and became mothers. Within the hierarchy of women's bodies as designated by the church, the most privileged females were those who remained virgins; next came chaste widows who refused remarriage; and finally wives, whose role was enhanced through the production of new virgins.

Scientists since Hippocrates, the fifth–fourth-century BCE Greek doctor, believed that all bodies – male *and* female bodies – had humors or bodily fluids. These four humors comprised black bile, yellow bile or choler, phlegm, and blood. If one humor dominated the individual, it could cause psychological or physical problems. Too much black bile would make you melancholy or sad; too much yellow bile made you angry; too much blood made you sanguine, happy, or even passive; and too much phlegm made you phlegmatic (slow and lethargic). Thus, blood-letting became an integral part of medieval medicine to balance the humors.

Women's bodies were seen as particularly problematic. A major issue for male medical theorists was menstrual blood. Aristotle argued it lacked "the principle of Soul".[12] Church Fathers similarly felt an aversion to women's periods. Isidore of Seville compiled an encyclopedia, for which he has been considered the patron saint of the internet. Isidore spoke soberly and confidently about the menses. "From contact with this blood, fruits fail to germinate ... plants die, trees lose their fruit, metal is corroded with rust, and bronze objects go black. Any dogs which consume it contract rabies."[13]

So that explains rabies.

Not all thinkers were so misogynistic. Medical writings suggested that menstruation was key to women's health. If your period was out of whack, then so was your entire body. Focusing on menstrual complaints, afflictions affecting the womb, and childbirth and its complications, many cures attributed to the woman doctor Trota were commonsensical and based on empirical observation. For example, there was emphasis on being sure that

---

Male and female bodies

Men were believed to be hot and dry, better able to excrete foul fluids through their pores. Women were thought to be cold, moist, and unable to purge efficiently, thus suffering monthly menses. The second-century physician Galen even believed that the uterus had a dual-temperature control. The birth of a boy would mean that the warmer right side of the uterus affected his gestation and the cooler left for a girl. Left was seen as the sinister [from the Latin *sinister*] or negative side or direction, while right was the positive side or direction. As we will see, the doctor Trota took male and female differences as a fundamental basis for medical thought and read them positively. Both male and female balanced each other out as complements, not adversaries, to each other.

---

the afterbirth was expelled after labor for the sake of the mother's health. Some remedies for stopping the flow of blood were based on folk belief, including tying a hair of the afflicted woman around a tree or hanging a bag of burnt toads around her neck. One manuscript suggested a combination of prayer and charm for the woman in labor. After writing out a charm on a piece of parchment, it should be cut up and given to the woman in labor to drink. A woman should tie it around the laboring mother a large scroll on which had been written the *Magnificat,* the hymn the Virgin Mary is said to have uttered to her cousin Elizabeth, pregnant with John the Baptist.[14] It begins, "My soul doth magnify the Lord ..." Medical writings also suggested that the common age for menstruation to begin was fifteen, older than today, perhaps due to nutritional issues.

While mystical visions may seem like fantasies, we can learn a lot about the historical situation of women's everyday lives from them. In Saint Birgitta of Sweden's vision, the Virgin Mary described how she gave birth: "I was alone in the stable, praying ... I had given birth without any help ... I stood and gave birth ... my knees were bent and I was alone in the stable".[15] Women gave birth squatting using birthing stools. Gravity helped the child emerge more quickly; lying in bed was more convenient for the doctor, but not for the laboring mother.

Doctors tried, using the theories of the time, to help women's bodies.

Food habits

Since women have traditionally been seen as the preparers of food, they used food as a means of power. Food was a highly potent symbol that could be used for political or spiritual purposes. Misogynistic thought led some ascetics to fast and police their female bodies. Sarah Kilfoyle has linked food practices, particularly tragic self-starvation habits, of the holy anorexics of the Middle Ages to the suffragettes of the early twentieth century. Suffragettes fought for women's right to vote and likewise starved themselves to provoke social progress.

Although some thinkers considered menstruation to be polluting, others showed compassion. Pope Gregory the Great in the early seventh century wrote to the missionary Augustine in Anglo-Saxon England, that women should be permitted to enter a church while menstruating, "for the workings of nature cannot be considered culpable, and it is not just that she should be refused admittance, since her condition is beyond her control."[16] People knew that pregnant women did not menstruate. Why? The menstrual blood was thought to speed through a vein to the breasts as it cooked, becoming purified into breast milk. Needless to say, these contentions were false. But many smart people accepted these views about women and their bodies.

Learn more
- See here for a discussion of the humoral theory from Hildegard von Bingen's perspective. http://www.fordham.edu/halsall/med/hildegarde.asp#melancholy.
- Browse the Index of Medieval Medical Images at the University of California, Los Angeles (UCLA): http://digital.library.ucla.edu/immi/.
- Images at the Wellcome Library focus on medicine: http://wellcomeimages.org/.

Notes
1. Alcuin Blamires, ed., *Woman Defamed and Woman Defended: An Anthology of Medieval Texts* (Oxford: Clarendon Press, 1992), 40.
2. Blamires, 45.
3. Blamires, 51.
4. Blamires, 57
5. Jo Ann McNamara, 'The *Herrenfrage*: The Restructuring of the Gender System 1050–1150', in Lees, 18.
6. Barbara Newman, *From Virile Woman to WomanChrist: Studies in Medieval Religion and Literature* (Philadelphia: University of Pennsylvania Press, 1995), 23.

7. Vern L. Bullough and James Brundage, *Sexual Practices and the Medieval Church* (Buffalo, NY: Prometheus Books, 1982), 32.

8. Newman, 247.

9. Mark Atherton, trans., *Hildegard von Bingen: Selected Writings* (London: Penguin Books, 2001), 118.

10. All Jerome quotes from Saint Jerome, Letter XXII. To Eustochium, at http://www.ccel. org/ccel/schaff/npnf206.v.XXII.html.

11. Writings would have been put onto rolls; the technology of the book was still being developed.

12. Blamires, 40.

13. Blamires, 44.

14. Alexandra Barratt, ed., *The Knowing of Woman's Kind in Childing: A Middle English Version of Material Derived from the Trotula and Other Sources* (Turnhout, Belgium: Brepols, 2001), 64, 66.

15. Barbara Obrist, 'The Swedish Visionary: Saint Bridget', in *Medieval Women Writers* edited by Katharina M. Wilson (Athens, GA: University of Georgia Press, 1984), 245.

16. Leo Sherley-Price, trans., *Bede: Ecclesiastical History of the English People*, revised by R. E. Latham; Introduction D. H. Farmer (London: Penguin Books, 1990), 83–84.

Poster advertising the Suffragette newspaper, 1912, by Hilda Dallas (1878–1958). Dressed as Joan of Arc, the patron saint of suffragettes, this woman was illustrated using the suffragette colors of purple, green and white (Museum of London; photo credit: HIP/Art Resource, NY)

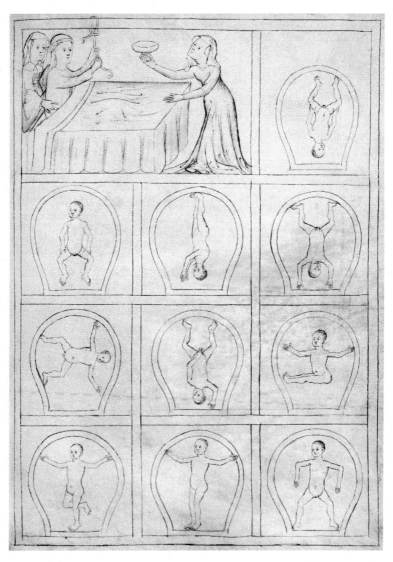

In this medical text, a woman in labor sits up in bed, pulling a cord to help her give birth, assisted by two female aides. The page includes images of the many possible presentations of a baby in childbirth (Ms Laud Misc, 724, f. 97r, c. 1400; with permission of the Bodleian Library, Oxford University)

CHAPTER 11

Trota of Salerno
(Twelfth Century)

COMPASSIONATE PHYSICIAN

Medieval women participated in medicine. Healers worked in female-only spaces such as nunneries, in a family business as a wife or daughter of a doctor, as midwives, or as a servant whose tasks included medical duties. Women tended herb gardens, made pills and concoctions for patients, and acted as consultants or therapists. They were also doctors. Fabiola founded the first public hospital in fourth-century Italy; hospitals named after her exist today. Medical centers like these were later founded at pilgrimage shrines to tend to those making a holy journey for the purposes of healing. Shrines set up cradles for women who gave birth on pilgrimage.

One champion of women's medicine was Trota of Salerno, a twelfth-century Italian woman from the coastal town of Salerno, south of Naples. We know little about Trota's life, though she may have been married to a doctor named Copho, who also wrote in the early twelfth century on gynecology. She was not the only woman practicing medicine and therapy here. Salerno had a well-known reputation as a prestigious medical hub. At least one woman was known to lecture on medicine. One legend contends that Sigelgaita, the wife of a Norman duke, had had training in poisons in Salerno. Her attempt to murder her brother-in-law failed and she had to provide her victim with an antidote to cure him, one she had likewise mastered in Salerno.

There was both lively interest in helping women's complaints and respect for women's empirically based treatments founded in experiment and practice. Generally avoiding the theoretical for the practical, Trota focused on how to actually help her patients with cures, therapies, and treatments using ingredients that would have been locally sourced. Numerous manuscripts called the *Trotula* were credited to Trota. These writings fascinated physicians in the Middle Ages and continue to give us insight into the medical habits, observations, and treatments of late medieval Europe.

On Treatments for Women treated everything from difficulties with bladder control and incontinence to chapped lips from too much kissing. Freckles could be reduced by a concoction that included "cuttlefish [squid] bones"[1] and rosewater. Myrtleberry helped with bad breath. *On Women's Cosmetics* included recipes for depilatory (removing body hair), teeth whiteners, hair shampoos and conditioners, as well as treatments against lice and sunburn. And forget any rumors you may have heard about people not bathing in the Middle Ages. Baths, steaming, and fumigation (letting herbal steam draw poisons out through your pores) were frequently prescribed. For constipation, Trota recommends pills, bloodletting, bathing, and mint tea. Sounds yummy – except for the bleeding.

Most significantly, Trota worked in the field of gynecology, the field of medicine focused on women's reproductive health. Her *Book on the Conditions of Women* not only diagnosed and treated complaints relating to women's unique physiology, but also actually suggested touching patients to feel for tumors, wounds, and growths, something few male doctors would have dared. Trota was able to do what no man could: function as both a doctor and a sympathetic woman when treating female patients. As Trota wrote, women's "misfortune, which ought to be pitied [has] impelled me to give a clear explanation regarding their diseases in caring for their health." The division between the sexes heightened women's shame in encountering male doctors. How could a woman tell a male doctor of an intimate problem if she felt embarrassed? Trota spoke to women about sensitive topics as a compassionate fellow woman. As she pointed out, "[If] the menses flow out either more or less than they ought to, many sicknesses thus arise."[2] One treatment for the excessive flow of menses stipulated: "[M]ake a plaster of the dung of birds or of a cat [mixed] with animal grease and let it be placed upon the belly and loins."[3]

Many recipes and treatments dealt with conception, pregnancy, labor, and post-partum issues. The development of fistula or tear was a danger in childbirth, still today in developing countries. Trota described how to sew up ruptures using silk thread. Advice for how to care for an infant includes "[O]ne should use nursery songs and simple words ... After the hour of speech has approached, let the child's nurse anoint its tongue frequently with honey and butter."[4] She was also credited with *Practica* (*Book of Practical Medicine*), demonstrating her expertise in general medicine. One way we can see Trota as a feminist is in her fearless honesty, talking openly and without

> ### *Arabic medical texts*
>
> The Middle Ages was the golden age of Arabic writings in science, medicine, astronomy, and physics. Many crucial contributions helping women medically came from Arab scientists who described gynecological surgical procedures. After all, what if a mother died in labor but the child was still alive? How could the child be extracted safely? Highly sophisticated Arabic medical writings, particularly those by Avicenna, were beginning to be translated into Latin for the Christian West starting in the eleventh century. Arabic texts treated women's issues integrated with all other parts of the body, while the Latin tradition tended to separate out female specific issues.

discomfort about medical matters that some might have found mortifying to acknowledge. "I have labored assiduously to [discuss women's] diseases."[5] Her perspective was that all of us have bodies and there is nothing shameful in them. Rather than covering things up, she practically addressed issues of importance for women and men.

Non-Christian women practiced healing. Muslims and Jews, sometimes living in separate areas of a city from Christians, developed their own medical licensing systems. In fourteenth-century Valencia, Spain, documents attested to Muslim women working as general practitioners. Muslim midwives worked at the court of Navarre. A law there from 1329, however, demanded that "no woman may practice medicine or give potions, under penalty of being whipped through the town; but they may care for little children and women to whom, however, they may give no potion."[6] At the same time in Frankfurt, Germany, Jewish women worked as eye doctors. Sarah of Saint-Gilles, a Jewish woman in Marseilles, France, actually had a male apprentice in 1326. Hebrew translations of *Trotula* appeared, along with a pregnancy and birth manual. A malpractice trial in 1403 in Marseille, France, against a Jewish midwife named Floreta d'Ays, offered insight into childbirth rooms and labor practices, as well as evidence that anti-Judaic sentiment was becoming increasingly common in this late medieval period.

Many women were mentioned as healers by name. In the thirteenth century, Stephanie, the daughter of a French physician in Lyon, was called a *medica* (doctor). Other documents referred to women in Italy and England

> ### Surgeons
>
> Today surgeons are often seen as the rock stars of the medical world. Not so in the Middle Ages. In 1215, Pope Innocent III called the Fourth Lateran Council to establish many rules and stipulations concerning theology, proper behavior, and church functions. Canon 18 stated, "No subdeacon, deacon, or priest shall practice that part of surgery involving burning and cutting." Thereafter, surgery fell in status below healing through herbs and drugs. As the deaf Spanish nun Teresa de Cartagena described medical intervention, "in order to heal a physical ailment we will suffer great torments, swallowing bitter draughts of medicine or submitting our bodies to burning instruments or the surgeon's blade or even consenting to amputation if required to save our lives."[8] Since it was a less-prestigious field, women were able to establish themselves in it, particularly in Italy and England. The Kingdom of Naples alone noted 24 women surgeons.

as healers. In 1286, Katherine, the daughter and sister of surgeons in London, was identified as one herself. Fava, the matriarch of a Jewish medical family with three generations of practitioners, was named as a surgeon in Manosque, a southern French town. Women became members of medical guilds, including those of surgeons, barbers, and apothecaries (like today's pharmacists).

Between Trota's era and the fourteenth century, the medical field became increasingly bureaucratized. Christian practitioners had to become licensed. Fearing that a baby would die shortly after birth before baptism, midwives in France licensed by the church could perform an emergency baptism if necessary. In 1238, the medical faculty at the University of Paris insisted that doctors be licensed, which effectively prevented women from gaining official approval for medical work. Women were not permitted to attend universities. The dean of the medical faculty in Paris prosecuted two women for not being certified. Clarie of Rouen, the wife of a medical practitioner, was not only arrested and fined in 1312, but excommunicated as well. In 1410 Perretta Petone was confronted by the Royal Tribunal in Paris for having practised unlicensed medicine. Joan, an Englishwoman in the early fifteenth century, petitioned King Henry IV for a license to practise medicine "without hindrance or disturbance from all folk who despise her by reason of her said art".[9] By the fourteenth century and the rise of universities, men were beginning to dominate in gynecology and infertility treatments.

How could women become certified if they were not admitted to university in the first place? If those trained in universities were the only ones qualified to function as doctors, then how could women be healers? In 1322, Jacqueline (or Jacoba) Felicie de Almania was arrested for acting as a male physician would. A legal complaint attested that she visited many gravely ill people, "after the manner of physicians and doctors", "inspecting their urine ... and touching, feeling, and holding their pulses, body, and limbs".[10] Urine study and uroscopy – the observation of urine – were vital elements in the doctor's kit – just as they are today. Think of how people routinely still give a urine sample to be tested for white blood cell counts, sugar levels, or pregnancy tests. Jacqueline was reputed to have said to patients, "I shall make you well, God willing, if you will have faith in me."[11] And cure them she did.

One of her clients, Jean Faber, had an illness in his head and ears that she healed with green and clear potions. Another patient, treated with an herbal sauna, became better. Other patients likewise testified on her behalf. Jacqueline protested that the statute that forbade women from treating patients was intended for those who were ignorant. She saw herself as different from "illiterates and empty-headed ignoramuses".[12] Since she, Jacqueline, was "expert in the art of medicine and instructed in the precepts of said art", she should be "excepted" from the rule that should not be "binding"[13] on her. Furthermore, Jacqueline argued:

Barbers

Medieval barbers actually undertook basic surgery and dentistry. Even bloodletting constituted an accepted practice – hence the red (for blood) and white pole you might see in your neighborhood designating a barber shop. One such male barber treated Joan of Arc after battle. He put olive oil and bacon fat on her wound. This may sound strange, but it had some efficacy. Don't try it at home though. The olive oil may be needed for salad dressing and the bacon for a bacon, lettuce, and tomato sandwich.

[I]t is better and more becoming that a woman clever and expert in the art should visit a sick woman, and should see and look into the secrets of nature and her private parts, than a man ... [A] woman would allow herself to die before she would reveal the secrets of her illness to a man, because of the virtue of the female sex and because of the shame which she would endure by revealing them.[14]

While this argument was dismissed as "worthless" and "frivolous",[15] Jacqueline contested that she should be allowed to continue, especially considering that she cured patients certified men failed to heal. Nevertheless, as she had not attended university lectures, she was not certified. As a woman, she was not even legally permitted to appear as a witness in her own trial. Ultimately, she, two men, and three other women – one a convert to Christianity and one who was Jewish – were found guilty of unlicensed practice, fined, and excommunicated.

The issue of what medical texts were available and what information could be included were topics of vital importance and intense debate in the Middle Ages – and even today. When you pick up a cookbook to make chocolate chip cookies, give a little nod to the women healers of the Middle Ages. The recipe book was a genre of medieval women's writing stemming from the longstanding exchange among women of medical recipes. Just as midwives were seen as specialists in a field where many women acted in that capacity, recipe writers increasingly saw themselves as experts in the realm of household management. Creating healthy meals lay on the same spectrum as creating recipes for potions to cure sickness. Those chocolate chip cookies are like antibiotics – of the soul.

Learn more
- The stipulations established by the Fourth Lateran Council in 1215 can be read here: http://www.fordham.edu/halsall/basis/lateran4.asp.
- To find out more about Avicenna's medicine, look here: http://www.fordham.edu/halsall/source/1020Avicenna-Medicine.asp.
- Novelist Karen Cushman brings medical issues to life: *Matilda Bone* (NY: Yearling, 2002) and *The Midwife's Apprentice* (NY: HarperCollins, 1996).

Notes
1. Monica H. Green, *The Trotula: An English Translation of the Medieval Compendium of Women's Medicine* (Philadelphia: University of Pennsylvania Press, 2001), 101.
2. Green 2001, 66.

3. Green 2001, 71.

4. Green 2001, 83.

5. Green 2001, 65.

6. Monica H. Green, 'Women's Medical Practice and Health Care in Medieval Europe', *Signs* 14.2 (1989), 448.

7. Twelfth Ecumenical Council: Lateran IV 1215 at http://www.fordham.edu/halsall/basis/lateran4.asp.

8. Teresa de Cartagena, *The Writings of Teresa de Cartagena: Translated with Introduction, Notes, and Interpretive Essay*, translated and edited by Dayle Seidenspinner-Núñez (Cambridge: D. S. Brewer, 1998), 57.

9. Labarge, 179.

10. James Bruce Ross and Mary Martin McLaughlin, eds., *The Portable Medieval Reader* (Harmondsworth: Penguin, 1977), 636.

11. Ross and McLaughlin, 636.

12. Monica H. Green, 'Getting to the Source: The Case of Jacoba Felicie and the Impact of the *Portable Medieval Reader* on the Canon of Medieval Women's History', *Medieval Feminist Forum* 42.1 (2006), 56.

13. Ross and McLaughlin, 638–639.

14. Ross and McLaughlin, 639.

15. Monica H. Green, *Making Women's Medicine Masculine: The Rise of Male Authority in Pre-Modern Gynaecology* (Oxford: Oxford University Press, 2008), 16.

Portrait of Hildegard of Bingen (miniature from the Lucca Codex, c. 1410. Biblioteca Statale, Lucca, Italy; with permission Werner Forman Archive/ Bridgeman Art Library)

CHAPTER 12

ildegard von Bingen (1098–1179)

AUDACIOUS INNOVATOR

ould you be walled up into a cell next a church as a young girl with a holy woman as your spiritual teacher and companion? Don't worry: you would have plenty of air to breathe and sufficient food to eat, but little heat or exercise. What would you do all day? Pray, meditate, and read holy books. Not interested in this lifestyle?

One girl did just this. Hildegard von Bingen, born in the wine-growing region of Bermersheim, Germany, was the tenth child of Hildebert and his wife Mechthild. As a child, she saw visions. "[I]n the third year of my life I saw so great a brightness that my soul trembled; yet because of my infant condition I could express nothing of it."[1] At the age of four or five, she saw a pregnant cow and accurately predicted how the calf would be marked and colored, "all white with dark patches on his forehead, feet, and back."[2] She described how "until I was fifteen I saw numerous visions",[3] amazing people she told about them. She dared to ask her nanny if she could see anything "apart from outward objects. 'Nothing', [the nanny] then replied, because she saw none of them. Then, seized by a great fear, I did not dare to tell about these things to anyone."[4] Hildegard was renowned as the Sibyl on the Rhine, another prophetess in a long line of women of faith, starting with Jewish heroines like Miriam, Deborah, and Hannah.

Her visionary aptitude propelled Hildegard into a religious life. "[H]er parents wondered about her, and, perceiving that her ways were different from those of other people, made arrangements for her enclosure in a monastery".[5] The church was seen as a haven for those of intellectual and artistic promise. "[I]n the eighth year I was offered to God [and] given over to a spiritual way of life."[6] Not long afterwards, Hildegard was walled up in the rite of enclosure with the holy woman Jutta of Spanheim at the Benedictine monastery of Disibodenberg. Like Christina of Markyate, Hildegard and the older Jutta were sealed into a room or cell called an 'anchorhold'. When a holy anchorite

---

Jutta of Sponheim

The life of Jutta, Hildegard's mentor and teacher, reads like a model history for devout young women. Her mother made sure Jutta learned the 'sacred scriptures,'[7] which she memorized. Coming down with a grave illness at age 12, she promised to devote herself to God should she survive. Convinced by her brother to become enclosed with several other holy sisters and devote her life to God, she wore humble clothes, ate only the leftovers rejected by paupers, recited the psalter daily, and wore no shoes in the coldest of winters. Hildegard, her loyal student, had the life of Jutta written so that many could read of her devoted teacher's holy life.

---

achieved fame for her spirituality, similarly inclined women gathered nearby. Over time, a small Benedictine nunnery formed, whereupon Hildegard took the veil as a Benedictine nun when she was in her teens. When Jutta died in 1136, Hildegard was chosen to head the convent.

In 1141 she suddenly experienced a series of revelations and heard the divine command, "Shout and tell!"[8] A severe illness she suffered at this time disappeared only once she started writing and sharing her visions. Out of a combination of bodily suffering and ecstasy, she fashioned works known for their religious insight, erudition, beauty, and compassion. She created texts in the realms of mysticism, theology, letters (to monarchs, popes, monks, and nuns), a cosmology (model of the universe), medicine, and music. Just as J. R. R. Tolkien did for his *Lord of the Rings* series, she even created a secret language.

For ten years Hildegard wrote *Scivias* (*Know the Ways of the Lord*). In this work she gave the theological meaning of fundamental elements in our universe, like the sun, the moon, and the stars. After describing a vision, she then proceeded to analyze it and explain what it meant. Her understanding and explanation came, she said, from a divine source. While she remained physically lucid and awake, a divine voice she called 'the Living Light' spoke to her:

> I hear them not with my physical ears, not with my heart's thoughts, nor do I perceive them by bringing any of my five senses to bear – but only in my soul, my physical eyes open, so that I never suffer their failing in loss of consciousness; no, I see these things wakefully.[9]

She explained, "I am taught inwardly, in my soul",[10] validating her authority through the experiences of her own body. She used simple, everyday images to explain complicated religious ideas. For example, she explained how human will inspired actions, just as fire caused bread to bake in an oven. Pope Eugenius authorized her visionary expertise at the Synod of Trier in 1147–8. Indeed, being a woman heightened her authority: "[T]he inspiration of the Holy Spirit would not have dwelt in her so powerfully."[11]

While she called herself a "fainthearted woman"[12] and "poor female",[13] Hildegard was simply using the modesty topos common to so many women of the Middle Ages, as we have seen with Hrotsvit of Gandersheim. Putting themselves down, these women could say exactly what they wanted to. Hildegard was no weakling. Critical of corruption in the church, she clearly asserted that her writings needed to be noticed:

> Thence, let no man be so audacious as to add anything to this writing, or to take anything away from it, lest he be blotted out from the book of life, and from all happiness under the sun ... And who should presume otherwise, he sins against the Holy Spirit. And then neither here nor in the future world shall it be forgiven him.[14]

Those were strong words indeed – she was basically saying that if you mess with her writing in anyway, you are a sinner who will be eternally punished. After all, like the Virgin Mary, she was a vessel for God's word: "[G]od gave out this book ... through a simple and unlearned woman, as it pleased Him in a wonderful way to do."[15] While she apparently did not draw images herself, she supervised the illustrations that accompanied her visionary writings. Hildegard elaborated on theological ideas as well as church policy, forcefully arguing that children should not be dedicated to the church by their parents without the child's consent. After all, being a member of the church was "a servitude which [the parents] themselves are not willing to undergo."[16] If parents were not willing to make such a sacrifice themselves, they should not force it on a young child.

Hildegard was not afraid to defy convention. For example, in the New Testament, St Paul said, "Women should remain silent in the churches. They are not allowed to speak ... If they want to inquire about something, they should ask their own husbands at home; for it is disgraceful for a woman to speak in the church" (1 *Corinthians* 14:34–35). This passage was used to enforce how women were not supposed to preach. In her typical defiance of tradition, Hildegard went on several highly successful preaching tours.

Her life was not without its crises. Monks resisted her desire to build her own nunnery – she won that battle. She lost two beloved nuns who went to run their own religious institutions. In her final years, Hildegard allowed a nobleman, who had been excommunicated, to be buried on her convent's grounds. Although she claimed he was a Christian in good standing, the convent was put under interdict or prohibition. If nuns would not dig up the corpse of the man, they would be excommunicated and no longer be allowed to hear mass or receive the Eucharist. Likewise these devout women would no longer be allowed to sing the Holy Office, the prayers and chants that were the lifeblood of Hildegard's nunnery. In a famous letter to the male church leaders who punished the nunnery by stopping its musical tradition, Hildegard argued that "The body is the vestment of the spirit, which has a living voice, and so it is proper for the body, in harmony with the soul, to use its voice to sing praises to God."[17] She wrote that God's desire for justice exerted itself, with "a female warrior battling against injustice, so that it might fall defeated."[18] While at first the prelates ignored her plea, the prohibition was eventually lifted so that Hildegard could participate in heavenly music before her death.

Hildegard attained miraculous achievement in all the arts. "I brought forth songs with their melody, in praise of God and the saints, without being taught by anyone, and I sang them too, even though I had never learnt either musical notation or any kind of singing."[19] The harmony of the cosmos demanded that she and her nuns sing. In her letter to another mystic, Elisabeth of Schönau, Hildegard suggested that humans were like a trumpet, bringing forth sound but not causing it; only God could do that. "So too I ... resound a little, like a small trumpet-note from the living brightness."[20] The Living Light (God) commanded her to make music. Her songs included *Antiphons* (short religious chants) to the Virgin Mary, whom she praised as "the lucid [clear] matter / Through whom the Word [God] breathed forth everything of value".[21] For Hildegard, the Virgin Mary exemplified the best of womanliness. "Your womb contained joy / Just as the grass was infused with / Greenness, when the dew sank into it; / Therefore Mother everything joyful has been Created through you".[22] Hildegard associated the 'matter',[23] from which God created all creatures, with the Latin word *mater* for *mother* or *maternal*. Rather than suggesting that matter, long connected to female flesh, as the source of all evil, Hildegard redeemed it and, thus, women's bodies.

Hildegard was considered to be Germany's first woman scientist and doctor. This 'greenness' or *viriditas* that Hildegard saw the Virgin Mary embodying

---

Elisabeth of Schönau (1129–1165)

Can you imagine reciting Latin every day from religious works starting from when you were 8 years old? Elisabeth did this. Influenced by Hildegard's writings, Elisabeth, likewise a mystic and visionary, presided as the *magistra* (Latin for *mistress* or directress) of nuns at a Benedictine double monastery. Her visions radically imagined the Virgin Mary taking on the male duties of priest and Christ as a young virgin woman. Yet her writings were avidly read and accepted.

---

was a key principle for her natural cosmology and medical writings. Gardening knowledge and agricultural symbolism saturated her medical philosophy. Her book *Causae et Curae* [*Causes and Cures*] (*c.* 1155) confirmed the humoral theory which saw the body as needing to have balance among blood, phlegm, black bile, and yellow bile. Moisture was key to health, both physical and spiritual. Since in the humoral theory of the body, men were hot and dry and women cold and wet, her praise of greenness and moisture was rooted in the praise and endorsement of the female body. "Just as a tree flowers and puts forth leaves by means of its *viriditas*, so a woman brings forth flowers and leaves in her womb by means of the *viriditas* of menstruation."[24]

Her scientific writings proved that medieval people did not believe the world was flat. With her idea of the 'cosmic egg',[25] Hildegard imagined the earth as a sphere wherein humans were a microcosm for the macrocosm of the cosmos. "Each human being contains heaven and earth and all of creation and yet remains one whole figure, and within every human being all things lie concealed."[26] Like our contemporary concept of the fractal, in which the smallest section is replicated in the whole, Hildegard's vision of the cosmos could be reduced in the individual: "The firmament contains stars just as a man has veins that hold him together."[27] Indeed, in her *Liber Divinorum operum* (*Book of Divine Works*; *c.* 1163–1674), Hildegard argued that each human was a tiny microcosm or little world reflecting the macrocosm or totality of the cosmos. In one of many letters that still exists, she wrote to an abbot that even "the grace of God shines like the sun and sends its gifts in various ways: in wisdom, in viridity, in moisture."[28] When Hildegard sent one of her books to the Abbot Ludwig, she asked him to think of it as a unicorn that he had to care for and protect.

Hildegard, who was a virgin, nevertheless wrote in *Causes and Cures* about all sorts of biological aspects of the human body. She gained this knowledge while functioning as the infirmarian or head nunnery doctor before she became an abbess. While not all her analysis was correct according to present day medical and scientific knowledge, for her time she was revolutionary, writing lyrically of women's physiology. Hildegard used poetic language to describe reproduction from a woman's point of view. She argued that the strength of love felt by the man and woman helped to determine the gender and character of the child they had. Although a nun, she did not *judge* such activity, rather *observed* as a scientist would in the twenty-first century. Like other writers at her time, she saw men as representing strength and women frailty. However, she interpreted this positively. She even suggested that it was a good thing that it was Eve who caused the fall rather than Adam. Referring to original sin – when Adam and Eve ate from the Tree of the Knowledge of Good and Evil in the Garden of Eden in *Genesis* – Hildegard argues that had it been initiated by Eve's male counterpart, Adam, he would have been so stubborn that he would never have wanted to be nor been able to be saved.

In her own time, important churchmen and politicians addressed her as "exalted maiden of Christ", "[w]ise woman,"[29] and "dearest mother".[30] Multiple miracles are ascribed to her, including the healing of those with epilepsy and fevers. Today Hildegard is a medieval woman superstar. Pope Benedict XVI declared her a saint in 2012 and named her a Doctor of the Church, the highest possible designation given to only the greatest of thinkers of doctrine and theology. The three other female Doctors are the saints Teresa of Ávila, Catherine of Siena, and Thérèse of Lisieux. There are countless recordings of Hildegard's musical works, films of her life, cookbooks and organizations devoted to her, and New Age inspired healings accredited to Hildegard. Revered by traditional Catholics, feminist scholars, and Wicca practitioners, she has even been made the namesake for a minor planet: 898 Hildegard.

Hildegard's song of praise imagined St Ursula being mocked for her mystical visions by men who say, "In her simple, girlish ignorance / she does not know what she is saying".[31] Hildegard saw herself as Ursula, mocked but ultimately justified. She knew that girls can experience things that elders might dismiss, only to be validated later on.

12. Hildegard von Bingen

This reliquary was said to hold the relics of a companion of St Ursula (made in the sixteenth century in present-day Belgium; Metropolitan Museum of Art, Gift of J. Pierpont Morgan, 1917 (17.190.728) © The Metropolitan Museum of Art. ARTstor: MMA_IAP_10310749702)

Learn more
- Read some of Hildegard's letters: http://epistolae.ccnmtl.columbia.edu/woman/115.html.
- You can hear many beautiful versions of Hildegard's music on YouTube.
- This discography lists many recordings of her music: http://www.medieval.org/emfaq/composers/hildegard.html.
- The luminous film *Vision* (2009) directed by Margarethe von Trotta stars Barbara Sukowa as the visionary leader.

Notes

1. Peter Dronke, *Women Writers of the Middle Ages* (Cambridge: Cambridge University Press, 1984), 145.
2. Mark Atherton, trans., *Hildegard von Bingen: Selected Writings* (London: Penguin Books, 2001), 201.
3. Atherton, 190.
4. Anna Silvas, *Jutta and Hildegard: The Biographical Sources* (University Park, PA: Pennsylvania State University Press, 1998), 159.
5. Silvas, 267.
6. Dronke, 145.
7. Silvas, 67.
8. Atherton, 11.
9. Dronke 168.
10. Atherton, 4.
11. Elizabeth Alvilda Petroff, *Medieval Women's Visionary Literature* (NY: Oxford University Press, 1986), 156.
12. Atherton, 22.
13. Atherton, 38.
14. Petroff, 157.
15. Petroff, 156–157.
16. Atherton, 78.
17. Joseph L. Baird and Radd K. Ehrman, *The Letters of Hildegard of Bingen*, Volume 1 (NY: Oxford University Press, 1994), 79.
18. Baird/Ehrman, 79.
19. Dronke, 145.
20. Dronke, 149.
21. Petroff, 157.
22. Petroff, 158.
23. Atherton, 166–167, 210.
24. Sweet, 400.
25. Atherton, 89.
26. Atherton, 95.
27. Victoria Sweet, 'Hildegard of Bingen and the Greening of Medieval Medicine', *Bulletin of the History of Medicine* 73.3 (1999), 390.
28. Baird/Ehrman, 195.
29. Atherton, 181.
30. Atherton, 184.
31. Carolyne Larrington, *Women and Writing in Medieval Europe: A Sourcebook* (London: Routledge, 1995), 239.

CHAPTER 13

Heloise d'Argenteuil
(c. 1100–1164)

SCANDALOUS NUN

A pregnant teenager. The teacher who seduced her. Despite attempts to break them up, she defiantly persisted in their affair. A scandalous headline ripped from the manuscripts of … 1118. By the time they met when she was about 17, Heloise was renowned as the most educated woman in Europe. Peter Abelard was the most brilliant philosopher of his time. In his 30s, he had already caused an uproar among the intellectual classes. No diplomat, Peter alienated respectable older theologians, making enemies.

Heloise's Uncle Fulbert was a clergyman at the church of Notre-Dame on the Île-de-France in Paris. Fulbert hired Peter, who gladly took on the role of tutor to this young girl, 20 years younger than himself. He would not be the first older teacher to take advantage of a woman who admired intelligence and maturity. As Peter admitted, he took the job intending to break his lifelong chastity and seduce the student entrusted to him. This love affair became the gossip of Paris and soon resounded as the biggest scandal of the medieval European world.

Uncle Fulbert was flattered by Peter's fame as a logician without equal. To obtain him as his niece's instructor was a coup for his own reputation. Blinded by pride, Fulbert could not see that their lessons included more than book learning. Barely did they meet before amorous glances ensnared Heloise and Peter, looks that transformed into touches. As Peter openly confesses, "My hands strayed oftener to her bosom than to the pages". They soon were enjoying carnal embraces. "[O]ur desires left no stage of lovemaking untried, and if love could devise something new, we welcomed it."[1] Heloise's uncle remained oblivious, until he caught the lovers together.

Meanwhile, Heloise was thrilled to learn she was pregnant. She traveled to Peter's sister in Brittany, northwestern France, to give birth. They named the boy Astrolabe, for the cutting edge scientific instrument predicting the position of the sun, planets, and stars, thus enabling sailors to determine

Heloise and Abelard. From the wildly popular poem, The Romance of the Rose, *by Guillaume de Lorris and Jean de Meun. Read about Christine de Pizan's critical view of this literary work in her chapter (this image dates from c. 1370. Ms 482/665 f.60v. Museé Condé, Chantilly, France, with permission Giraudon/ Bridgeman Art Library)*

where they were at sea. It would be like calling your child 'Computer' or 'iPhone' today. Little is known of Astrolabe, though it is believed that, once grown, he entered a religious vocation.

Furious, Fulbert insisted that Heloise marry Peter. Marriage, however, would destroy Peter's career in the church. Only celibate (unmarried) priests could advance up the ladder of success. Heloise adamantly insisted that they remain unwed. She cited multiple misogamist (anti-marriage) works written by male scholars over the years, scholarly writings that she knew inside-out. How could a man devote himself both to philosophy and a wife? If a woman were "bent on sacred or philosophical thoughts" – a woman like herself – how would she "be able to bear the constant filth and squalor of babies".[2] Just like today, many women were mothers, wives, and had occupations to support the household. Women were often torn between becoming domestic engineers (housewives and mothers) or focusing on the scholarly pursuits a nun engaged in. The possibility to balance both paths did not seem easily possible in Heloise's era.

After the birth of their son and despite her entreaties not to marry, upon Heloise's return to Paris, they took their marital vows in a private and secret ceremony so that Peter's career would not be damaged. He bundled Heloise off to the convent where she had been educated as a girl. Fulbert thought Peter was pulling a fast one on him and insisted on trumpeting the nuptials of his niece to all who would listen. Periodically, the lovers met secretly.

One night, infuriated by what he saw as Peter's reluctance to publicly acknowledge his marriage to Heloise, Fulbert acted. Under cover of darkness, he sent two men to Peter's apartment. They stealthily entered, finding Peter asleep. Before he could react, they cut off "the parts of my body whereby I had committed the wrong of which they complained."[3] Peter claimed later to have suffered more pain from the shame than from the physical torment. He then insisted that Heloise take vows of permanent chastity as a nun before he did so as a monk. This she later resented, as it suggested he mistrusted her.

Helpful wives

While few writings by medieval Jewish women have yet come to light, we can still learn about them. Eleazar ben Judah of Worms, Germany (d. 1232) praised his wife, Dulcia, in his poem as "[a] woman of valor, her husband's crown ... renowned for her good deeds."[4] Killed by thieves along with her two daughters, Bellette and Hannah, Dulcia received her husband's loving and grieving tribute. While anti-marriage (misogamist) Christian literature urged men not to marry in order to study, Jewish texts welcomed marriage since the wife could help the husband work for God. Dulcia "feeds her husband (so he can) study Torah."[5]

Ultimately Heloise became abbess at the Paraclete, a religious hermitage where Peter's supporters and students had gathered some time after the devastating attack. Originally consisting of rather primitive buildings, Heloise and her fellow sisters were supported by Pope Innocent II in 1129. She was to have contact with Peter in an emotional exchange soon enough.

About 1132, over a decade after their love affair ended, Heloise came upon Peter's long letter called 'The History of My Calamity' to 'A Friend', a public declaration retelling his life story, where he described tribulations, from being forced to burn the book he wrote to being threatened by murder from fellow monks. She could no longer remain silent and had to contact Peter, even though it had been well over ten years since she had held him in her arms. After all, hadn't they had a child together, one who had been raised by Peter's sister? Weren't they still married? Didn't they still mean something to each other?

So begins the most famous letter exchange of the Middle Ages. Heloise lamented that, while people think of her now as a chaste nun, in fact she was a hypocrite since she still desired Abelard. The honesty with which she expressed these views only brought her more admirers amongst those who read her letters. Devastated by his heart-rending personal history, Heloise suggested that Peter owed her, she "who is yours alone".[6] She wrote to him that he was "the deeper in my debt because of the love I have always borne you, as everyone knows, a love which is beyond all bounds."[7] She pointed out she became a nun at his bidding, in order to show her passionate submission to his will. Although the word 'wife' may seem more sacred:

> sweeter for me will always be the word friend, or, if you will permit me, that of concubine or whore ... God is my witness that if Augustus, Emperor of the whole world, thought fit to honor me with marriage and conferred all the earth on me to possess for ever, it would be dearer and more honorable to me to be called not his Empress but your whore.[8]

While these words were shocking in the Middle Ages, just as they are today, Heloise went on to explain that the true prostitutes were those who married for money. She gave herself willingly to him of her own free will, thus making her actions ethical and genuine. Intention, which only God could understand, determined the sin, not the action itself.

Peter responded to her letter coolly, now that he was a monk, not acknowledging what they were to one another and were still – husband and wife. Whereupon Heloise reprimanded him and lamented how Fortune had

> ## Medieval Japanese women writers
>
> Just as Latin was a dominant and male associated language in medieval Europe, Chinese remained wedded to men's public discourse in Heian and Kamakura Japan (794–1333 CE). Japanese court women wrote both prose and poetry in their native language, the most famous being Murasaki Shikibu (active *c.* 1000), author of *The Tale of Genji*. She related how she proficiently succeeded in understanding Chinese classics while her brother could not. Her father lamented, "What a pity she was not born a man!"[9] Ono no Komachi expressed her passion in a poem in which she described missing her lover: "My breast a fire raging, exploding flame / While within me my heart chars".[10] For these women, as for their European counterparts, letters, diaries, poetry, and narrative became ways to express their longings and experiences in comparably restricted cultures.

treated her. While once she was the luckiest of women, she was now the most degraded. Was there no love between them as she had believed? If only he would acknowledge the love that existed between them. Impotent to acknowledge Heloise's feelings, Peter answered that she was the true martyr since she could still feel erotic desire. It must have been lust rather than love that drove him to passionate heights. Peter could not go back to the past with her.

After Peter Abelard's death about 1142, the Abbot Peter the Venerable wrote to Heloise a letter glowing with compliments. She "surpassed all women in carrying out your purpose, and have gone further than almost every man."[11] Both in learning and holiness, she remained unrivaled. Heloise continued to head the Paraclete, a religious foundation with daughter houses, six of which were set up under Heloise's rule. She remained abbess until her death in 1163 or 1164.

One legend suggested that Heloise was welcomed by Peter's skeleton with open arms when the two bodies were laid together in her abbey church. Later they were interred by none other than Josephine Bonaparte, the wife of Napoleon Bonaparte, in a sarcophagus in the cemetery of Père Lachaise Cemetery in Paris. In death, their love was immortalized in *The Romance of the Rose*, a hugely popular medieval romance. Even today, lovers from the world over visit their gravesite to lay flowers in memory of the violent, stormy, and tragic love of Heloise and Peter who live on in countless art works of literature, music, poetry, film, and paintings.

While Heloise could only understand her feelings based on Classical ideas of passion and sexuality, a new mode of articulating the worth of erotic love was coming on the scene soon after her death: that of Courtly Love.

Learn more

- You can read letters and to and from Heloise: http://epistolae.ccnmtl.columbia. edu/woman/28.html.
- The 1988 film, *Stealing Heaven*, based on the novel by Marion Meade, interprets the passionate tragedy of these two lovers.

Notes

1. Betty Radice, trans., *The Letters of Abelard and Heloise*, revised edition by M. T. Clancy (London: Penguin Books, 2003), 11.
2. Barbara Newman, *From Virile Woman to WomanChrist: Studies in Medieval Religion and Literature* (Philadelphia: University of Pennsylvania Press, 1995), 67.
3. Radice, 17.
4. Elisheva Baumgarten, *Mothers and Children: Jewish Family Life in Medieval Europe* (Princeton: Princeton University Press, 2004), 213.
5. Baumgarten, 215.
6. Radice, 50.
7. Radice, 50.
8. Radice, 51.
9. Barbara Stevenson and Cynthia Ho, eds., *Crossing the Bridge: Comparative Essays on Medieval European and Heian Japanese Women Writers* (NY: Palgrave Macmillan, 2000), 1.
10. S. Lea Millay, 'The Voice of the Court Woman Poet', in Stevenson and Ho, 97.
11. Radice, 218.

CHAPTER 14

Marie de France
(Late Twelfth Century)

RHYMING ROMANCER

While many details of Marie de France's life are unknown, her writings have been vital to the reading habits of girls and women until today. The *Twilight* phenomenon could not have taken place without the foundation laid by Marie. Why? She wrote about love, passion, romance – and even werewolves. Unlike Bella Swan in *Twilight*, though, Marie was an ardent feminist, seeing women as capable of making choices in their personal emotional lives even when threatened with physical danger.

What little we do know of Marie is the following: highly learned, she knew Latin, French, Breton (the language of Brittany in northwestern France), and perhaps some English. She was a native French speaker who wrote in

Marie de France writing (from an Anthology of French Poems, c.1280–1290. Ms.3142 fol.256. Bibliotheque de L'Arsenal, Paris, France, with permission Giraudon/Bridgeman Art Library)

Anglo-Norman for the court of Eleanor of Aquitaine and Henry II from about the 1170s through 1190 in England. Her three major works were dedicated to nobility: a king – probably Henry II – and a Count William. Yet she made clear that her priority was to make these tales available to an audience unfamiliar with Latin. Marie wrote *Fables*, her own version of Aesop's animal fables, and *Saint Patrick's Purgatory*, in which a knight visits the afterworld. Her most famous work is a collection of 12 poems called the *Lais* (English *lay* or short romance).

In each one of her three major works, Marie strongly named herself so that she got credit for her masterpieces. "Hear, my lords, the words of Marie, who, when she has the opportunity, does not squander her talents."[1] She was authoritative, insisting that her writings be remembered as *hers*. She had an obligation to speak since she had a talent that could not be denied. "Anyone who has received from God the gift of knowledge and true eloquence has a duty not to remain silent; rather one should be happy to reveal such talents."[2] Those who dared to slander were "spiteful tittle-tattlers", acting like a "vicious, cowardly, treacherous dog which will bite others out of malice."[3] She dedicated the *lais* to a "noble king", to whom she bid not "consider me presumptuous if I make so bold as to offer you this gift. Now hear the beginning."[4] She practically forced him to listen.

Marie insisted that the stories she told were known "to be true".[5] Throughout the *Lais*, the female characters write, read, and speak as fleshed out characters. In fact, telling a story or writing a letter often leads to a happy ending, something all budding writers should find heartening. Marie did not sugarcoat the female sex. She suggested that women were *human*, not simply bland ideals of virtue or hideous seductresses. Her women could be adulterous married women, virgins, loyal or neglected wives, challenged lovers, or a twin daughter abandoned by her untrustworthy mother. The tales were magical, since they were adaptations of Breton fairytales from northwestern France. These stories took place within a courtly and feudal society where women had to marry the men their fathers insisted on. We can learn a lot about Marie's culture, the lives of women, and the role of marriage through reading her short romances.

Marie's plots and characters cemented the romance as a genre often identified with girls and women until this day. Some of these characteristics that we can even see in a *Harlequin* romance include the importance of the woman's point of view; romance as spiritually ennobling; and magic – literal or symbolic – that comes about with romantic love. Love provided access to an imaginary world of joy that could sustain even the most defeated and down-hearted person in times of trial and woe. Some her *lais* ended happily, others sadly, but altogether they constituted the vast array of possibilities that have been used by later writers, from Charlotte Brontë in her novel *Jane Eyre* to J. K. Rowling's *Harry Potter* series, where love is literally tied to magic.

Marie begins *Bisclavret* [*The Werewolf*] by assuring us that:

> In days gone by one could hear tell, and indeed it often used to happen, that many men turned into werewolves and went to live in the woods. A werewolf is a ferocious beast which, when possessed by this madness, devours men, causes great damage and dwells in vast forests.[6]

A baron happily lived in Brittany (northwestern France) with his wife. Only one thing disturbed their perfect happiness: the husband departed for three days every week, never telling his beloved where he went. The wife coaxed out what his secret was. "Lady, I become a werewolf ... I go about completely naked". He feared telling her where he hid his clothes: "[I]f I lost them and were discovered in that state, I should remain a werewolf forever."[7] Fearful of her bestial husband, the wife secretly contacted a knight who had long loved her in vain. She vowed to become his beloved if he fetched her husband's clothes. The knight did so. Her husband was never seen again and the unfaithful wife married her knight.

After a year, a wolf came up to the king and kissed his "foot and leg". The king saw that the "beast possesses understanding and intelligence".[8] After this, the king and Bisclavret were inseparable. One day, there was a festival to which Bisclavret's wife and new husband were invited. Although normally as gentle as a lamb, the wolf attacked the knight. As Marie commented, "No wonder Bisclavret hated him." One day, the king visited the wife. Upon seeing his former wife, Bisclavret "tore the nose right off her face".[9]

A wise counselor pointed out that the wolf had been calm and peaceful with everyone save the wife and her husband. Perhaps there was a reason the wolf hated her. After being cruelly tortured, the wife revealed all and returned Bisclavret's clothes. To preserve the wolf's modesty, he was put alone into a room with his clothes. When they returned, Bisclavret had transformed back into a man. The wife and knight were banished, Bisclavret got his lands back, and the wife was punished most amazingly: "She had a good many children who were thereafter recognizable by their appearance. Many of the women in the family, I tell you truly, were born without noses and lived noseless."[10]

Such a tale entered the lore of werewolves, advising women not to betray promises or husbands. While we see the story from the perspective of the pitiful werewolf, Marie also acknowledged the terror of the wife at having a shape-changing husband.

Disloyal men victimized knights in vicious power plays. In *Lanval,* knights at King Arthur's court ignored the young knight Lanval, making him "very sad and forlorn".[11] Wandering off into a lovely meadow, he witnessed the arrival of two stunningly beautiful maidens. Their splendor was nothing compared to that of their mistress, "who surpassed in beauty the lily and new rose when it appears in summer."[12] She loved him on one condition – their love must remain secret. If he disobeyed this command, he would lose her forever. He agreed to this condition and returned to court. While there, Queen Guenevere spied Lanval and found him to be attractive. Suggesting that he become her boyfriend, he refused out of loyalty to the king. Angered, the queen suggested Lanval only desired men, whereupon he said, "I love and am loved by a lady who should be prized above all others I know."[13] In fact, his beloved – even her servants – "is worth more than you, my lady the Queen, in body, face and beauty, wisdom and goodness."[14] He even revealed that the queen propositioned him. Oh dear, not a smart idea to speak in haste.

Now that he had told his secret, he bewailed his fate: his beloved would never return and he would put on trial for lying. The only way he could free himself from death would be if his lover returned. Just when all hope was lost, the two maidens and their mistress appeared. "There was none more beautiful in the whole world."[15] All were amazed at their exquisite perfection; his beloved declared that the queen lied. Vindicated and freed from the court, Lanval "went with her to Avalon, so the Bretons tell us, to a very beautiful island."[16] No one heard anything further about them.

Marie's characters populated a hostile world placing demands on them. Only true love could provide freedom and self-fulfillment. Marriages between young women and old men were fated to fail. Imprisoned in loveless marriages, the women became literally imprisoned in *Guigemar* and *Yonec*. A rich old man locked away his beautiful, young wife in a tower in *Yonec*. Desperate after seven years of her trials, she lamented:

> I have often heard tell that in this country one used to encounter adventures which relieved those afflicted by care: knights discovered maidens to their liking, noble and fair, and ladies found handsome and courtly lovers, worthy and valiant men.

Six degrees of separation

In Marie's *The Two Lovers* [*Les Deus Amanz*], a king would not allow anyone to marry his beautiful daughter unless that suitor could carry her in his arms up to the top of a mountain without stopping to rest. When the damsel fell in love, she reassured her beloved that a special potion would help. She said, "I have a relative in Salerno ... who has practiced the art of physic [medicine] so much that she is well-versed in medicines."[17] After fetching the potion, her beloved carried his true love, insisting he needed no medical aid. Reaching the mountaintop, he collapsed and died, whereupon the girl kissed his dead corpse and expired as well. One lesson was: always obey your woman doctor – like Trota from Salerno.

Upon praying that she might see such a man, a hawk immediately entered the window of her prison and transformed into a knight who declared, "I never loved any woman but you, nor shall I ever love another."[18] Happily, they enjoyed each other's company; the knight visited her whenever she thought of him.

After some time, suspicious, the old husband uncovered their affair and put razor sharp knives on the window, mortally wounding the hawk-knight on his next visit. As he died, he reassured his beloved that she would bear his child whom she should name Yonec. Their son would avenge his death. Many years later, what the magical hawk-knight foretold came to pass. Yonec beheaded the evil husband and tenderly buried his dead mother in the tomb of his father. Perfect love needs constant vigilance – haters want to destroy the beauty and happiness of others. Protect your love. Acts of destruction will ultimately be punished.

While Marie's own life is shrouded in mystery, her works were vital to the history of medieval women. Translations of her works existed in multiple medieval languages – Old Norse, Middle English, Middle High German, Italian, and Latin – testifying to her influence and popularity. Romances became the hot genre, demanded by readers in all European countries. There was even a Hebrew version of Marie's *Lais*, testifying to the appeal of her stories to diverse audiences, including a Jewish one in the thirteenth century. Marie's stories have become woven into the narratives that women today rely on to fulfill their dreams, act out their desires, and persevere for happiness.

Learn more

- Read some of Marie's *Lais*: http://people.clas.ufl.edu/jshoaf/marie_lais/.

Notes

1. Marie de France, *The Lais of Marie de France*, translated by Glyn S. Burgess and Keith Busby (Harmondsworth, England: Penguin, 1999), 43.
2. de FranceBurgess and Busby, 41.
3. de France/Burgess and Busby, 43.
4. de France/Burgess and Busby, 41.
5. de France/Burgess and Busby, 43.
6. de France/Burgess and Busby, 68.
7. de France/Burgess and Busby, 69.
8. de France/Burgess and Busby, 70.
9. de France/Burgess and Busby, 71.
10. de France/Burgess and Busby, 72.
11. de France/Burgess and Busby, 73.
12. de France/Burgess and Busby, 74.
13. de France/Burgess and Busby, 76.
14. de France/Burgess and Busby, 77.
15. de France/Burgess and Busby, 80.
16. de France/Burgess and Busby, 81.
17. de France/Burgess and Busby, 83.
18. de France/Burgess and Busby, 87.

PART IV

ON-CONFORMISTS

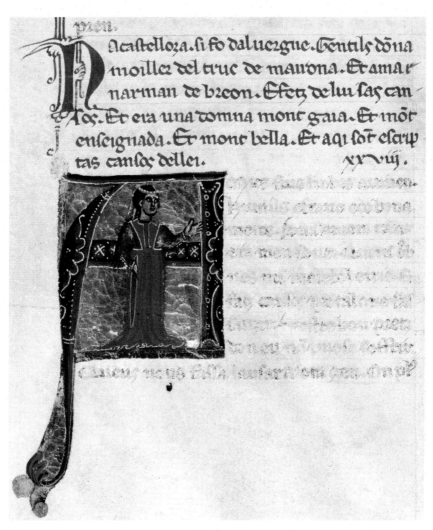

Castelloza, one of the most famous of the women troubadours or trobairitz (B. N. fr. 12473, chansonnier K f.110v Castelloza. Bibliothèque nationale de France)

CHAPTER 15

𝕎omen Troubadours
(Late Twelfth/Early Thirteenth Century)

CLEVER COMPOSERS

𝕀magine: You are with a fellow knight, speeding through the dark of the evening to get to your beloved ladies as you had promised. Suddenly, you hear several "despondent" knights lamenting, wishing "for a place to stay". What should you do? "[O]ne of them turned back to help the gentlemen, / the other one ran straight on to his lady: / which of them did as he should?" The female poet Guillelma de Rosers posed this question in the middle of the thirteenth century. In the poem, one of the ladies chastised her lover: "[A] man who keeps his word is worth much more / than one whose plans are constantly revised".[1] He responded that chivalry comes from love, therefore it is best to act as chivalric gentleman ought to. That truly proves his love. Who do you think is right?

The women troubadours – known as the *trobairitz* in their language Occitan or Provençal – were the first known women composers of secular music in the West, writing passionate, angry, and funny songs about love. They defied male troubadours who only presented the male point of view of romantic entanglements. These women wanted their private feelings acknowledged and made public. Even though they may have been defeated or challenged in love, the *trobairitz* candidly admitted their desires. Speaking with 'I', they audaciously demanded to be heard. Whether the speaker uttered exactly what really happened to her or not, the game or pose of the *trobairitz* allowed her to claim that she spoke the truth. They established, through these songs, the first documented popular music – not church music, like that of Hildegard. We hear echoes of their themes in the poignant laments and authentic anguish voiced today by Beyoncé, Taylor Swift, and Rihanna.

These songs were often considered to be examples of courtly love or *fin' amors*. Some characteristics included the love between noble people. It must be secret. It could be adulterous – between a married woman and a lower status man. After all, as Andreas Capellanus wrote in his twelfth-century *The*

Courtly love

Whether this type of love *really* existed or not is much debated. Perhaps it was just a realm that existed in the ideal and never in reality. Literature may have created the myth of a young lover loyal to a married noblewoman to sustain people emotionally. Showing adoration of his lord's wife – without any real hanky-panky – would tie him in a closer bond to the lord himself. This political game had real-life consequences that the women troubadours commented on and suffered from.

Art of Courtly Love: "Marriage is no real excuse for not loving".[2] Whether or not this adultery was a fantasy or not remains an open question. The vocabulary used to describe the loyalty between two lovers echoed that of the feudal system, where the king was obeyed by his knights. The same kind of freely given eternal loyalty was expected between lovers, but could be betrayed due to vicious outsiders or a lover's own weakness.

The word *troubadour* came from the word to *invent*, *find*, or *compose*. Given the proximity of southern France to the Iberian peninsula of Spain and Portugal where Christians, Jews, and Moors (Muslims) lived, it was likely that Hispano-Arabic love poetry influenced the development of the troubadour lyrics. Male troubadour poetry may on the surface seem positive, having men praise women as a lady-lord or *domna* who had complete power over the poet's life. Yet, if that praise was conditional on her acting only in the way he liked, then love would become a prison. Faultless women did not exist – just as ideal men did not. Describing a woman as so extraordinary that she could not sometimes act 'normally' put pressure on the female beloved to be like a goddess, not a flesh-and-blood human being. Rather than being ethereal and flawless beings, these women demanded attention from their lovers. Poetry may have been a way not only to express authentic emotion, but to gain power in terms of social status or for poetic fame.

About eight named female *trouvères* or *troveresses* (literally *finders*) were known from northern France, including Eleanor of Aquitaine's granddaughter, Blanche of Castile (1188–1252), who was the French queen. An extraordinary number – at least 20 – *trobairitz* appeared in southern France in the second half of the twelfth and the early thirteenth centuries. This area was unusual in that its inheritance laws were more advantageous for women than in the north. While a husband could *use* a wife's land, he could not *pass it on* to his heirs. She could *keep* her land. For women in Occitania, land signified power; power meant military strength. The Crusades left many estates without their lords, so that the women had to take over and control the property. If the lord were away on Crusade, the lady acted in his stead, much as women on the home front took over many men's jobs during World War II. The *trobairitz* were often relatives or friends of the male troubadours, even the objects of affection for whom the men had composed. Others were patrons to fellow *trobairtiz* and troubadours. These poems would have been sung. Only a little of the music for the *trobairitz* poems exists, so, if you like to write or sing, make up your own tunes and musical arrangements for this wonderful material.

The little we know about the *trobairitz* comes from the *vida* (or *life*) accompanying some of their verses. Since we only have small details of the lives of these women, they are best looked at in terms of *prosopography* – group or collective history. This is an especially useful methodology when examining the lives of those for whom we sometimes lack sources, such as those marginalized due to class, gender, age, or religion.

Castelloza, which means 'Castle Lady', was from the Auvergne in southern France. She lived in the first half of the thirteenth century, wife to a Crusader named Turc de Mairona. According to her *vida*, she "loved N'Arman de Breon and made up songs about him. And she was a lady very gay and very accomplished and very beautiful."[5] She showed no shame in expressing her

---

Muslim women's literature

Arabic poetry by medieval Muslim women was composed by elite women, courtesans, and even slave girls. In one charming story, a prince walking by a river began a poetic couplet: "The wind rippled a mailcoat in the water". A slave girl washing laundry in the water responded: "What a shield it would make if it froze".[3] Enchanted, the prince freed, married, and made her queen of Seville. She became famous as the poet Itimad ar-Rumaikiyya (twelfth century). The noblewoman Hafsa bint Hajj ar-Rakuniyya composed love verse from the same time period: "Shall I visit you or shall you visit me? For my heart always bows to what you long for."[4]

Beatriz, Contessa de Dia (B. N. fr. 12473, chansonnier K f.126v. Bibliothèque nationale de France)

feelings – even her physical desires – and did not smooth over her angry words with courteous display. "[Y]ou were mean and sly and villainous". Guilt seemed immaterial to the world conjured up by the *trobairitz*. There's no reason a woman should not court a man: "[W]hoever says that isn't very bright".[6] Even though she was socially below the man she loved, he would be wise to trust her. After one glimpse of him, she was his: "[W]hen a lady's mind / is set on love, she ought / to court the man, if she shows strength and chivalry".[7] Yet he had betrayed her: "[N]ow I see I was a fool…you returned bad for good."[8] She was direct in her speech. Her culture seemed receptive to women's straightforward attitude and openness to bodily longings.

Wife of Guillem (William) de Poitiers, the Countess of Dia, whose given name was Beatriz, had a twin sister. Their father died in battle when they were still young. One poem praised women "who [love] openly". "[S]he should dare to love him face to face".[9] Beatriz wrote about having been betrayed. Her consolation was thus: "At least in love I have my victory, / since I surpass the worthiest of men".[10] His treachery was all the more intense because they had exchanged poems. Her poem of lament was itself a messenger, asking "why I deserve so savage and so cruel a fate".[11] She called out those spies who tried to destroy her secret love. Not unlike Facebook bullies, these "sneaky" and "nasty-worded" underminers "are out to do me harm … [N]o one will find honor / who has anything to do with them."[12] Her crisp dialogue suggested that, even when heart-broken, she refused to humble herself.

Maria de Ventadorn from Limousin, born about 1165, was:

> the one who did most good and most kept herself from evil. And her good sense always helped her, and folly never made her do foolish things. And God honored her with a pretty, graceful body that was unequalled.[13]

In addition to composing, she generously served as patron to troubadours. Typical for noblewomen, her marriage to Viscount Eble V of Ventadorn was carefully thought out so that her family would profit in terms of prestige, lands, and wealth. Maria had two sons, thus ensuring a secure lineage for his family. She wrote a dialogue with Gui d'Ussel, asking Gui:

> [W]hen a lady
> freely loves a man, should she do
> as much for him as he for her,
> according to the rules of courtly love?

Gui answered that:

Female friendship

Men were not the only objects of the attention of the *trobairitz*. The thirteenth-century Bietris de Romans addressed her *chanson* to Lady Maria:

> [I]f it please you, lovely woman, then give me
> that which most hope and joy promises
> for in you lie my desire and my heart
> and from you stems all my happiness,
> and because of you I'm often sighing.[14]

This lovely tribute suggests that deep, abiding, and intimate friendships of same-sex love were documented in the Middle Ages. As Bietris wrote, Maria possessed within "All good things one could ask of a woman."[15] A memorial brass commemorating two women in fifteenth-century England depicted Elizabeth Etchingham and Agnes Oxenbridge next to each other in positions similar to those of married couples.

> the lady
> ought to do exactly for her lover
> as he does for her, without regard to rank;
> for between two friends neither one should rule.[16]

She then pointed out that the man knelt down before the woman to offer to serve her when he declared his affection:

> [T]hus to me it's nothing short of treason
> if a man says he's her equal *and* her servant.

The poem ended with Gui's comment that:

> it's embarrassing
> to argue that a lady should
> be higher than the man with whom
> she's made one heart of two.[17]

What do you think? Should the woman do as much for the man as he does for her?

This poem must have been written before 1209, for in that year the pope forbade Gui to write. How could that be? This heyday of women's power and expression was doomed. Pope Innocent III hated any deviation from orthodoxy, what he saw as the proper and right way to worship the Christian God. In southern France, various heresies were becoming popular. To stamp

---

Heresy

Multiple heresies fell under suspicion in the later Middle Ages. The crusade launched in France in the early thirteenth century was intended to cleanse it of heresy. Cathars, also known as Albigensians, were slaughtered, though women resisted the attacks. The leader of the crusade, Simon de Montfort, 5th Earl of Leicester, was supposedly killed by a catapult launched by a group of ladies. Cathars believed in one good god and one evil god. Since they held that the spirit was good and the flesh evil, they rejected a fundamental tenet of the Church that Christ was incarnated (became man). Vegans, they rejected sexual contact and developed their own religious ritual for perfecting believers. Men and women were equally able to be leaders, so-called *perfects* – a problematic assertion at this time.

them out, the pope called for a Crusade – not to the Holy Land, but within France itself. In less than 50 years, cities lay in ruins and the Occitan culture and language was taken over by the French of the north. Maria witnessed her husband taking vows to enter an abbey as a monk in 1221 and, along with him, became a member of the Cloister of Grandmont.

This shift from secular court to sacred monastery paralleled a shift in the literature too. *Trobairtiz* and troubadour poetry changed as well – rather than praising a flesh-and-blood woman, the woman to adore became the Virgin Mary. In one poem by three women – Alais, Iselda, and Carenza, of whom nothing else is known – the state of marriage was rejected for becoming the bride of Christ by entering a nunnery. After all, as one of the ladies said:

> [T]o be married would please me
> but making babies seems a huge penitence:
> then your breasts hang down limp
> and your belly's wrinkled and horrible.[18]

The poem made becoming a nun an attractive proposition. Heresies and threats of heresies were not stamped out in the thirteenth century. Our next medieval woman was caught in a fatal battle between politics and her soul when the Inquisition, the official judicial group of the Catholic Church charged with combatting heresy, replaced Crusades to conquer heresies starting in 1232.

Learn more
- Discography and information about women composers and their music: http://earlywomenmasters.net/cds/.
- This novel fictionalizes a female troubadour: Mary Hoffmann's *Troubadour* (NY: Bloomsbury, 2009).
- For a masterwork of world literature, be sure to read the Arabic prose masterpiece *One Thousand and One Nights*, in which the lovely Scheherazade saves her own and other women's lives through relating a cornucopia of tales about Sinbad, Ali Baba, and Aladdin.

Notes
1. Meg Bogin, ed. and trans., *The Women Troubadours* (NY: W. W. Norton, 1980), 135.
2. Capellanus, Andreas. *The Art of Courtly Love* at http://www.fordham.edu/halsall/source/capellanus.asp.
3. Bogin, 175.

4. Segol, 158.
5. Bogin, 119.
6. Marla Segol, 'Representing the Body in Poems by Medieval Muslim Women', *Medieval Feminist Forum* 45 (2009), 152.
7. Bogin, 125.
8. Bogin, 127.
9. Bogin, 83.
10. Bogin, 85.
11. Bogin, 87.
12. Bogin, 91.
13. Bogin, 168.
14. Bogin, 133.
15. Bogin, 133.
16. Bogin, 99.
17. Bogin, 101.
18. Carolyne Larrington, *Women and Writing in Medieval Europe: A Sourcebook* (London: Routledge, 1995), 95.

CHAPTER 16

Marguerite Porete
(d. 1310)

HEROIC HERETIC

What was heresy? Typically, it was the perceived deviation from what were considered the acceptable beliefs of a system. In connection with medieval women, heresy would be an accusation leveled at those people considered promoters of rituals, actions, and ideas that the orthodox or central church did not agree with. Why was this problematic? After all, we praise diversity of opinion in our culture. At least, we say we do.

The church controlled or at least influenced many aspects of medieval life – from huge tracts of land and monastic foundations to the prayers everyday parishioners would utter. To have some people publicly declare their deviation from these norms was frightening and threatening. What if many people decided to follow these new ideas? Cynically, one might say the church wanted to quash new creeds out of a selfish desire for financial and political power. On the other hand, some members of the orthodox church might have truly believed that those people who promulgated ideas that

Marguerite Porete was put on trial for heresy. This image shows the only known life portrait of Marguerite's fellow sufferer, Joan of Arc, from a page of transcribed testimony, written down when Joan was questioned by authorities. Both French women were burned to death as heretics over 100 years apart (Registre du Parlement de Paris, 10 May, 1429. Archives Nationales Paris; photo credit: CCI/Art Archive at Art Resource, NY)

Beguines

Two Beguines, adherents of the highly successful Northern European spiritual movement for women, wrote their visions in the thirteenth century. "Now am I a naked soul,"[1] wrote Mechthild of Magdeburg, who lived at the convent at Helfta, a center of feminine spirituality. Her writings, called *The Flowing Light of the Godhead*, were threatened. "I was warned about this book and was told by men / that it should not be preserved / but destroyed by fire."[2] Fortunately, she – and the authorities – did not burn it. Hadewijch of Brabant used courtly love imagery in her visionary writings that are now foundational writings in the history of Dutch literature. She declared, "I am a free human creature."[3] She addressed her female reader: "O heroine, because you are so heroic and never yield, you are called the greatest of heroines."[4]

---

deviated from tradition were possessed by the devil or at least seriously misguided, enough that they had to be chastised, excommunicated, or even cut from society permanently.

There were many heresies over the course of the Middle Ages. Some early ones include Arianism, which denied the eternity of Christ as the Son of God, and Pelagianism, which emphasized human will over God's grace to do good. Waldensians, another group, believed in voluntary poverty and the virtue of wandering preachers, a lifestyle rejected by Pope Alexander III in 1179. They also were accused of allowing anyone – even a woman – to consecrate the Eucharist during mass.

One group that periodically came under scrutiny was called the Beguines. These strictly female members of a religious movement were laywomen who lived in urban communities together, starting in 1200 in present-day Holland and Belgium and later spreading to other European regions. These communities – complete with chapels, hospitals, and homes – were called *beguinages* that you can still visit in Antwerp, Ghent, Leuven, and Bruges. While some communities might have just a few members, the one in Mechelen had as many as 1500 residents. They lived in communal religious societies without taking formal and permanent vows as a nun would. These women preferred flexibility in their spiritual practices. They could live informally, sometimes temporarily, with groups of like-minded women who endeavored to do charitable work with the poor or taking care of the sick.

While they did not take vows of poverty, they did take vows of celibacy and obedience to the *beguinage* head. Yet they were free to leave and marry should they choose to do so. Beguines were expected to support themselves through their wealth or work. A member kept her income upon leaving the community. Beguine devotion centered on Christ's crucifixion, the Eucharist, and the Virgin Mary. Knowing God mystically – though deep spiritual contemplation – was a hallmark of Beguine writings.

While many people praised such women for the supernatural authority they gained through visions of God and the saints, others found them threatening. Their way

Beguinage [Begijnhof] in Bruges, Belgium (photo by Jan Darthet, with permission)

of knowing God personally slipped away from a male priest's guidance. Avoiding the necessity of male priestly guidance undermined the power of the church. Yet papal approval of Beguines was informally granted in the early thirteenth century. A Beguine finding a religious man to approve of her visions or writings was protected from attack.

Not every Beguine had such guardians, alas. Even if you had one, such as in the case of Marguerite Porete, he might not be able to save you from death. Born in Hainault, Belgium, Marguerite became associated with a sect

---

Christ dolls

Christ dolls allowed women to have a directly personalized relationship with God. The family of a new nun might donate such a doll to her convent. The doll was not just an object, but was filled with spiritual qualities. This active participation with God was epitomized in this dialogue between a theologian and a Beguine who said, "You talk, we act."[5]

This fifteenth-century Crib of the Infant Jesus would have cradled a Christ doll beloved by Beguines (South Netherlandish. This beautiful work was made from materials including silver-gilt, painted parchment, silk embroidery with seed pearls, gold thread, and translucent enamels; Metropolitan Museum of Art, Gift of Ruth Blumka, in memory of Leopold Blumka, 1974 (1974.121a-d). © Metropolitan Museum of Art. ARTstor: MMA_IAP_1039651934)

called the Free Spirits. As it came increasingly under suspicion, so too did Marguerite. Not all Beguines lived in elaborate communities. Marguerite lived a solitary life, apparently wandering from place to place.

Her book entitled *Mirror of Simple Annihilated Souls and Those Who Only Remain in Will and Desire of Love* about 1290 caught the attention of authorities. Her arrest in 1306 coincided with an open attack on her book. Even though three churchmen – including a friar, a monk, and a theologian – supported her and endorsed her writings, her book was publicly condemned and burned. Burning her book in a sense substituted for her. Rather than remaining quiet on pain of excommunication, Marguerite insisted on continuing to spread her beliefs and she was rearrested in 1308. She was imprisoned for a year and a half.

Refusing to speak to her inquisitors, to ask for absolution (forgiveness) of her transgressions or to take the vows necessary for the trial examination, Marguerite contended that only God had power. She contrasted the human-run Catholic church, "Holy Church the Little", with the loving community of Free Souls, "Holy Church the Great". Earthly justice was meaningless since only divine justice had any significance. That bothered those possessors of earthly justice, such as priests and theologians who were to decide her fate.

She had a defender, Guiard of Cressonessart, who sensed in Marguerite a "true adherence to God".[6] He was even jailed for his defense of her. The theologians determining the orthodoxy of her book had their own rivalries and differing opinions. Yet the prologue to her treatise said, "theologians and other clerics / you will have no understanding of [this book] at all ... unless you shall proceed humbly / and Love and Faith together/cause you to rise above reason".[7] Unfortunately for Marguerite, medieval theologians were the supreme masters of reason. Her accusers quoted many of her arguments out of context, twisting her meaning, finding 15 of her points heretical. Her life could still have been saved, but Marguerite refused to apologize. She ultimately was declared a relapsed heretic based on her book. After she was released to secular authorities, all copies of her book were to be seized. Though never called a Beguine in the final sentence, Marguerite's death as a *mystical* heretic was the first such execution recorded in Christian history.

Hildegard created a new vision of divinity, crediting the 'Living Light' or God for sharing it with her. Other female Beguines who wrote mystical works, such as Marie of Oignies (d. 1213), managed to attain approval. Marguerite's writings caused a stir. What did she write that was so controversial? Erotic imagery of the *trobairitz* was not limited to love poems. Marguerite's religious writing carries many beautiful allusions to lyric poetry. This imagery allowed her to visualize the divine and the Church. Privileging love over reason, Marguerite infused bridal imagery into her description of the fusion of soul and God. Courtly imagery wafted sweetly with divine love. The soul united with God's love "feels no joy, for she herself is joy, and swims and floats in joy without feeling any joy, for she inhabits joy and joy

---

Na Prous Boneta (c. 1296–1325)

"If this pope and the cardinals should say that the things she holds and claims are erroneous and heretical she would neither believe nor obey them."[8] This follower of the Spiritual Franciscans, whose policy of radical poverty was declared heretical, became a visionary leader who opposed the church's burning of lepers in 1321 and 1322. In fact, she went so far as to compare the present Pope to "Caiaphas, who crucified Christ."[9] Burnt to death in 1325, Na Prous gave trial testimony before the Inquisition, articulating her beliefs.

inhabits her."[10] Marguerite's diction was dramatic: "Thus it is fitting and necessary that the soul pulverize by breaking and shattering itself, in order to enlarge the place where Love wishes to be."[11] "Gracious love" even makes the Soul "completely drunk".[12] Finally, she suggested that the utterly passive soul could not sin on earth if united with God.

Dangerous words for a woman to espouse.

In Marguerite's schema, the soul could become merged with God without the intervention of anyone else. This union with the divine eliminated the need for any intercessor to help the individual understand God. She stripped everyone, even powerful bishops, of worldly power. She found authority for her beliefs in herself, not in the writings of the Church Fathers.

She did not use the modesty topos, putting herself down as we saw in Hrotsvit who spoke of her "little talent".[13] Rather, Porete wrote boldly, "I have promised, says this Soul, with regard to being taken by Love, to say something about the seven states that we call beings – because that is what they are."[14] Concerning the first state achieved by the Soul on its pilgrimage, Marguerite contended, "[I]n this state I have found myself for some time. Now I in no way fear to gain the height, nor should anyone if you have a gentle heart and are full of noble courage."[15] Her fearlessness and confidence conflicted with the humility more seemly for female writers. She insisted on publicly expressing her view, including to other women. As a public figure, Marguerite refused to be a victim, almost embracing her role as a trailblazer even unto death.

When she was burned at the stake June 1, 1310, the crowd was said to have been sympathetic to her. They cried in recognition of her courage and her steadfastness in refusing to deny her beliefs. She was burned alongside a relapsed Jew – who had converted to Christianity and was suspected of having returned to Judaism – one of many Jews killed in the Middle Ages for their faith. Marguerite's final moments were recorded:

> She showed many signs of penitence at her end, both noble and devout, by which the hearts of many were piously and tearfully turned to compassion, as revealed by the eyes of the witnesses who beheld this scene.[16]

Shortly after her death, a decree was formulated suggesting that "some beguines ... seem to be led by a particular insanity". Yet "faithful women" may "live a life of penance".[17] In 1318 Pope John XXII softened the wholesale condemnation of Beguines by supporting "numerous women ... who lead

---

Burning people and books

Burning a book may not seem so shocking – after all, you could just go to a bookstore or order another online, right? In the Middle Ages, each book was handwritten and created. It symbolized hundreds of hours of work. Totalitarian governments like the Nazis have burned books. As the nineteenth-century German poet Heinrich Heine wrote, "[W]here they burn books, they will ultimately burn people also."[18] This was certainly true for Marguerite. Perhaps those of you in the USA could celebrate Banned Books week, observed annually at the end of September, by reading about Marguerite and other writers whose works were destroyed.

---

lives beyond reproach." After all, "[r]ight reason does not permit that the innocent be judged equal to the guilty."[19] Nevertheless, those who persisted in false contentions must be removed "from the error of their ways [so that] no more healthy sheep become infected."[20]

Marguerite's accusers commanded that all copies of her book be given up. But theirs has not been the last word. Despite attempts at curbing the beliefs of the Beguines and even though Marguerite was burnt, her book lived on in various translations and continued to be read for centuries. The last known Beguine died 700 years later, in 2013.

Learn more

- Na Prous Boneta's actual testimony: http://www.fordham.edu/halsall/source/naprous.asp.
- The testimony of her sister, Alisseta Boneta: http://www.history.vt.edu/Burr/heresy/beguins/Alisseta_Boneta.html.
- You can see some Christ dolls at the Bishopric Augsburg, Germany: http://www.bistum-augsburg.de/index.php/bistum/Nachrichten/Ein-Buendel-voller-Hoffnung_id_100366.
- Flemish Béguinages have been declared members of the UNESCO World Heritage Site: http://whc.unesco.org/pg.cfm?cid=31&id_site=855

Notes

1. Elizabeth Alvilda Petroff, *Medieval Women's Visionary Literature* (NY: Oxford University Press, 1986), 220.
2. Carolyne Larrington, *Women and Writing in Medieval Europe: A Sourcebook* (London: Routledge, 1995), 121.
3. Petroff, 198.
4. Barbara Newman, *From Virile Woman to WomanChrist: Studies in Medieval Religion and Literature* (Philadelphia: University of Pennsylvania Press, 1995), 248.
5. Kathleen Ashley, 'Cultures of Devotion', in *The Oxford Handbook of Women and Gender in Medieval Europe*, edited by Judith M. Bennett and Ruth Mazo Karras (Oxford: Oxford University Press, 2013), 514.
6. Sean L. Field, *The Beguine, the Angel, and the Inquisitor: The Trials of Marguerite Porete and Guiard of Cressonessart* (Notre Dame: University of Notre Dame Press, 2012), 120.
7. Field, 143.
8. Petroff, 289.
9. Petroff, 286.
10. Peter Dronke, *Women Writers of the Middle Ages* (Cambridge: Cambridge University Press, 1984), 218.
11. Petroff, 296.
12. Petroff, 296.
13. Katharina Wilson, trans., *The Plays of Hrotsvit of Gandersheim* (NY: Garland Publishers, 1989), 3.
14. Petroff, 294.
15. From Heinrich Heine. http://www.egs.edu/library/heinrich-heine/biography/. Born Jewish, he later converted to Christianity due to discrimination he faced. Criticized by authorities in his own time for political criticism, the Nazis burned his writings 100 years later.
16. Petroff, 295.
17. Field, 162.
18. Elizabeth M. Makowski, 'When is a Beguine not a Beguine? Names, Norms, and Nuance in Canonical Literature', in *Labels and Libels: Naming Beguines in Northern Medieval Europe,* edited by L. Böhringer, J. Kolpacoff Deane, and H. van Engen (Turnhout, Belgium: Brepols, 2014), 94.
19. Makowski, 99.
20. Makowski, 100.

CHAPTER 17

St Birgitta of Sweden (1302/3-1373)

RIGHTEOUS REFORMER

The only woman canonized in the fourteenth century, fewer than 20 years after her death, Birgitta of Sweden lived an active life. She was born in Sweden to a powerful and important family. The legal proceedings determining her sanctity relate various events in her youth showing her religious nature from early on. We are told that even before she was born, she saved her mother threatened by a storm at sea. At her birth, a priest had a vision of the Virgin Mary who says "A daughter is born ... whose voice will be heard throughout the world with admiration."[1] Birgitta claimed to have met the Virgin Mary at age seven, helping her to fashion lovely embroidery. Her first mystical vision of Christ being crucified occurred when she was only 10 years old.

Birgitta's father, Birger Persson, was a judge; her mother, related to the royal court, died when Birgitta was only a girl. Thereafter, her aunt and godmother, Katarina, took care of Birgitta. Swedish law not only prohibited a girl from marrying against her parents' will, but also against her own will. Birgitta married 18-year-old Ulf Gudmarsson when she was about 13 years old, spending the first year as chaste companions. He served as a judge and member of the king's council, so she became a woman with powerful connections. An intimate of the Swedish royal court between 1335 and early 1340s, she encouraged King Magnus Eriksson and his wife Blanche to be morally upright. Birgitta never minced her words, warning the king's brother "if you do not improve your way of life, neither will you be king, nor will you live long".[2] He died a short time later.

Birgitta and Ulf had eight children, four boys (Karl, Birger, Benedict, and Gudmur) and four girls (Martha, Katarina, Ingeborg, and Cecilia). Birgitta highly valued learning. Though never officially taking religious vows, she was educated in religious writings and the Christian tradition. Two of her boys were taught at home, one at a monastery, and the youngest at a school in

et mēbris tuis egris refrigeria
prestari fac nos,ppicuis ipsius
meritis a gehenne incendijs libe
ratos integros mente et corpe ti
bi feliater in gloria presentari
per dnm. Oro deuota ad dnm
ihesum xpm Omine ihe
su xpnste.
Ego cogno sc
co me graui
ter peccasse
et libenter
volo me e
mendare
per graciam
ergo tuam
et ppter amaram passione tuā
miserere mei in hora mortis mee.

Bridget (Birgitta) of Sweden depicted in a prayer book, c. 1500 (© British Library Board, Yates Thompson 18 f. 234)

Stockholm. Birgitta's daughters were sent to convents to be educated. As was standard in the lives of the saints, her activities as a pious wife and mother described her as instructing her children in religion, taking care of the family estate, and helping the poor and needy through charity. She also encouraged her husband to be devout, teaching him "to say the hours of our Lady (and say them every day) and directed him to works of mercy and good deeds, and made him willing to seek Saint James, and she with him, in great travail."[4]

Pilgrimage was in her blood. Not only had her father travelled to Santiago de Compostela in northwestern Spain, but also many generations of the family before him had visited the Holy Land. When her youngest boy, Gudmar, died, she and Ulf, still grieving, made their way to visit the shrine of St Olaf in Trondheim, Norway. Birgitta convinced Ulf to go with her to Santiago in 1341. He did, only to die three years later after their return to Sweden.

Deeply emotional and spiritually impressive visions led her to found her own religious order – the only order of nuns from Northern Europe – dedicated to the Virgin Mary. It was called the Order of the Holy Saviour (or Birgittine Order) in 1346.

She related these visions in her *Revelations* as coming from God, Christ, the Virgin Mary, and various saints, such as John the Baptist and Saint Agnes. A number of male editors and transcribers copied and translated Birgitta's works from Swedish into Latin to enormous success. Early versions of her *Revelations* circulated in Sweden and were even presented in 1346–7 before an international company of dignitaries.

Moving to the court in Stockholm in 1347, she gained the approval of both the king and clergy. The king and queen even gave her a castle for her religious order, which focused on women, with an abbess to rule over the double monastery. Ultimately Birgitta's own daughter, Katarina, took on this prestigious role. The order was especially dedicated to study and learning. Though poverty was a vow to uphold, members of the order could retain as many books as they liked. Perhaps not surprisingly for a woman from the cold climes of Scandinavia, Birgitta stipulated practical garb for members of her order – including winter clothes lined with wooly sheepskin. The Birgittine nuns worshipped with a unique divine service focused on the Virgin Mary.

Seeking papal approval for the order she founded in Vadstena, Birgitta arrived in Rome in 1349. She made contact with the pope and became actively engaged in church politics. Even though Pope Urban V was reluctant to approve her

The Bishop of Assisi Handing a Palm to Saint Clare (German (Nuremberg) (c. 1360); Metropolitan Museum of Art, The Cloisters Collection, 1984 (1984.343), © Metropolitan Museum of Art. ARTstor: MMA_ IAP_10311574928)

order, it ultimately got approval – perhaps because she said Christ Himself ordered her to found it. In Birgitta's vision, Christ assured Birgitta that He had brought her "the rules of the order that has to be founded and begun in Sweden, at Vadstena. It has come forth from my mouth".[5] Surely God surpassed an earthly man's power, even if the Pope did lead the worldly church.

Birgitta stayed on in Rome for the Jubilee Year of 1350 where those flocking to Rome could receive forgiveness for their sins. She spent the last 24 years of her life in this Italian city. The Romans came to respect and admire her for helping the poor. Though at times her *Revelations* came under suspicion, Birgitta maintained that Christ was all-powerful. He could decide to reveal himself to whomever he

St Clare of Assisi (1194–1253)

"The little plant of the holy Father".[3] A companion to St Francis and inspired by his leadership in the early thirteenth century, St Clare founded the Poor Clares, a religious monastic order committed to serving the poor and sick. Guided by a voice from God, she was said to have frightened off Saracen (Muslim) troops threatening to attack her convent. Despite papal pressure, Clare insisted that the principles laid down by Francis needed to be followed. Ultimately, Pope Innocent IV agreed to her stipulations.

chose – whether the poor, the mentally handicapped, or female. Indeed, by situating her humble position as a mere woman in a sinful world, Birgitta's stance made her the ideal medium through which God wished to contact and transform the corrupt world. Unlike Hildegard's works which described how church theology and even the cosmos worked, Birgitta's was more an etiquette book of the soul, a how-to book: how to save your own souls and those of others.

Her *Revelations* described horrific scenes of suffering in hell. Better to reform yourself now, than feel pain later for all eternity. Just like the traditional intercessor or mediator in the church – the Virgin Mary – Birgitta set herself up as a representative on earth through whom sinners could contact God and be saved. She enthusiastically endorsed indulgences, the means whereby sins could be forgiven for the dead to get them more quickly out of purgatory. She urged the living to pray for the dead, thus hurrying them through punishments after death making them worthy of heaven.

By the end of her life, Birgitta was said to have experienced over 700 mystical visions, dealing with moral behavior, theological problems, visions from the Holy Land, and political insight. Birgitta agitated against corruption in the church. Both ecclesisastical (church) and secular authorities like kings and Swedish aristocrats were chastised for their ills and were strenuously urged to act in an upright fashion. She was fearless in expressing her opinion, even

St Birgitta (Bridget), with a book, presents a message from Christ to a bishop (image taken from Revelations [Liber Celestis] of St Bridget of Sweden, c. 1410–1420 © British Library Board, Cotton Claudius B. I, f. 117)

St Catherine of Siena (1347–1380)

"Let us rise above every imperfection."[6] One of four women Doctors of the Catholic Church and a patron saint of Italy and Europe, this fourteenth-century mystic resisted her family's attempts to marry her off. She preached publicly, something not allowed for women at this time. An advisor to popes, Catherine's theological writings advocated reform. Considering herself the bride of Christ, she practiced self-starvation and died at the age of 33 as one of the so-called Holy Anorexics. To read more about medieval women's relationship with food, including the phenomenon of 'holy anorexia' or 'anorexia mirabilis', two standard books provide fascinating details. These books are Caroline Walker Bynum's *Holy Feast and Holy Fast: The Religious Significance of Food to Medieval Woman* (Berkeley: University of California Press, 1987) and Rudolph M. Bell's *Holy Anorexia* (Chicago: University of Chicago Press, 1985).

---

proposing to end the conflict that became the Hundred Years War (see Chapters 19 and 20). A prophetess, she predicted the Black Plague that killed up to half the population of Europe in the late 1340s and the death of Pope Clement VI in 1352. Birgitta even arranged for an unprecedented meeting between Emperor Charles with Pope Urban V in 1368. While her visions could have gotten her into trouble, she always wisely sided with the Church's power over secular authority.

A catalyst for change both religious and political, Birgitta wielded influence on the highest levels of society. Due to political agitation, the popes had lived in Avignon in the south of France since 1304. Birgitta convinced Pope Urban V to return to Rome in 1367. After 3 years, he left, finding the situation in Rome unpleasant. It took Saint Catherine of Siena to convince the next pope, Gregory XI, to return to Rome.

Birgitta became a pilgrim, travelling to major sights, including in Cologne, Germany, and the Holy Land. Her children periodically accompanied her. It was best to travel in a group on pilgrimage. Robbery, theft, and murder were known to have taken place against pilgrims. Birgitta's daughter Katarina feared being raped when she went to meet her mother in Rome, where she stayed for many years. In 1372, her children Karl, Birger, and Katarina decided to accompany Birgitta to the Holy Land. Birgitta's life woven into her family circle reflected and helped promote interest in the Holy Family (Saint Anne, Saint Joseph, and the Virgin Mary) who became increasingly represented in art in the later Middle Ages. Birgitta embodied how sanctity could become part of everyday family life.

She and her children associated with nobility. In Naples, Italy, Birgitta was especially nervous for her son, Karl, whom she suspected of having an affair with Queen Giovanna. They decided to wed, even though he was already

Saint Catherine of Siena Receiving the Stigmata (Giovanni di Paolo, Italian (Sienese) (c. 1400–1482); Metropolitan Museum of Art, Robert Lehman Collection, 1975 (1975.1.34); photo by Malcolm Varon © The Metropolitan Museum of Art. ARTstor: MMA_IAP_10312707921)

Crime on Pilgrimage

Pilgrims were not immune from crime while on pilgrimage. A case from 1398/9 told of Emma, "wife of William Bole of Walsingham,"[7] who was raped and robbed while on pilgrimage to Canterbury, as was a prioress on her way to Jerusalem. Agnes Paston wrote about how "enemies ... seized two pilgrims, a man and a woman, and they robbed the woman and let her go."[8] Other women were known to have been kidnapped. Nefarious sea captains even sold their passengers into slavery. Despite the dangers, many men and women undertook these hazardous journeys, suggesting deep devotion to their faith.

---

married. Tragically, Karl died of illness, but Birgitta continued to the Holy Land. While in Jerusalem she stayed in the humble pilgrims' hospice rather than the Franciscan monastery, the elite pilgrim hotel.

Birgitta died in 1373, whereupon her remains were sent to Vadstena, Sweden, site of her original Birgittine Foundation, where they are still the goal for pilgrims devoted to her memory. Birgitta was said to have saved people's lives with miraculous cures. Her *Revelations* became well-known throughout Europe and appeared in many languages, including Middle English. Numerous Birgittine houses popped up all over Europe. England was especially fond of Birgitta. The English Birgittine Syon Abbey was founded in 1415 by King Henry V and maintained close ties with royalty. It was renowned for the learning the nuns mastered until the institution was closed by King Henry VIII in 1539. Legend tells us that, when the body of this destructive monarch was taken there on the way to burial in Windsor after his death, dogs chewed his corpse.

The official designation of sanctity made her a key figure for women in the Middle Ages. Not a virgin – she was the mother of eight children – she obviously had known intimacy with her husband. Her status as a married mother, then a chaste widow, was hugely influential for other women. Birgitta was a model for how a married woman living a life with a large family could still attain sainthood. As we shall see with our next medieval woman, Margery Kempe saw Birgitta as a model to aspire to – in her visions, her pilgrimage activity, and her public renown or, in Margery's case, notorious infamy.

While many luminaries defended Birgitta – emperors, kings, and queens – in 1415 the intellect Jean Gerson referenced her activities as suspect.

Teenagers and women in particular may have religious enthusiasms that were "overheated, versatile, [and unbridled]" and visions "false, illusionary, [and] frivolous".[9] Well over 100 years after her death, Martin Luther, the founder of the Protestant faith, thought of her as 'crazy Bridget'. Fortunately, their views were in the minority. Birgitta not only became canonized as a saint in 1391, but also as the patron saint of Sweden in 1396. In 1999, she became canonized as one of six patron saints of Europe, along with two other women – St Catherine of Siena and Edith Stein (Saint Teresa Benedicta of the Cross).

Learn more

- Birgitta was described in the *Acts of the Saints* as a virgin, wife, and widow. To read a fictional life of a comparable Scandinavian woman, delve into a trilogy by the Norwegian Noble Prize-winning woman, Sigrid Undset. Her famous series follows the life of *Kristin Lavransdatter*. King Magnus, who was a key champion of Birgitta, appears in this imaginative book series.
- Director Franco Zeffirelli's stunning film *Brother Sun, Sister Moon* (1972) recreates the friendship of St Clare and St Francis, infusing it with the 'flower power' sensibilities of the 1960s and 1970s counter culture.

Notes

1. Birgitta of Sweden, *Saint Bride and Her Book: Birgitta of Sweden's Revelations,* translated by Julia Bolton Holloway (Cambridge: D. S. Brewer, 2000), 3.
2. Barbara Obrist, 'The Swedish Visionary: Saint Bridget', in *Medieval Women Writers,* edited by Katharina M. Wilson (Athens, GA: University of Georgia Press, 1984), 248.
3. Elizabeth Alvilda Petroff, *Medieval Women's Visionary Literature* (NY: Oxford University Press, 1986), 243.
4. Nanda Hopenwasser, and Signe Wegener, '*Vox Matris*: The Influence of St. Birgitta's *Revelations* on *The Book of Margery Kempe*: St. Birgitta and Margery Kempe As Wives and Mothers', in *Crossing the Bridge: Comparative Essays on Medieval European and Heian Japanese Women Writers,* edited by Barbara Stevenson and Cynthia Ho (NY: Palgrave Macmillan, 2000), 63.
5. Obrist, 245–246.
6. Petroff, 269.
7. Susan Signe Morrison, *Women Pilgrims in Late Medieval England: Private Piety as Public Performance* (London: Routledge, 2000), 57.
8. Diane Watt, trans., *The Paston Women: Selected Letters* (Cambridge: D. S. Brewer, 2004), 27.
9. Obrist, 236.

Margery Kempe often went on pilgrimage, including to Walsingham, England, where this stained glass comes from. It shows the Annunciation, when the angel Gabriel tells Mary she, as a virgin, will bear Jesus (St Mary's Church, Little Walsingham, England; photo by John A. Twyning, with permission and thanks)

CHAPTER 18

Margery Kempe
(c. 1373–after 1438)

PEERLESS PILGRIM

argery Kempe went mad after giving birth to her first child at the age of 20 in about 1393. In late fourteenth-century England, there would be no diagnosis of post-partum depression. Rather, her anxiety and fear of damnation was channeled into what the culture understood at the time. She was out of her head; demons seemed to attack her. She wanted to die, but her husband and family kept her bound to protect herself. Only a vision of Jesus Christ, coming, she claimed, "half a year, eight weeks and some odd days"[1] after the crisis first began, cured her spirits. Her wits became stable and her husband handed her back the buttery or pantry keys, symbolizing her ability to take on her proper domestic role as housewife again.

Considered the writer of the first autobiography in the English language, Margery dictated her story to a series of male scribes who took down her words. Though her father was both a mayor and alderman, prestigious positions, she was most likely illiterate. This did not preclude her from being a 'writer', since she created a narrative of her life with the help of a secretary. It was important that the person writing down her story in the third person was a credible male, so that her life story would be believed.

And what a life she had! She gave birth to 14 children, though she only wrote at length about one particular son after he grew up. She ran a brewing business, a common occupation for women in the Middle Ages. Unfortunately, her business failed. She had a horse mill to grind grain, but the horses refused to do their work. People said she was cursed. Open about her faults and weaknesses, Margery appeals to modern readers and legions of scholars.

Margery wanted to be chaste because of her love for Christ. Yet she was no nun and had to pay her marital debt to her husband, the debt of companionship in bed. Finally, after 14 children, she asked if they could live together as brother and sister. Saying "You are no good wife",[2] John agreed to her demand on one condition: that she pay his debts and not fast on Fridays as she liked to do in

Walsingham

A shrine dedicated to the Virgin Mary, Walsingham was said to have a drop of the Virgin's milk. Legend says Mary was breast-feeding the baby Jesus on the flight to Egypt. Some milk spurted to the floor of the cave they were sheltered in, which eventually found its way to this popular English shrine sought out by women who wanted to get pregnant or had problems with lactation and breastfeeding. In order to pray to the Virgin for a male child, Henry VIII accompanied his wife, Catherine of Aragon, to Walsingham, years before he was responsible for having it destroyed in 1538 during the Protestant Reformation. Today it has been revived as a popular pilgrimage goal and center that strives for understanding among differing denominations.

honor of the day of the week Christ died. Husband and wife continued to live together throughout their lives. But they did not stay put at home in Bishop's (now King's) Lynn, Norfolk. Margery wanted to show her love for God by going on pilgrimage. Margery traveled throughout England, including to a shrine called Walsingham, about 25 miles (40 km) from her home.

Margery, despite not being able to read, nevertheless knew many important writings, including the Bible and visionary works written by other devout Christians such as Saint Birgitta. How did she know them? Through listening. Preachers would quote the Bible. Kind literate people would read aloud to those wanting to listen and take in inspirational stories – like a live audiobook.

In addition to local pilgrimages in England, Margery went abroad to the most famous pilgrimage sites in Europe and the Holy Land, today's Middle East. Travel back then was not so easy: you had to get permission from your parish priest to depart on such a trip. You would arrange with a lawyer about your earthly possessions should you die while gone. It would be about a year's journey to and from the Holy Land from England. Such a journey would entail sailing to the continent, traveling overland through Germany to Italy, and picking up a ship in Venice, Italy. The more you paid, the better the care and food you received, such as getting a donkey to ride upon as opposed to walking.

Jerusalem was a key site to visit, and Margery went to the Mount of Calvary where Christ was said to have been crucified. She cried and wailed in sadness at the memory of his death, which seemed to be taking place right before her in a vision of ecstatic passion. Margery visited the famous Spanish pilgrimage shrine in Santiago de Compostela, as well as Rome, home to the pope and key to Christian history. While there, Kempe visited sites that were significant to her role model Saint Birgitta, including the room she died in and the very stone upon which Birgitta had had a revelation of Christ. Margery even made sure to meet a woman who had been Saint Birgitta's maid: "[T]he maiden said that her lady, Saint [Birgitta], was goodly and meek to every creature and that she had a laughing countenance."[3]

Margery also visited Julian of Norwich, a well-known anchorite in nearby Norwich. Anchorites were meant to spend their time thinking about God, meditating, and praying. A visitor like Margery sought a kind of blessing or sanction of her own visions of Christ from the respected Julian. Julian's writings, now known as the *Showings* or *Revelations of Divine Love*, described her own mystical encounters with Christ. Margery likewise had all sorts of visions including of the birth of the Virgin Mary herself. Margery's crying and tears were key elements in her story. She saw the world through a Biblical lens. If she saw a woman holding a baby, Margery 'read' them as the Virgin Mary and baby Jesus and began to cry. If she saw a man beating an animal, she interpreted the violence as the whipping of Christ. This spiritual eye with which she saw the world was typical of visionaries.

The way Margery interpreted everyday life caused her to sob

Pewter pilgrimage badge portraying the Annunciation with the Virgin Mary and angel Gabriel. Pilgrims would buy and wear such badges as souvenirs (from the Shrine of Our Lady of Walsingham, England, fourteenth century, with permission the Museum of London)

Julian of Norwich (c. 1342–1416)

"Jesus is our true mother by nature."[4] This English mystic lived in a cell as an anchoress for much of her life. She wrote over her entire lifetime about the series of visions she experienced at the age of thirty, developing a theology in which she pictured Christ as a merciful mother and compassionately argued for universal salvation. Sin was good since it brings us closer to God. Whatever your faith, Julian's comfort and compassion are exemplified in these famous words, "[A]ll shall be well, and all shall be well, and all manner of things shall be well."[5]

---

and roar. Some people took this public display of emotion to be a sign of her sanctity. Others, not believing she saw God, accused her of being possessed by the devil. They thought she was a hypocritical liar, just wanting a lot of attention. One priest even forbade her to be in church when he preached. To Margery's credit, she did not deny that her noisy behavior could be annoying. Yet another priest, urged by his mother, read holy books such as Birgitta's with Margery, and found *himself* spiritually inspired by *her*.

Margery got in trouble with the law – church law. Accused of being a Lollard, an English heretic, she could have been burnt at the stake. Yet she managed to wriggle out of such dangerous situations. One of the clerks of the Archbishop of York accused her of being of the devil because "she speaks of the gospel".[6] Since Margery openly spoke about God and her visions and beliefs, she appeared to be publically teaching. This was forbidden to women. Accused, Margery said, "I preach not, sir, I go in no pulpit. I use but communication and good words, and that will I do while I live."[7] A master of language, Margery was able to free herself from possible accusations by saying she was just using "good words". In fact, the Archbishop even took a shine to her tale about priests who misbehave.

Margery suffered the cruelty of her fellow pilgrims when she was in a dangerous position – a lone woman travelling across Europe who could not speak the local tongues. They took her maid away from her, she had to eat apart from them, and they bought no wine or bedding for her. Yet some did come to her rescue. Again and again in Margery's story, she would be spitefully attacked, only to find consolation in fellow travelers who came to believe in her visions and her special grace. Whether she really saw visions of Christ or not, we can never know. What matters to us was that Margery clearly believed it.

Her story was one of many life stories told by medieval women and men about their spiritual encounters with saints, the Virgin Mary, and God. Margery lived an extraordinary life – full of travel, danger, anguish, and comfort. That she defied male authority even at the risk of death itself speaks to the conviction of her beliefs. Her perseverance despite her persecutors pays heed to her resolution and will. Her story provides a model for anyone bullied or oppressed who wishes to bear witness to her own pain and find solace in the knowledge of her own truth. Now considered one of the most important early writers in English literature, Margery's book is required reading in many English classes in colleges and universities.

Learn more
- Margery's book is digitized: http://www.bl.uk/manuscripts/FullDisplay.aspx?ref =Add_MS_61823.
- Rebecca Barnhouse's *The Book of the Maidservant* (New York: Random House Books for Young Readers, 2009) imagines Margery Kempe's life from the perspective of her servant Johanna.
- Candace Robb (pen name Emma Campion) has written numerous dazzling novels set in fourteenth-century England. Focusing on the women – fictional and historical – who influenced events and experienced love and betrayal, these books bring to life the lives of medieval women, such as the 'Fair Maid of Kent' in *A Triple Knot* (New York: Broadway Books 2014) and Alice Perrers, who really was *The King's Mistress* (New York: Broadway Books 2011).

Lollards

Followers of the Oxford University theologian John Wyclif (d. 1384), Lollards promoted the use of the vernacular (English rather than Latin) to spread God's word – even though the accepted Bible was itself a translation by St Jerome (late fourth century CE) into Latin. While many Lollards in the early years were academics or aristocrats, after a purging of Lollardy in the 1410s the vast bulk of Lollard activity was among lay people. Critics of the Lollards disliked women disputing fine theological points from the Bible that was now in a language they could understand. Many Lollard beliefs were similar to those promoted in the Protestant Reformation of the sixteenth century.

Notes

1. Margery Kempe, *The Book of Margery Kempe*, edited and translated by Lynn Staley (NY: W. W. Norton, 2001), 7.
2. Kempe/Staley, 18.
3. Kempe/Staley, 69.
4. Julian of Norwich, *Revelations of Divine Love (Short Text and Long Text)*, translated by Elizabeth Spearing (London: Penguin Books, 1998), 140.
5. Julian/Spearing, 80.
6. Kempe/Staley, 93.
7. Kempe/Staley, 93.

PART V

"MY MOST HONORED LADIES"[1]

Christine de Pizan, *The Book of the City of Ladies*

Christine de Pizan giving instructions to her son, Jean (© British Library Board, Harley 4431, f. 261v)

CHAPTER 19

Christine de Pizan
(1364–c. 1431)

VOCAL FEMINIST

young woman sits reading in her study. Suddenly, she feels deeply depressed. The books she reads – works that everyone says were important, true, and good – maintain that "the behavior of women is inclined to and full of every vice".[2] She comes to detest "myself and the entire feminine sex, as though we were monstrosities in nature". She even pleads with God. "[W]hy did You not let me be born in the world as a man, so that ... I ... would be as perfect as a man is said to be?"[3] Even though this young woman knows many girls and women who were virtuous and upstanding, these famous men could not all be wrong in what they write. Could they? "I relied more on the judgment of others than on what I myself felt and knew."[4] This story reminds us not to pay attention to the harsh judgment of others when we know the worthy truth of our own and others' characters.

Christine, born in Venice, Italy, in 1364, began her early years in nearby Bologna. When she was just a tiny baby, her father Thomas voyaged to Paris to become the court astrologer to King Charles V, known as the 'Wise'. For several years the family could not join him. Then, the happy day arrived when they could be sent for, to join him in royal circles in France when Christine was only four. Dressed in rich garments typical of the area they came from in Lombardy, Italy, Christine's mother and family first met the king on a cold December day at the Louvre palace. A close advisor to Charles, Christine's father associated with the highest of nobility. Because of his profession, he established himself with royalty as did his family. Christine became familiar with princesses and courtiers.

Best of all, Thomas supported Christine's desire to study and learn. Not every girl was given this opportunity. While a noble family might hire a tutor to teach girls in the family, the only other way a young female could become proficient in Latin, rhetoric, and other subjects was to enter a convent as a child or young teenager. Thereafter, she might take a vow to be a nun or simply leave the convent once a marriage had been arranged for her. Thanks to her father, Christine did not have to leave home for her high-powered educational training.

At age 15, she was considered ready for marriage in 1379. Numerous knights, clerics, and scholars desired her hand in marriage. Her father, rich in knowledge and intellect rather than wealth, sought out a fellow scholar for her. Though it was an arranged marriage, it became a love match between Christine and her husband, Etienne de Castel. The king, in turn, hired him to be a notary and financial secretary. They had three children, two sons – Jean and a boy who died – and a daughter, Marie. All was perfect in their lives. Etienne even encouraged her studies. As Christine tells it, Fortune beamed happily on her and her family.

Then, tragedy struck. First, the king died unexpectedly at the age of 44. This meant Christine's father was out of a job. Even worse, the money from books and other items the king had promised Thomas verbally had not been attested to on paper. So Thomas's salary was sadly shrunken. He had not saved much money, preferring to share what he had with the poor. In the wake of this financial hardship, Christine's father sickened and died. Christine's husband became the head of the household. Incredibly, only five years later Etienne died in 1390, succumbing to the plague at the age of 34.

Twenty-five-year-old Christine was left in charge of her children and the de Pizan household, including her mother and niece. In despair, she did not even want to go on living. If that heart-break were not enough, Christine had been left with no knowledge of how the financial accounts were arranged. She was even cheated by people claiming false debts:

> For it was the custom for married men not to talk about or declare the complete state of their affairs to their wives, from which often comes harm as it was to happen to me in my experience, and it makes no sense unless women, instead of being ignorant, learn wise management of such matters.[5]

Thus she initiated a feminist critique of marriage that still is undertaken today. Though she had been happily married, she did not want to rewed, having promised her beloved husband never to unite with another man again.

Christine had had an elite upbringing at the most admired court in Europe. Her father had given her an extraordinary education, particularly for a female. Yet here she was, barely out of her teenage years, essentially destitute with heavy financial obligations. She had few options. "Now it

> ### *The first professional woman writer*
> Christine is often called the first woman to be paid for her writing talents. Many women had written before Christine's time. But most were in the church or of the nobility. They did not need – or expect – to be recompensed for their poems, commentaries, or stories. They may have had a patron at court, a person of wealth who would support them while they wrote. Most writers used scribes, female and male, to copy their works.

was necessary for me to go to work, something which I, nurtured on the finer things of life, had not learned."[6] Initially, she copied manuscripts as a scribe. Then she did what she could with her talents: she became the first professional woman writer.

Christine's first famous writing came in the form of a series of letters. Letters were not always private writings in the Middle Ages. Often, they were meant to be shared and discussed. She began a writing exchange with Jean de Montreuil, secretary to the King, about the most popular French poem at the time, *Roman de la Rose* (*The Romance of the Rose*). An allegory in which personified characters such Jealous Husband and Reason appear, a Lover seeks out his beloved, a rose in a garden. Along the way, he meets many characters who talk with him. Sometimes they tell the Lover very rude things about women – they even lie about how women are all bad and just want to be unfaithful to their husbands. One of the most notorious characters is the Old Woman, who tells the Lover how women trick their husbands, find young lovers, and get money from men.

Some readers found these passages amusing. Christine did not. She felt that this poem slandered women by telling lies about them. The women she knew were nothing like that. She knew *she* was nothing like that. So she decided to fight back the best way she knew how – through words. And so the famous *Querelle des Femmes* (*Quarrel about Women*) began. John would write one letter defending the poem *Romance of the Rose* and Christine would challenge him by breaking down every argument he constructed. Fearless, Christine had no shame about publicly calling a man a liar.

She also wrote in a clever, subtle way. Sarcastically she twisted the modesty topos.

[I]nasmuch as the feebleness of my paltry intellect would enable me …
I … mean to say, divulge and manifestly uphold that, your good grace
notwithstanding, you have committed a great error without reason in giving
such perfect praise of [*The Romance of the Rose*], which could better be called
utter idleness than a useful work, in my judgment.[7]

When the poem suggested that a man should never tell a woman a secret,
Christine called such a sentiment "hodgepodge, rubbish, and wasted words".[8]
She even accused the poem's author of only frequenting bad women's
company since apparently that was all he knew about women.

Ouch.

Every argument raised, she smashed with her pen. Concerning love, she
wrote: "[I]t is less bad to be deceived than to deceive."[9] She concluded:

And may folly, arrogance, or presumption not be imputed to me for daring,
I a woman, to take up and refute such a subtle author and whittle down the
praise of him, when he, only one man, dared to undertake the defamation and
blasphemy, without exception, of an entire sex.[10]

For Christine, to say someone was like a woman was a compliment, not an
insult.

This public letter exchange made Christine famous. She already had her
supporters – all the women she would have known at court. Christine even
bound together the letters from the exchange debating women and presented
them to the French queen, Isabeau de Bavière, in 1402. When Christine
decided to write a longer work, there was lots of interest. While she wrote a
number of books, the one she is most famous for today is called *The Book of
the City of Ladies*, written 1404–5.

The book is divided into three parts, each one dominated by one of three
women, named Reason, Rectitude, and Justice. Prompted by questions from
the protagonist, also named Christine, each allegorical figure tells multiple
stories of extraordinary women from the beginnings of mythological and
recorded history all the way up to the early fifteenth century in France. A
collection of all the most frequently cited tales and historical actors known
up to Christine's time, it provides a lesson in Western civilization and culture
– from a woman's perspective.

Lady Reason helps Christine build the foundations to an allegorical city
of ladies she will found, one that "will never be destroyed".[11] Rather than
mentioning negative things about her female characters, Christine changes
myths and history to include only the best of women's lives. Lady Rectitude

Christine de Pizan before the personifications of Rectitude, Reason, and Justice in her study, and with other ladies building the City of Ladies (© British Library Board, Harley 4431, f. 290r)

The printing press

Printing, which began in China in the eleventh century, did not come to Europe until the 1450s with Johannes Gutenberg's printing press in Germany, enabling the creation of multiple copies of identically printed books and pamphlets. Before this time, each book was hand-crafted. The most luxurious volumes were made from vellum, or sheepskin, that had been scraped and treated so that it could absorb the ink and paint the scribe and illuminator might use. Each word and image was a singular creation, carefully inscribed by the artist or writer. It might take weeks, months, even years to copy one book. After all, the Bible was a very popular book to read – and it is very long. Imagine writing it out by hand, and then including images as well.

carries a ruler that divides good from evil. She will help Christine measure the buildings and towers for Christine's city. Lady Justice, who determines wisely who ends up in Heaven or Hell, concludes the book with multiple tales of heroines and saints. Justice helps Christine make the golden roofs of the city, hands Christine the keys to the city gates, and populates it with worthy women. At the end, the Ladies leave Christine, who has found consolation in their lesson.

What is also remarkable about the book was that Christine determined how it would look. Not only did she carefully watch the scribes, but she also told the illuminators and artists exactly how she wanted the illustrations to be painted. Christine intended to have total control over her masterpiece. And she got it.

Christine wanted her readers to not only see stories and history in a new way, but to acknowledge that a woman could create such a transformative image of the world, one "so resplendent that you may see yourselves mirrored in it."[12]

Christine went on to write other important works, such as the *Book of Three Virtues* that illustrated how a woman should act in her culture. Princes accepted her volumes and soon the books were discussed all over France. Many of her works were popular in other countries as well. Numerous English translations of her writings were made in the fifteenth century.

Just as Christine was writing with most confidence, there were hard times for France. A long war had been taking place on French soil for over 75 years.

Christine writing with her puppy dog by her side (© British Library Board, Harley 4431, f. 4)

The Hundred Years War was fought between England and France, starting in 1337. The English king at that time, Edward III, felt he should also be king of France. King Philip VI of France, of course, disagreed. Battles raged off and on until 1453. During Christine's heyday, the English King Henry V invaded France and a famous battle called Agincourt was fought in 1415. Many men on both sides died, but some say the English victors massacred the French. Christine's son became a royal secretary to the future French King Charles VII. In 1418 Paris fell to troops sympathetic to the English. Christine fled to the royal convent of Poissy, where her daughter Marie was a nun.

Onto this chaotic scene, a young woman came who epitomized all that Christine praised and found worthy about women. This young woman was brave, pure, religiously devout, and fearless. Christine's last poem in 1429 praised this young woman: "A woman – a simple shepherdess – braver than any man ever was in Rome! ... Oh! what honour for the female sex! ... A little girl of sixteen (isn't this something quite supernatural?)".[13]

This young woman was, of course, Joan of Arc.

Learn more

* Explore Christine's fabulous manuscript with sumptuous images created under her supervision, presented to Queen Isabeau of France in 1414. http://www.pizan.lib.ed.ac.uk/.
* Jess Wells reimagines Christine de Pizan's life in her novel *A Slender Tether* (Whittier NC: Firebrand Press 2013).

Notes

1. Christine de Pizan, *The Book of the City of Ladies*, translated by Earl Jeffrey Richards (NY: Persea Books, 1982), 254.
2. de Pizan/Richards, 4.
3. de Pizan/Richards, 5
4. de Pizan/Richards, 4.
5. Elizabeth Alvilda Petroff, *Medieval Women's Visionary Literature* (NY: Oxford University Press, 1986), 338.
6. Petroff, 338.
7. Petroff, 341.
8. Petroff, 343.
9. Petroff, 342.
10. Petroff, 346.
11. de Pizan/Richards, 11.
12. de Pizan/Richards, 254.
13. Christine de Pizan, 'Ditié de Jehanne D'Arc', translated and edited by Angus J. Kennedy and Kenneth Varty, *Medium Ævum Monographs* New Series IX (1977), accessed May 20, 2013. http://faculty.smu.edu/bwheeler/Joan_of_Arc/OLR/crditie.pdf

CHAPTER 20

▓oan of Arc
(c. 1412–1431)

SAVIOR OF FRANCE

▓oan of Arc was killed while still a teenager, yet her legacy dominates images of the Middle Ages – and, indeed, images of women in the Middle Ages. She had visions (just as many mystics did); she was a farm girl (as the vast majority of people, male or female, would have been familiar with); she fought in battles dressed in men's armor (just as many female saints resorted to male dress); and she was killed by a system designed to oppress behavior that threatened power structures (as with heretics). While her tale has themes we have seen in other women's stories, her story is unique.

Born on January 6, 1412, Joan lived a conventional life as a farmer's daughter in Domrémy, France. Often characterized as a shepherdess, she did housework and "learned to spin and sew".[1] She told in her trial testimony about a Fairies' Tree near her home, though she herself saw no fairies. Starting with puberty at age 13, she began to hear the voices of St Michael, St Catherine of Alexandria, and St Margaret of Antioch. "The first time, I was terrified".[2] With this miraculous connection to divinity, Joan determined to remain a virgin. This was not an unusual thing to decide to do, given the hierarchy that privileged virginity as a state for women to maintain over marriage. Her nickname, *la Pucelle*, the maiden, emphasized her virginity, a means to gain power and legitimacy in her world.

The Hundred Years War (1337–1453), an ongoing conflict between England and France over who had the right to rule in France, caused the English army to periodically invade and at various times take French cities. There were periods of peace during this long period, but the war heated up again during Joan's time. The French royal family was itself divided. France suffered a civil war with the Burgundians who joined in an alliance with the English. Joan was implacable in her defense of Charles VII as the true heir to the French crown. St Michael "told me the pitiful state of the Kingdom of France".[3] She realized that she needed to meet with the king to help save France.

Joan of Arc: miniature. Franco-Flemish school, fifteenth century (from the Archives Nationales, Paris, France; photo credit: Bridgeman-Giraudon/Art Resource, NY

Joan left home despite her father's threats that he would drown her if she did so – especially if she left accompanied by men. Nevertheless, she defied her father's desires, much as the legendary virgin martyrs did in obeying their Heavenly Father (God) over their earthly and biological fathers. In February 1429, Joan convinced the nobleman and captain Robert de Baudricourt of the legitimacy of her voices. Though at first he called her a "poor girl",[4] he later helped by giving her a horse, male dress, a sword, and a small cadre of men to aid her – "a knight, a squire, and four serving-men".[5] She needed male dress as a disguise, for practical reasons, and to help prevent being meddled with sexually. She also kept her hair short, a problem later when she was put on trial. She miraculously knew a sword would be hidden behind an altar in a church dedicated to her beloved St Catherine. When it was found as she predicted, she joined a long list of warriors in legend and history for whom a sword signifies the bearer's mythic power. She was also likened to Jewish warrior heroines from the Bible, such as Esther, Judith, and Deborah.

One of the most famous legends in Joan's history is how she convinced Charles to pay attention to her. Arriving in Chinon in March 1429, she was tricked by being told the wrong man was the king. This low deception could not fool a messenger from God. Her voices told her who the true king was, whom she then approached. During this time, the city of Orléans was surrounded, under siege by the English. Joan declared she could change the course of the war. The court, while remaining dubious about this girl's determined and bold assertion that she could stop the siege of Orléans, agreed to give Joan male armor. The English had already been demoralized, so perhaps they would have lost anyway. Joan's fervor and boasting gave heart to the French. Her words inspired her soldiers so that they fought as though on a crusade for God. Although she forbade drinking, swearing, and womanizing among her troops, Joan in her white armor and carrying a religious banner roused them to achieve victory.

Her letter to the English, dated March 22, 1429, was probably dictated since Joan was undoubtedly illiterate. Her oral command of language is evident in this bold statement. She commanded the king of England and other worthies to "do right in the eyes of the King of Heaven".[6] She demanded the return of keys to the towns the English have taken since she was "sent by God" and "has come here by God's will to re-establish the blood royal".[7] She also addressed those of lower status, such as the archers and soldiers. Leave or "expect to hear news from the Maid who will shortly make you see great damage to yourselves."[8] She assured the king of the English that she would have killed any of his men who refused to leave.

After this victory, Joan urged the French king to extend the fighting to nearby cities under English control. French commanders supported her practical suggestions. After some success, Joan urged that the king move into Burgundian territory where the English held sway. If they succeeded in doing so, Charles could make it to Reims for the traditional royal coronation. One soldier pointed out that the endeavor was undertaken "solely at the recommendation of Joan the Maid ... because it was the desire and the will of God."[9] Charles was crowned in Reims on July 17, 1429. Joan and her parents joined him for this solemn, yet joyous, occasion.

Joan continued her military exploits, though she said she never killed anyone. Moving on Paris to take it back for the French, an eyewitness told that:

> after sunset, the Maid was struck by a crossbow bolt in the thigh. And since she was so stuck, she forced herself to cry more strongly that each man should approach the walls and that they should take that place.[10]

This attempt failed in September 1429. On May 23, 1430, Joan was captured by the enemy at Compiègne. She was pulled from her grey horse by the gold surcoat she wore. Charles, whom she had helped become anointed king, did not even bother to pay her ransom. Secretly, he had made a treaty with the Burgundian leader. Charles abandoned Joan to her fate.

The summer and fall of 1430 she was moved from prison to prison controlled by church authorities. She even jumped from a tower in a failed attempt to get free. At last, she ended up in Rouen. It was here that her trial for heresy took place between January and May 1431. The head of the prosecution was Pierre Cauchon, the bishop of Beauvais. Along with clerics from the University of Paris, Cauchon dominated the proceedings supported by Burgundians in cahoots with the English. Key issues at the trial were the divinity (or not) of her voices and her wearing of male dress. Men, who possessed the highest education possible, pitted themselves against an illiterate peasant girl. They asked questions attempting to trip her up. Concerning St Michael when he appeared to Joan and spoke to her, they asked, "Was he naked?" Joan replied practically, "Do you think that God has not wherewith[al] to clothe him?" "Had he hair?" "Why should it have been cut off?"[11] Her judges told her that she kept nothing "on your person which shows that you are a woman."[12] She said she was willing to wear women's clothing if she could return to her mother.

Joan placed her God over the worldly church. This seemed to be at the root of many accused heretics' beliefs: the primacy of what they perceive as God's will over man-made bureaucracy. Ultimately, the worldly church demanded to be acknowledged as powerful and right. Its power questioned, the church responded violently. As we have seen, female mystics with male religious figures who endorsed their visions were usually protected. In this case, Joan found herself in enemy territory with no champions to support her. Threatened with torture, she said, "[I]f I did say anything, afterwards I should always say that you had made me say it by force."[13] Offered a document to sign, she agreed to wear women's clothing. She also denied the

Joan of Arc as she was imagined in the nineteenth century, listening to her angelic voices. You can see the ethereal saints she hears hovering in the background; (Jules Bastien-Lepage, French (1848–1884; painting from 1879); Metropolitan Museum of Art, Gift of Erwin Davis, 1889 (89.21.1). © The Metropolitan Museum of Art. ARTstor: MMA_IAP_10310750416)

authenticity of her voices. On Thursday, May 24, 1431, she agreed to recant, since "I would rather sign it than burn."[14]

Remember, she was only 19. Would you be able to stand up to the threat of being burnt at the stake?

Four days later, on Monday, May 28, 1431, she put male clothing on and took back her recantation. "What I said, I said for fear of the fire … I was damning myself to save my life."[15] She wore the clothes at the command of God. The clerics declared:

that you blaspheme God and hold him in contempt ... You err in the faith. You boast in vanity. You are suspected of idolatry and you have condemned yourself in not wishing to wear clothing suitable to your sex.[16]

Joan was convicted of heresy for believing in her voices and of idolatry for resuming her male clothing against the court's demands. The court called her revelations "lies, fantasies, seductive and dangerous things ... all these revelations are superstitious, proceeding from evil and diabolical spirits."[17] And so they dismissed the strong words of a young girl. Joan was burnt at the stake for many reasons, including political worries by the Anglo-Burgundians that she was providing too much power for the French side. These highly educated and extremely important and powerful men were afraid of Joan's strength and her refusal to take back her beliefs. As she unwaveringly maintained, "I would rather die than do what I know to be sin."[18]

On Wednesday, May 30, 1431 in Rouen, Joan lamented, "Alas! Am I so horribly and cruelly used, that my clean body, never yet defiled, must this day be burnt and turn to ashes!"[19] As she was killed, she was forced to wear a cap with the following words written in it: *Heretic, Relapsed [Person], Apostate, Idolater*.[20] The actual words were in Latin, the language of the church. A relapsed person has gone back to an undesirable state; in this case, Joan was seen as going back to heretical beliefs. An apostate is someone who abandons her faith – which certainly isn't true for Joan. An idolater worships images, which is blasphemous in the Catholic Church. Her male clothing was interpreted as

---

Skeptics believe

Did she really hear voices and see angels? Religious skeptics such as the American writer Mark Twain and the Irish playwright George Bernard Shaw were highly moved by her story, enough so that each one wrote eloquently about her in prose and drama. Shaw's play premiered in 1923, shortly after her canonization. The drama *Saint Joan*, including the Preface, is most highly recommended. Here Joan learns that she will be condemned to permanent imprisonment:

[T]o shut me from the light of the sky and the sight of the fields and flowers ... is worse ... [B]y your wanting to take them away from me, or from any human creature, I know that your counsel is of the devil, and that mine is of God.[21]

Joan's afterlife

Since her death, Joan has been used by various, often diametrically opposed, forces to support their causes. She has appeared in countless artistic renditions dressed in everything from armor to Victorian dress. She has been used for political purposes on both the left and the right – republican and conservative or reactionary forces – including a US poster in World War I to encourage Americans to buy War Savings Stamps. Manufacturers have exploited poor Joan for advertising purposes, including on clothing, cheese graters, china patterns, fashion, and even cans of kidney beans. http://www.maidofheaven. com/joanofarc_pictures_index.asp.

---

idolatry in order to convict her. At the stake Joan asked to have an image of Christ on the cross held up for her to gaze at while she died.

Her final words were "Jesus, Jesus!"[22]

Joan had the kind of power that comes from a truly remarkable individual. She was able to inspire hope in her own male soldiers and fear in the hearts of enemy warriors. But the attempt to burn her memory from history backfired. After the Hundred Years War ended in 1451, evidence started to be gathered to exonerate Joan. Charles VII and Joan's mother agitated to have her vindicated. Miracles were ascribed to her even in her lifetime, such as a baby who had been dead for 3 days coming to life long enough to be baptized. A sorrowful Englishman, who helped burn her at the stake, claimed to have seen a white dove fly off at her death and was "very afraid that he was damned, for he had burned a holy woman."[23] In 1456, the French canceled Cauchon's conviction. In 1920, Joan was made an official saint of the Catholic Church.

As Christine de Pizan wrote before Joan's death, "It is perfectly obvious that God has special regard for [the female sex] when … the whole Kingdom [is] now recovered and made safe by a woman, something that 5000 men could not have done."[24] Joan would have been an ideal resident in Christine de Pizan's City of Ladies.

Learn more
• Carl Dreyer's silent film *The Passion of Joan of Arc* (1928), riveting and spectacular, caused a furor at its release in the wake of Joan's successful canonization proceedings. The highly evocative music of composer Richard Einhorn accompanies certain releases.

- You can read the film script of *The Passion of Joan of Arc* (1928): http://www. aellea.com/script/passionarc.txt.
- Many documents related to Joan, including her trial testimony, can be found here: http://faculty.smu.edu/bwheeler/ijas/guide.html.

Notes

1. Willard Trask, trans., *Joan of Arc in Her Own Words* (NY: Turtle Point Press, 1996), 3.
2. Trask, 5.
3. Trask, 6.
4. Trask, 7.
5. Trask, 19.
6. Carolyne Larrington, *Women and Writing in Medieval Europe: A Sourcebook* (London: Routledge, 1995), 182.
7. Larrington, 182.
8. Larrington, 182.
9. Deborah Fraioli, 'Joan of Arc', in *Women and Gender in Medieval Europe: An Encyclopedia*, edited by Margaret Schaus (NY: Routledge, 2006), 432.
10. Kelly R. DeVries, '"Because It Was Paris": Joan of Arc's Attack on Paris Reconsidered', in *Magistra Doctissima: Essays in Honor of Bonnie Wheeler*, edited by Dorsey Armstrong, Ann W. Astell, and Howell Chickering (Kalamazoo, MI: Medieval Institute Publications, 2013), 126.
11. Trask, 105.
12. Larrington, 183.
13. Trask, 132.
14. Trask, 135.
15. Trask, 139.
16. Larrington, 184.
17. Jane Marie Pinzino, 'Speaking of Angels: A Fifteenth-Century Bishop in Defense of Joan of Arc's Mystical Voices', in *Fresh Verdicts on Joan of Arc*, edited by Bonnie Wheeler and Charles T. Wood (NY: Garland, 1996), 174, n. 6.
18. Trask, 137.
19. Trask, 143.
20. Susan Schibanoff, 'True Lies: Transvestism and Idolatry in the Trial of Joan of Arc', in Wheeler and Wood, 31.
21. George Bernard Shaw, *Saint Joan: A Chronicle Play In Six Scenes And An Epilogue* (1924) at http://gutenberg.net.au/ebooks02/0200811h.html.
22. Trask, 144.
23. Larrington, 184.
24. Christine de Pizan, 'Ditié de Jehanne D'Arc', translated and edited by Angus J. Kennedy and Kenneth Varty, *Medium Ævum Monographs* New Series IX (1977), accessed May 20, 2013. http://faculty.smu.edu/bwheeler/Joan_of_Arc/OLR/crditie.pdf

CHAPTER 21

extile Concerns

HOLY TRANSVESTITES AND THE DANGERS
OF CROSS-DRESSING

lothing has been important since Adam and Eve became ashamed upon noticing they were naked. While they opted for fig leaves, garment options developed rapidly, a reflection of developing technologies and cultural change. Clothing could indicate your gender, class, religion, or sinful life. Your body, clad in material, would be read like a book by onlookers.

Blanche of Navarre helped the textile industry in her lands while simultaneously solidifying her own power. She – along with Marie de Champagne, Eleanor of Aquitaine's daughter – was able to not only spark a kind of 'commercial revolution',[1] but also enhance the economic vibrancy of her realm. Water-powered mills for grinding grain freed women from the labor-intensive work of hand grinding, thus enabling them to undertake other activities, such as preparing raw materials like wool, cotton, flax, and silk for material production. Technological innovations such as mills and, later, horizontal looms for cloth manufacture spurred a commercial and economic revolution for Western Europe.

Depicted in artworks as undertaking needlework, sewing, and spinning in material artifacts, women practiced many fabric handicrafts. The 224 ft (*c*. 68.25 m) long Bayeux Tapestry, embroidered by women, tells the story leading up to the Norman Conquest. Legend suggests that the wife of William the Conqueror, Matilda, and her ladies-in-waiting created this masterpiece. UNESCO designates it a 'Memory of the World'. In a French tale, one young woman weaves and sews better than another other woman in Europe. "She knows how to make banners, / Lace and fabrics and purses, / and cloths worked from silk and gold / that are well worth a treasure".[2] Geoffrey Chaucer's famous character, the Wife of Bath, was a cloth-maker. Frenchwomen's guilds for silk handkerchief weavers had rules, including not working on a feast day. Women sang cloth songs, often romantic in character, while at work.

In Marie de France's *Guigemar*, each young lover wore a piece of clothing tied so that only the other could undo it, proving their true love. While

Dedication to Queen Isabel of Bavaria, with Christine presenting her book. The long sleeves were considered particularly elegant (from the Collected Works of Christine de Pizan, called The Book of the Queen. © British Library Board, Harley 4431, f. 3)

chastity belts have been exposed as a mythic invention, many other aspects of attire remain to be explored. Clothes in the Middle Ages meant more than coverings from the natural elements. They carried political meaning. They could signify class, status, occupation, marital status (white for virgins), religion, and gender. Sumptuary laws determined what people were allowed to wear. Lower-class people could not wear certain colors or materials exclusively reserved for upper-class people lest the hierarchies of society get mixed up. As *The Good Wife Taught Her Daughter* reminds the reader: "With rich robes and garlands and any such thing, / Do not counterfeit a lady, as if thy lord were a king".[3] In her book *The Treasure of the City of Ladies* dedicated to a 12-year-old princess, Margaret of Burgundy, Christine de Pizan suggested how women of different classes – royalty, nobility, and commons – could use textiles to best represent their families and to earn money. Yet in *The Book of the City of Ladies*, Christine shied away from her mother's desire for her to stick to spinning rather than learning.

Clothes could have allegorical or symbolic meaning. Different groups might be marked publicly. In areas of Europe, Jews had to wear clothes that would distinguish them from Christians, such as a saffron-yellow badge, a red star, or a particular style of hat. Muslims were likewise singled out for sartorial branding and prostitutes in England wore striped hoods. One Lollard heretic who recanted, Joan Grebill, had a badge depicting sticks of wood, symbolizing how heretics would be burnt at the stake.

Margery Kempe alienated fellow villagers by wearing fancy clothes with tippets (loose hanging cloths) that were dagged (stylishly slashed):

> [S]he would not leave her pride nor her pompous array ... [S]he wore gold pipes on her head and her hoods with the tippets were dagged. Her cloaks were also dagged and laid with divers colors between the dags so that they should be more conspicuous to men's sight and she the more worshiped.[4]

Later she repented of this ostentatious display and wore a hairshirt under her garments. Made from animal hides, a hairshirt was worn with the bristly side against the skin. It was very uncomfortable, scratching her tender skin as a constant reminder of her sins. Other clothing choices came under attack. Margery's mistake was to wear white, the color associated with purity or virginity and traditionally reserved for consecrated virgins. As she was a mother with her fourteen children, she suffered mockery. The group of English people with whom she travels to the Holy Land act like brutal bullies. "They cut her gown so short that it came but a little beneath her knee and made her put on a white canvas in the manner of a sackcloth garment, for she would be taken as a fool."[5]

Clothing is never a neutral choice – just think about school dress codes.

Cross-dressing women popped up throughout medieval history. Literature not infrequently described women in male garb. In the Icelandic *Laxdaela Saga*, Gudrun desired Aud's husband, Thord. She deviously suggested to Thord that his wife Aud wore men's breeches. If true, this would give Thord legal justification to divorce her. When Aud found out that Thord had abandoned her, she said, "Kind of him to leave me so / and let me be the last to know".[6] Aud got her vengeance by visiting Thord when Gudrun was out. Now wearing men's breeches, Aud attacked her ex-husband with a sword, gashing him across the chest. She also wounded his sword-arm before riding away to freedom.

A contemporary Greek historian, Niketas Choniates, chronicled the European women who went on the Second Crusade. It is believed that this description portrayed Eleanor of Aquitaine:

> Females [rode] horseback in the manner of men ... bearing lances and weapons as men do; dressed in masculine garb, they conveyed a wholly martial appearance, more mannish than the Amazons. One stood out from the rest as another Penthesilea (Amazon queen) and from the embroidered gold which ran around the hem and fringes of her garment was called Goldfoot.[7]

Eleanor certainly was able to make a dramatic entrance, imprinting an unforgettable impression on people's minds.

Anna Komnene did not leave out the magnificence of the enemy in *The Alexiad*, her work in praise of her father's rulership. In particular, Anna mentioned the wife of the Norman invader Robert Guiscard. Sigelgaita, or Gaita for short, "was indeed a formidable sight" when she "donned her armour".[8] Anna compared her to the Greek goddess Athena. When Gaita saw her own men run away from battle in fear, she "[glared] fiercely at them, [shouting] in a loud voice ... 'How far will ye run? Halt! Be men!' As they continued to flee, she grasped a long spear and charged at full gallop against them."[9] Anna, the consummate historian, praised and admired her father's opponent; both writer and enemy warrior were women of determination.

The thirteenth-century Old French romance, *Le Roman de Silence*, told the story of a girl raised as a boy. While she ultimately took on a female persona at the end of the poem, it was clear that she was successful as a male minstrel and knight. One mid-fifteenth-century document told how a "young woman

Queen and her ladies entering the City of Ladies. Note the headdresses, girdles (belts), and tight-fitting bodices (© British Library Board, Harley 4431, f. 323)

who claimed to be a virgin attended the university [in Kraków, Poland] for two years in male dress, and came close to the baccalaureate in arts."[10] While she "lived in a student hostel", presumably with young men, she nonetheless "behaved properly toward others … and attended the lectures diligently".[11]

181

Her disguise was finally unmasked. When asked why she dressed like this, she answered, "For the love of learning."[12] Of unimpeachable character, she entered a convent where she became abbess. All these works sympathized with transvestite women acting as positive examples for all women.

But a couple of other cross-dressers ended up badly. The Pope, the head of the Catholic Church on earth, can only be male. A popular thirteenth-century legend told of a woman who became Pope Joan. Said to be English, she disguised herself as a man and made her way up through the ranks until she became the leader of the Christian Church. Her true identity became known at a procession when she suddenly went into labor and had a baby. While clearly a myth, the idea of Pope Joan took hold in the popular imagination. The renowned fourteenth-century Italian writer, Giovanni Boccaccio, wrote about her in his book, *Famous Women*: "Her unprecedented audacity made her known to the whole world and to posterity."[13] Versions of her appear on Tarot cards as the High Priestess, in novels and films, in art works, dramas, and even a musical – all retelling and interpreting her story.

While the book of *Deuteronomy* in the Torah forbade wearing the clothes of the opposite sex (*Deuteronomy* 22:5), there was a long tradition in Christianity that endorsed women wearing men's clothes in cases of necessity, such as remaining a virgin and living a religious life. Early Christian culture was particularly flexible when it came to gender roles, allowing women to participate in religious rites later restricted to men. Over 40 holy transvestites appeared in many stories, such as that Saints Pelagia, Thecla, Marina, Athanasia, and Euphrosyne. St Euphrosyne, for example, lived as a monk for almost 40 years. St Uncumber or Wilgefortis miraculously grew a moustache and beard to retain her chastity. Her father, angry because he wants her to marry the king of Sicily, crucified her in retaliation. Saint Eugenia, daughter of a pagan family, entered a monastery disguised as a man so she could lead a Christian life. Repulsing the advances of a widow who thought Eugenia was male, Eugenia was accused of attempting assault. Brought before her own father sitting in judgment, Eugenia bared her breasts, revealing herself to be a woman and confirming her innocence.

By becoming a man, at least in outward appearance, these saintly women were understood to be striving to be better people – which generally meant becoming male. By not disguising her true sex, Joan of Arc could not fit into the category of the holy transvestite who successfully hid the fact that she was a woman. Called *la Pucelle* with the feminine form of the French word for *maid*, Joan never hid the fact that she was a girl. Her cross-dressing suggested to her enemies that she was making herself into a false idol, and idol worship was a heathen act that needed to be punished.

Imagine if girls and women today lived back then, wearing their blue jeans and shorts without a thought. Would we be called idolaters? Would you?

Learn more

- Bayeux Tapestry: The history of this needlework is very mysterious. See some speculative theories at the website for the Bayeux Tapestry Museum. http://www.tapestry-bayeux.com/index.php?id=395.
- Chrétien de Troyes's twelfth-century romance, *Yvain, the Knight of the Lion*, depicts poverty-stricken and poorly clad female slaves incarcerated inside of sharp stakes where they sew using golden and silken thread for their evil masters in a textile sweatshop.
- In Tamora Pierce's series *The Protector of the Small Quartet* and *The Song of the Lioness*, a cross-dressed girl becomes a knight.
- Sarah Roche-Mahdi's translation of *Silence: A Thirteenth-Century French Romance* (East Lansing, MI: Michigan State University Press, 2007) delightfully draws the reader along with the trials and tribulations of Silence, raised as a boy so as not to lose her inheritance.
- Though fading as a custom in present day Albania, women still take on the roles of men: http://www.nytimes.com/2008/06/25/world/europe/25virgins.html?pagewanted=all.

Notes

1. Constance H. Berman, 'Gender at the Medieval Millennium', in *The Oxford Handbook of Women and Gender in Medieval Europe*, edited by Judith M. Bennett and Ruth Mazo Karras (Oxford: Oxford University Press, 2013), 549.
2. David Herlihy, *Opera Muliebria: Women and Work in Medieval Europe* (NY: McGraw-Hill, 1990), 57.
3. Nicholas Orme, *Fleas, Flies, and Friars: Children's Poetry from the Middle Ages* (Ithaca, NY: Cornell University Press, 2011), 52.
4. Margery Kempe, *The Book of Margery Kempe*, edited and translated by Lynn Staley (NY: W. W. Norton, 2001), 8.
5. Kempe/Staley, 46.
6. Keneva Kunz, trans., *The Saga of the People of Laxardal and Bolli Bollason's Tale*, edited by Bergljót S. Kristjánsdóttir (London: Penguin Books, 2008), 71.
7. S. J. Allen and Emilie Amt, eds., *The Crusades: A Reader* (Toronto: University of Toronto Press, 2010), 211.
8. Anna Komnene, *The Alexiad*, translated by E. R. A. Sewter; revised by Peter Frankopan. (London: Penguin Books, 2009), 43.

9. Komnene/Sewter, 121.
10. Michael H. Shank, 'A Female University Student in Late Medieval Kraków', in *Sisters and Workers in the Middle Ages*, edited by Judith, M. Bennett, Elizabeth A. Clark, Jean F. O'Barr, B. Anne Vilen, and Sarah Westphal-Wihl (Chicago: University of Chicago Press, 1989), 191.
11. Shank, 191.
12. Shank, 192.
13. Giovanni Boccaccio, *Famous Women*, edited by Virginia Brown (Cambridge, MA: The I Tatti Renaissance Library/Harvard University Press, 2001), 437.

PART VI

"EXPERIENCE IS RIGHT ENOUGH FOR ME"[1]

Chaucer's Wife of Bath, *The Canterbury Tales*

The Wife of Bath, a dynamic character from Chaucer's famous English poem The Canterbury Tales, *was partially deaf due to her husband's physical abuse. That did not prevent her from telling her side of the story. Like Teresa, she insisted that her personal experience was just as valid as writings by men for establishing her authority (EL 26 C 9 (The Ellesmere Chaucer), f. 72 r, with permission of the Huntington Library)*

CHAPTER 22

Teresa de Cartagena
(c. 1420/25–d. after 1465)

FOREMOTHER OF DEAF CULTURE

Saucy Teresa de Cartagena was the first Spanish feminist and foremother of the Deaf culture movement. Utterly without hearing due to an unknown illness suffered in her 20s, she insisted on using her body and experience to claim her authority. "[M]y own experience … makes me know more … than what I have learned from books."[2] This experience included three aspects of being marginalized in her culture of fifteenth-century Spain: being a woman, being deaf, and being from a *converso* (converted Jew) family. She took these 'disabilities' and used them to justify her special position of insight by writing the first pro-feminist treatise written by a Spanish woman. "[I]t is more within the reach of a woman to be eloquent than strong … easier for her to use the pen than the sword."[3] This could have been the theme song of many a medieval woman.

Teresa was born into a family that was prominent in both religious and political circles. Her grandfather (*c.* 1350–1435) had been the chief rabbi in the city of Burgos in Castile, Spain. He led the largest group of Jews in Spain and established a rabbinical school. Yet in 1390 he converted to Christianity. Later in his career, once he was a bishop and a political appointee, he wrote works criticizing Jews. His eldest son worked for the pope to make sure laws written against the Jews would be enacted. Why would they convert and then condemn their fellow Jews?

For much of the Middle Ages, Spain was a place with three religions: Islam, Judasim, and Christianity. At various times, members of these three groups got along, but friction was also apparent, ultimately leading to out and out condemnation and battle. Anti-Jewish feelings ran high, especially starting in the late fourteenth century. It is possible that Teresa's grandfather converted in the wake of verbal and physical violence committed against Jews. To protect himself and his family, conversion was the only way to safely protect them. Of his sons, two became churchmen, while Teresa's father was a knight. Her aunt was believed to be the grandmother of Fernando de Aragón – who, with his wife Isabella, expelled Jews from Spain in 1492. In 1604, descendants of Teresa's family were officially designated as having 'pure blood', allowing them access to certain privileges denied anyone with Jewish heritage. Much like African-Americans 'passing' as white in the days of Jim Crow laws, Jews who could be seen as Christian improved their status in society.

Teresa was born into this newly Christianized family as the third or fourth child of Pedro de Cartagena and María de Sarabia, in Burgos, Spain. Proclaiming to have studied at the University of Salamanca, she might have been tutored at home and sent to a convent to be educated, since women were not formally allowed to enroll at university. Her uncle Alsono left in his will money to his brother's children, including 100 florines (gold coins) to Teresa, "a nun."[4]

She opened her first writing, *Grove of the Infirm* (written after 1450), by saying that she was the composer, "being afflicted with grave ailments and, in particular, having lost completely [my] sense of hearing".[5] She saw herself as living on an island, scorned by mankind as an outcast. She wrote to console herself and fellow sufferers, never hesitating "to declare the reality of my truth".[6]

Uncle Alonso had been a bishop, like his father and brother. But he did not condemn Jews or *conversos*. Rather, his writings suggested how Jews and Christians had much in common. Teresa continued this conciliatory position. While she wrote directly to an audience of fellow sufferers, presumably those with infirmities, she might have also been consoling Jews and her fellow *conversos*. Teresa poetically called her conscience a city that could be besieged and attacked by bad desires. She described of being "in the city [where] a great noise is produced if some people rise up in revolt, and if all the people revolt, the city is in great danger and in mortal combat."[7] The city – her soul – was threatened by her longings. This violent image of a besieged city may refer to an attack on Jews in Toledo, Spain in 1449 focused against *conversos*, suspected of being false converts.

Anti-Semitism was, alas, rampant. Those who spoke against Jews slandered them, saying they were contaminated and filled with sickness, even as having impure or contaminated blood. In the most extreme cases, Jews were associated with heretics and lepers, groups that were burned to death by authorities. While anti-Semitic speech accused Jews of being 'deaf' to the 'true' God, Teresa showed how deafness could actually lead one *closer* to God. A faithful nun, she had empathy for the outcast and falsely accused in her society, defending them with her writings. An infirm or ill body did not reflect spiritual health. This was a strong statement in a culture where having a disease such as leprosy was seen as proof of sinful behavior. Teresa was even shunned by members of her family. "Worldly pleasures despise us, health forsakes us, friends forget us, relatives get angry, and even one's own mother gets annoyed with her sickly daughter."[9] Despite this rejection, Teresa insisted on finding worth in her heartache, firmly defending those with bodies not in line with the ideals of her time.

While deafness has been seen as a defect for much of human history, recent debate centers around endorsing a specific Deaf culture threatened by the advent of technical innovations such as cochlear implants, devices placed in the ear to give the sense of sound to the hearing impaired. Some deaf people contend they are not disabled and that hearing impairment should be seen as within the natural variation of human diversity. In fact, disabilities could open up new ways of seeing the world, enabling other sorts of knowledge. The well-known case of Temple Grandin demonstrates how her disability – autism – enables her to understand animal behavior. She invented the animal chute used at slaughter houses to permit a calmer and more compassionate end to livestock being butchered.[10]

Teresa was a foremother to the Deaf culture movement. "[S]uffering does not impede our thought, for although suffering makes the invalid powerless in outward deeds, it makes him powerful in inward thought."[11] When she was a hearing person, she was distracted from hearing God's voice by the daily nonsense and chatter bubbling up around her. She needed silence to hear the voice of God. Only in the quiet of the cloister as a nun and with "cloisters on my hearing"[12] could she listen to that quiet still voice in her heart. It was a blessing to be deaf: "[M]y longing is thus reconciled to my affliction, so that I no longer wish to hear ... What I used to call my crucifixion, I now call my resurrection."[13]

Why does divinity allow suffering? This is a fundamental question philosophers of all faiths have asked and attempted to answer. Teresa suggested affliction enhanced her life. Patience allowed her to face trials.

While this all seems like a philosophy that would be noncontroversial in late medieval Christian Spain, male writers viciously attacked Teresa. Disbelieving her authorship of *Grove of the Infirm*, they suggested she copied it, expressing their wonder that a mere woman could have penned such

This famous marble sculpture depicts Teresa of Avila experiencing a mystical vision accompanied by an angel (created by Gian Lorenzo Bernini c. 1651; Rome, Church of Santa Maria della Vittoria; Creative Commons)

a deep and meditative work. These attacks caused her to write a second treatise, *Wonder at the Works of God*, in which she strategically defended herself in the first feminist defense of all women by a Spanish woman. She began by mentioning that she wrote it "at the petition and request of Señora Juana de Mendoça, wife of Señor Gómez Manrique".[14] Gómez, a court poet, protected *conversos*, while Juana was a lady-in-waiting to the princess or *infanta* of Portuaga. By mentioning these prominent supporters, Teresa automatically lent herself authority.

Like other women we have met, she regularly used the modesty topos to put herself down. She called her writing "this slight and defective work".[15] She refered to her "weak womanly understanding",[16] "weak judgement", and "poor faculty". "[W]hat good words or devout works can you expect of a woman so infirm in her body and so wounded in her spirit?" She described her writing as "a brief work of little substance", "an insignificant thing",[17] and "a womanly text of little [worthy] substance". She went so far as to sarcastically call herself, "a small piece of dirt, [daring] to present to your great judgement these insignificant thoughts of mine". This seems to reinforce stereotypes of downtrodden women in the long-ago past. Yet Teresa's insistence on her lack of worth next to her highly sophisticated writing suggested that she scornfully rejected belittling herself.

By seeming to put herself down, she protected herself from being seen as too bold and so gained power. How? She stood up to the men questioning her writing. Men wondered at the ability of a woman – of all things! – being capable of writing such a deeply intellectual work as the *Grove of the Infirm*. Teresa refuted their amazement and attacked them for their condescension: "[A]lthough it is said that their wonder is flattering, to me it seems offensive and clear that they offer me scathing insults."[18] She told Juana, "most virtuous lady, that the reason that men marvel that a woman has written a treatise is because this is not customary in the female condition but only in the male."[19] She said this is presumptuous. Men were given their gifts from God and God alone. Men had to learn, just as women do. Just as God infused men with understanding, He could give women the same ability. Do men dare to blaspheme and question God's power? "[W]hy should we women not receive the same [ability] when He judges it necessary and appropriate?"[20] Why should it be a surprise when women excel? As Teresa suggested, we should not be shocked at women being able to be good thinkers and writers.

Teresa of Ávila

Teresa de Ávila (1515–1582) was another prominent Spanish nun of Jewish heritage. A mystic who experienced visions, she was canonized 40 years after her death. In 1970, she was made a Doctor of the Catholic Church. Teresa wrote these consoling words, "Let nothing make me afraid."[8]

Judith with the Head of Holofernes
(by Lucas Cranach the Elder, German,
1472–1553; Metropolitan Museum
of Art, Rogers Fund, 1911 (11.15),
© The Metropolitan Museum of Art.
ARTstor: MMA_IAP>10311574688)

True, Teresa admitted, men and women were different. God made us this way. But only humans made a hierarchy saying men were better than women. God never said that. She used the beautiful image of a tree with hard bark on the outside and soft 'medulla' on the inside. Men were like the bark – given to activities in the outside, public realm, while women:

> encased or enclosed in their homes give strength and vigor and certainly no little support to the males with their industry and work and domestic labor. And thus human nature ... preserves and sustains itself, for without these complementary exercises and labors it could not survive.

None of this was "to the detriment of women" nor should it "confer greater excellence to the male". Men and women should help each other as complements, not antagonists. Teresa rejected men's "worldly and vain arrogance". "[W]hat excuse is there to doubt that a woman can understand some good and know how to write treatises or any other praiseworthy good work?"[21]

How many women can use a sword, Teresa asks? Although most commonly associated with men, a sword was wielded by a mighty holy woman. Judith, a Jewish heroine and virtuous widow, defended her people oppressed by Assyrian forces.

Their leader Holofernes desired Judith. She tricked him and, while he slept, she beheaded him with a sword. Returning to her people, she inspired them to victory. God made this happen, said Teresa, and could do so again.

Teresa's pen was a type of sword with which she defended herself and other women, defeating those who maligned her. While accepting certain attributes of traditional misogyny – men were created first, men's natural realm was outside, men were brave with women the opposite – Teresa twisted them into something positive. Like a Ju-Jitsu master, she took the strength of her opponent – misogynist beliefs – and turned them against her rivals. She flipped the hierarchy placing men first to highlight women's insight and power. Women's suffering, in particular, lent them a special insight, bringing them closer to God.

Another medieval Ju-Jitsu master was Margaret Paston, who resisted attacks on her home and family, even when she was oppressed by legal and political opponents. She got back up again to defeat her enemies.

Learn more

• Teresa's attackers accused her of plagiarism. How could a deaf woman write so intelligently? Another famous deaf woman, Helen Keller (1880–1968), likewise was accused of plagiarism – at the age of eleven. People couldn't believe that someone deaf could read and write. You can read Helen's defense in her book, *The Story of My Life* (1903): http://www.afb.org/MyLife/book.asp?ch=P1Ch14

Notes

1. Geoffrey Chaucer, *The Riverside Chaucer*, 3rd edition, edited by Larry D. Benson (Boston: Houghton Mifflin, 1987), 105; amended by the author.
2. Teresa de Cartagena, *The Writings of Teresa de Cartagena: Translated with Introduction, Notes, and Interpretive Essay*, translated by Dayle Seidenspinner-Núñez (Cambridge MA: D. S. Brewer, 1998), 52.
3. Cartagena/Seidenspinner-Núñez, 93.
4. Cartagena/Seidenspinner-Núñez, 9.
5. Cartagena/Seidenspinner-Núñez, 23.
6. Cartagena/Seidenspinner-Núñez, 25.
7. Cartagena/Seidenspinner-Núñez, 31.
8. John Kirvan, ed., *Teresa of Avila. Let Nothing Disturb You: A Journey to the Center of the Soul with Teresa of Avila* (Notre Dame, IN: Ave Maria Press, 1996), 100.
9. Cartagena/Seidenspinner-Núñez, 46.

10. See more about her at http://templegrandin.com/.
11. Cartagena/Seidenspinner-Núñez, 64–65.
12. Cartagena/Seidenspinner-Núñez, 28.
13. Cartagena/Seidenspinner-Núñez, 29.
14. Cartagena/Seidenspinner-Núñez, 87.
15. Cartagena/Seidenspinner-Núñez, 26.
16. Cartagena/Seidenspinner-Núñez, 86.
17. Cartagena/Seidenspinner-Núñez, 87.
18. Cartagena/Seidenspinner-Núñez, 88.
19. Cartagena/Seidenspinner-Núñez, 89.
20. Cartagena/Seidenspinner-Núñez, 90.
21. Cartagena/Seidenspinner-Núñez, 92.

CHAPTER 23

Margaret Paston
(1423–1484)

MATCHLESS MATRIARCH

The Real Housewives of Norfolk, England in the 1400s. We meet them in the hundreds of family documents known as the Paston Letters. They reveal dozens of everyday details lying like jewels in a genie's cave. The Virgin Mary, who embodied the image of the compassionate, forgiving, and nurturing mother, was a role model for women, especially in the late Middle Ages as her cult gained widespread popularity. But not all of these Real Housewives follow Mary's lead. Margaret Paston's mother-in-law, Agnes Paston, hardly fulfills the role of the loving mother.

Agnes's son, John I, received a letter dated June 29, 1449, that his cousin instructed him to burn after reading. Luckily, he didn't – that is how we have it today. The letter exposed how mother Agnes attempted to force her daughter Elizabeth to marry the well-connected Sir Stephen Scrope. Scrope was a desirable choice for a son-in-law – rich, well connected, and smart – he even translated one of Christine de Pizan's writings. Yet, for Elizabeth, a woman 30 years younger, Scrope, disfigured by smallpox, was not so appealing. Resisting such a union, she was confined to her house by Agnes and "cannot speak to anyone". Poor Elizabeth was "since Easter ... been beaten once or twice a week, and sometimes twice in one day, and her head has been broken in two or three places."[1] Agnes physically and emotionally tormented this abused young adult over potential marriage partners.

These marriage negotiations fell through, though Elizabeth finally married at age 29 in 1458, only to have that husband killed in battle three years later in 1461. A letter to her domineering mother seethed with resentment underneath her seeming humble demeanor. Her second marriage to Sir George Browne ended with his execution in 1483. Elizabeth's only consolation was material: she became an extremely wealthy widow. As vivid as a Jane Austen novel written over 300 years later, we learn how "sorrow often causes women to bestow themselves in marriage on someone they should not."[2]

The Paston family had close political and financial ties to Sir John Fastolf, who ordered the creation of a manuscript from which this picture comes. Prudence stands in the middle with maidens on either side. At far left stands Reason, Intelligence, and Circumspection. At right, Docility, Providence, and Caution (by the Master of Sir John Fastolf. Livres des quatre vertus, c. 1450. Ms. Laud Misc. 570, with permission of the Bodleian Library, Oxford University)

Imagine finding a collection of over 1000 letters by family members – sons, wives, daughters, servants, and cousins – written over decades starting in the 1420s. A treasure chest of evidence about how a medieval upper-middle class family lived, we hear how a road Agnes built, blocking a religious procession, caused an angry neighbor to curse: "May all the devils of hell drag her soul to hell because of the road she has made!'"[3] Agnes matter-of-factly suggested her son Clement should be whipped if he did not start working harder at school. Her will showed how savvy she was in legal matters, making sure her youngest sons inherited certain estates that her husband's will neglected. The Paston women filled the roles of estate manager, political adversary and ally, and legal advisor.

The Pastons themselves came from humble origins. The son of a farmer, William Paston I (1378–1444) became a lawyer and married an heiress, the unstoppable Agnes Berry (*c.* 1400–1479), a union that enhanced his land-holding property. With this new prestige and increased financial security, they were able to purchase an estate near Paston in Norfolk, England. By 1429 he became a justice, holding a respectable and prominent position. By his death in 1444, when their oldest son, John Paston I, became the head of the family, the Pastons had gained a strong place in society and substantial property. A lawyer, John I (1421–1466) married the heiress, Margaret Mautby (*c.* 1420–1484). Their sons, John II and John III became knighted. Since infant mortality was very high, it was not uncommon for two sons in a family to have the same name in case one of them died. Within three generations, the family had become prominent citizens and members of the gentry.

Margaret Paston wrote voluminous letters recounting familial, business, and political matters, most probably dictated to a secretary, a common practice for men and women in a family this prominent. The extensive detail the letters provided could have been a means for the family to have evidence concerning legal affairs in the future, should a challenge to property have arisen. As Margaret reminded her eldest son, "Your father, may God absolve him, in his troubled period set greater store by his documents and deeds than by any of his moveable goods."[4] Margaret had a subtle and technical knowledge of the intricacies of legal terminology and law process. She acted as a substitute for her lawyer husband, who was detained for long periods of time in London dealing with complicated property matters, essentially functioning as his legal assistant in his absence. John encouraged her, "I pray you to see to the good governance of my household … concerning my

---

Jewish and Christian Encounters

Invited by William the Conqueror shortly after the Norman Invasion in 1066, Jews lived openly in England until their expulsion in 1290 under Edward I. While some Jews were involved in moneylending, others had occupations as wide-ranging as fencing master, doctor, coin engraver, and day laborer. The story of Licoricia of Winchester, the strong matriarch of an extensive family unit much like Margaret Paston, included a complicated marital history and run-ins with the law. She married David of Oxford after his fraught divorce from Muriel. Once widowed, Licoricia continued in her business of financial transactions, finding favor with King Henry III. Sadly, in 1277 Licoricia was found murdered along with her Christian maid Alice, though the co-habitation of Christians and Jews had been forbidden since 1179. Jews and Christians often lived, traded, and shopped with each other.

---

profit."[5] Margaret did that – and more. This strong-willed woman sometimes obeyed her husband's advice, but often followed her own desires. The Paston family was, for all practical purposes, run by Margaret.

The Paston family's fortunes reflected the uncertain times they lived in: the century dominated by the conclusion of the Hundred Years War in France and the violence of the War of the Roses, the civil war on English soil. At this time, you could not be free of politics. You had to take sides. Civil war impacted everyone's life. Tenants could not pay their rent. Stories of "robbery and manslaughter" filled Margaret's pages and the political disruption caused many to "act as if they were expecting a new world".[6] Many letters showed how Margaret wheeled and dealed to protect the family's property, along with acting as go-between among various family members whose actions caused strife. As with Teresa de Cartagena's vision of men and women working in complementary ways, Paston married couples were teams, striving to advance the family's fortunes.

Margaret's letters give us a peephole into everyday life. She requested that her husband send various goodies from London, including clothing items like stockings, shoes, and caps for the children, but also exotic fruits like oranges, almonds, dates, and spices. Childbirth and pregnancy recured in letters. Shortly after her marriage, Margaret Paston wrote to her husband how she "cannot fit into any of the waistbands or girdles [belts] I have except one".[7]

She reassured him that her midwife, though ailing, "has sent a message ... that she should come here when God should grant the time [of birth], even if she must be wheeled in a [wheel]barrow".[8] She also asked him to wear a ring with the image of St Margaret, the patron saint of childbirth. After a family member died, it was proper to mourn by avoiding certain games at Christmas: "[N]o masquerading, nor harp nor lute playing, nor singing, nor any loud pastime, only backgammon and chess and cards."[9]

Women of great households fulfilled their roles as medical providers, sharing recipes for potions and medicines. In fact, they perceived London doctors as adversaries, not properly tending loved ones medically. Moreover, licensed doctors were highly expensive to hire. Part of the process of healing included turning to God, such as when Margaret worried about John I's illness in 1443. She told him how mother Agnes vowed to send "another image of wax of the weight of yourself to Our Lady of Walsingham". Margaret herself "promised pilgrimages to be made for you to Walsingham and to St Leonard's [Priory, Norwich]". Margaret may have been one tough cookie, but she clearly loved her husband, John:

War of the Roses

An incredibly complex dynastic struggle resulted in civil war in fifteenth-century England. One source of the conflict lay in the marriage in 1420 between Catherine of Valois, daughter of the French king, and the English king Henry V, a union meant to resolve tensions from the Hundred Years War. Henry died 2 years later. Their son Henry VI eventually came to the throne. Since he suffered from mental illness, his queen, Margaret of Anjou, tried to keep the kingdom together. From about 1453 through the 1470s battles and opposing forces waged war. Ultimately, the Yorkists succeeded in gaining the throne with Edward IV, who married a woman from the gentry class, Elizabeth Woodville – mother to Elizabeth of York. She, in turn, became queen of Henry VII, a Tudor who defeated the Yorkist King Richard III. This marriage ended the War of the Roses, a time when, as Margaret Paston wrote, "Little store is set by a man's death".[10] Ultimately Elizabeth of York became mother to Henry VIII. Henry VII's grandfather had been Owen Tudor, who had secretly married the widowed Catherine of Valois.

By my troth, I never had so heavy a season from the time that I knew of your sickness until I knew of your amending, and still my heart is not at great ease, nor shall be until I know that you are truly well.[11]

John's marriage to Margaret not only brought additional lands into the Paston family, but her steadfastness even when under physical threat shows her to have been a force to be reckoned with. Their rival Lord Moleyns came and tried to take possession of one of the Paston estates, expelling them from the manor at Gresham in 1448. A henchman of Moleyns accused Margaret and her mother-in-law Agnes outside the church of being "flagrant whores", along with other "offensive language".[12] Stereotypes we may have of women as submissive and passive servants shatter when we read Margaret bidding her husband to send weapons, like crossbows, axes, and protective garments, should enemies attack. Like her Viking foremothers, she was fearless in confronting trouble, acknowledging "ruffians"[13] who may "abduct me and imprison me".[14] Margaret warned her husband to take care while eating and drinking in case of poison.

Powerful men would try time and again to deprive them of their estates and property. John I, chosen as an executor of Sir John Fastolf's will, immediately took control of Fastolf's property in 1459 to fulfill the dead man's wishes. Yet another executor sued him and there was legal turmoil up to the time of his death in 1466. In 1465, the Duke of Suffolk, deciding to take a manor the Pastons inherited in the Falstolf bequest, gathered a force of over several hundred men to attack Margaret and John II. The Duke did not attack that day, but for the next year he and his followers tormented and plundered property belonging to the Pastons. Margery succeeded in giving testimony at a court proceeding and the judges were "very gracious and patient with me in my business".[15] Nevertheless, the Duke and 500 men destroyed their estate and stole "feather beds and all our possession".[16] Shamelessly, they even ransacked the church. Margaret, the dominant administrator of their property, blamed her husband's death on the trouble these vast estates provoked.

John I and Margaret's seven children provided much of the liveliness of detail in the letters. A stern mother, Margaret frequently chastised her eldest son, John II, for his bad conduct. Expert at emotional blackmail, Margaret sent John II gold cloth to sell for money with which he should build his father's tomb. She grimly warned, "If you sell it for any other purpose, then on my word of honour I shall never trust you as long as I live."[17] She asked him to send the finest quality fabric for his sister Anne who was living with a high-class family: "I am put to shame ... because she has none."[18] Despite this seeming care, Margaret admitted that Anne would "often annoy me and cause me great anxiety"[19] if she did not occupy herself properly. Margaret worried that favorite son Walter would take holy orders before he had really contemplated what that would mean. "I would rather he were a good secular man, than a foolish priest."[20] One son revealed in a letter "[i]t is not easy to avoid being chastised [by my mother Margaret] by the time we go to bed."[21] She was unrelenting.

The love stories of daughter Margery Paston with Richard Calle and that of second son John III with Margery Brews particularly delight readers. Letters show how marriage negotiations were not only affairs of the heart, but also the pocketbook – and could cause great strife between parents and children. Daughter Margery fell in love with Richard Calle, the Paston estate manager and bailiff, whose station in life her mother Margaret found too low for their status. Though he loyally oversaw the Paston property, Richard owned no estates himself. Suggesting that Richard had run a shop, John III (Margery's brother) condescendingly and unkindly said that "he should never have my good will for to make my sister to sell candle and mustard in [the town of] Framlingham."[22] Despite their claim to have made secret vows to one another that constituted a solemn, unbreakable pledge to marry, mother Margaret was determined to break their betrothal. She bullied her daughter, separating the lovers. Richard had to sneak a letter in to Margery, in which he passionately confessed to the painful life they led. He felt as though they had not spoken for 1000 years. Margaret threw Margery out of the house, ordering her "servants not to admit her into the house". The Bishop of Norwich thoroughly questioned the two lovers, finding no reason they should not remain together. They officially married the next year. Margaret continued to employ Richard, but cut off ties with her own daughter, admitting that "[Margery] would never be in my heart as she used to be."[23]

She was one harsh mother.

John III successfully wed Margery Brews, but only after much negotiation with her cheapskate father over what dowry he would settle on her. The mother of his beloved promised John III that a "greater treasure" she could bestow upon him than money or land was "an intelligent gentlewoman ... a good and a virtuous one."[24] Margery wrote passionately to her "Valentine", the first known use of this word addressed to one's beloved. She confessed "no one knows what pain it is I suffer".[25] "My heart commands me to love you truly above all earthly things for evermore".[26] If he decided to marry another woman for more money, she requested him to visit her no longer. Fortunately, they happily wed. When he had to be away on a trip, she wrote to him urging him to return soon: "[I]t seems to me a long time since I lay in your arms".[27]

In her will, Margaret bequeathed gifts to those places one might expect from a devout woman of the late Middle Ages: religious institutions like monasteries and churches, as well as hospitals. She only recognized her daughter, Margery, and her husband with one bequest: £20 was to go to their oldest child, the same amount she left for the illegitimate child of her oldest son, John II. The insight of Margery Brews, John III's wife, that "one word of a woman would do more than the words of twenty men",[28] held true in these rare letters. The letters the Paston women wrote and collected allow us to share in the memory of this extraordinary and vigorous family.

Learn more

- Read the Paston Letters amid beautiful color illustrations: Roger Virgoe's *Private Life in the Fifteenth Century: Illustrated Letters of the Paston Family* (NY: Weidenfeld and Nicolson, 1989). Famed English novelist, Virginia Woolf, vividly imagines the Pastons' world in *The Common Reader* (1925): http://ebooks.adelaide.edu.au/w/woolf/virginia/w91c/chapter2.html.
- BBC History has more information and images: http://www.bbc.co.uk/history/british/middle_ages/pastonletters_01.shtml.
- Countless novels depict the savage era of the War of the Roses, from Philippa Gregory's *The Cousins' War* series (NY: Simon and Schuster, 2009) about Elizabeth Woodville, Margaret Beaufort and Anne Neville (now in a Starz mini-series) to Josephine Tey's mystery *The Daughter of Time* (NY: Scribner, 1951). More recently, George R. R. Martin's *Game of Thrones* draws on the War of the Roses mayhem to violent effect in his wildly popular *A Song of Ice and Fire* fantasy series, now filmed for HBO.

Notes

1. Diane Watt, trans., *The Paston Women: Selected Letters* (Cambridge: D. S. Brewer, 2004), 116.
2. Watt, 117.
3. Watt, 29.
4. Watt, 91.
5. Joanna H. Drell, 'Aristocratic Economies: Women and Family', in *The Oxford Handbook of Women and Gender in Medieval Europe*, edited by Judith M. Bennett and Ruth Mazo Karras (Oxford: Oxford University Press, 2013), 327.

6. Watt, 68.
7. Watt, 44.
8. Watt, 46.
9. Watt, 64.
10. Watt, 105.
11. Roger Virgoe, ed., *Private Life in the Fifteenth Century: Illustrated Letters of the Paston Family* (NY: Weidenfeld & Nicolson, 1989), 44; quoted in Susan Signe Morrison, *Women Pilgrims in Late Medieval England: Private Piety as Public Performance* (London: Routledge, 2000), 18.
12. Watt, 51.
13. Watt, 55.
14. Watt, 56.
15. Watt, 82.
16. Watt, 88.
17. Watt, 113.
18. Watt, 95.
19. Watt, 101.
20. Watt, 108.
21. Watt, 153.
22. Frances and Joseph Gies, *Women in the Middle Ages: The Lives of Real Women in a Vibrant Age of Transition* (NY: HarperPerennial, 1978), 223.
23. Watt, 97.
24. Watt, 122.
25. Watt, 127.
26. Watt, 127–128.
27. Watt, 130.
28. Watt, 130.

CHAPTER 24

Looking Forward

CONTEMPORARY FEMINIST THEORY AND MEDIEVAL WOMEN

Medieval women's lives and writings prefigure many issues that have arisen in more recent times. Indeed, the medieval period helped form current beliefs and attitudes towards women. The Middle Ages need to be integrated into considerations of current women's situations, including developments in feminist and gender approaches to literature and culture, since medieval women helped shape how women act and are treated today.

Nobel laureate Toni Morrison writes: "Canon building is Empire building".[1] The canon constitutes of that group of literary texts a culture decides is worthy of being taught and extolled in schools and universities. Until the past few decades, the vast majority of 'canonical' texts were by white males. Morrison suggests that the act of preferring a certain a group of texts over another group constitutes a *political* act, like that of 'Empire building'. Morrison chastises those non-African-American writers who write about African-Americans, imaging what 'they' think. Boldly, she proclaims, "We have always been imagining ourselves." 'We' – meaning African-Americans – "are not, in fact, 'other.'"[2]

Morrison works out of *intersectional feminism*, whereby one does not look just at gender, but also race, class, ethnicity and nationality, to see how all these factors play into the lives of actual people. While many of the European medieval women's lives are – due to available evidence – necessarily skewed away from knowledge about women of color, we can take insights by African-American critics and see how they resonate with the lives of medieval women, an often forgotten group who likewise "have always been imagining" themselves. Ann DuCille challenges conventional ideas of what constitutes 'authentic' experience for African-American women, alerting us to the dangers of imposing a grand narrative onto people's lives – historical or imagined. As she points out, all imagined lives are the product of representation.[3] We can use her ideas on twentieth-century black women to think about medieval women – and be cautious about assuming, for example, a debilitating lack of agency.

Take the concept of 'signifyin(g)', for instance, which Henry Louis Gates, Jr has argued has been an element in African-American writing. 'Signifyin(g)' is the act of paying homage to earlier writings, all the while revising them in order to show that earlier work's limitations. Gates writes: "Signifyin(g) is black double-voicedness; because it always entails formal revision and an intertextual relation."[4] This technique works as a kind of critique. By quoting, using, and reusing an earlier author, the new writer alters the original meaning. We could see this as a technique used by medieval women writers. The modesty topos, in which the woman writer superficially puts herself down only to establish her authority as a writer, works as 'signifyin(g)' does for African-American writers. Revisions of stories – such as Heloise's version of their love affair after Abelard makes his history known – allow the female to oppose the original (male-authored) work, and undermine, and subvert it. Hildegard von Bingen similarly revises misogynist theories of women's base matter by lyrically extolling the Virgin Mary's 'lucid matter'.[5]

Medieval women do not exist in a vacuum. Their experiences reverberate across the centuries and across geographical locations. The modesty topos so common in medieval women's writings – from Hrotsvit von Gandersheim to Christine de Pizan – reappears centuries later in the writings of the first American woman poet: Anne Bradstreet. In *Prologue*, written in the 1640s, Bradstreet concedes that her words may only be "mean and unrefined ore". She points out that if she does write beautifully, men will find excuses for it: "If what I do prove well, it won't advance, / They'll say it's stol'n, or else it was by chance". She resists expectations that a woman should sew rather than write: "I am obnoxious to each carping tongue / Who says my hand a needle better fits".[6] Like Hrotsvit and Christine, Bradstreet insists that her work is worthy, despite what men may think. The nineteenth-century writer and activist Harriet Martineau wrote under a pseudonym, a mere initial, to hide her identity and gender. When her brother learned of her authorship, he fully endorsed her vocation, saying, "'Now, dear, leave it to other women to make shirts and darn stockings; and do you devote yourself to this.' I went home in a sort of dream, so that the squares of the pavement seemed to float before my eyes. That evening made me an authoress."[7] As with Christine de Pizan, the loss of her family's position and economic security catalyzed and ultimately ensured Martineau's status as a professional woman author. As with Christine's father and husband, men frequently endorsed women's learning. Qasmūna Bint Ismā'īl lived in Iberia in the late eleventh- and early twelfth centuries. A Jew, she wrote poems in Arabic, the language of the king of Granada, who followed Islam. In a poignant lament on not yet being married, she writes, "Alas! Youth passes and is wasted, while one remains ... who is alone." Her father extolled her talent, crying out, "'By the Ten Commandments! You are a better poet than I!'"[8]

Simone de Beauvoir in her iconic feminist manifesto, *The Second Sex* (1949), argues that women are the 'Other' in society. Men are defined by what they are *not*, depending upon women as their negative opposite. "No man would consent to be a woman, but every man wants women to exist."[9] Women have only existed in relationship *to* men. We see de Beauvoir trace much of what is essential to medieval thought, noting the Aristotelian concept of woman as passive flesh and, thus, hierarchically lower than men; how menstrual blood and childbirth have been perceived as rendering women unclean; and how women have been seen as property. Yet, de Beauvoir points out, this horror of female flesh and its exudings stems from a *self-horror* by the male of his *own* animal nature that he displaces onto women. Sherry B. Ortner points out in her seminal essay 'Is Female to Male as Nature Is to Culture?' that "women are being identified or symbolically associated with nature, as opposed to men, who are identified with culture."[10] This plays out in writings as various as those by the Church Fathers to medieval medical treatises.

Gayle Rubin's famous study on 'The Traffic in Women' proves vital to illuminating works like Icelandic sagas. Gifts and gift-giving enhance the prestige of the giver, often humiliating the recipient. Things being gifted include women. While men might be traded due to their *status*, such as a slave, women are trafficked due to their *gender*. DNA evidence of men and women in Iceland today indicates that the patrilineal line is three-quarters Scandinavian and one-quarter Celtic, while the matrilineal line is roughly the opposite, suggesting that Viking males attacked the British Isles to obtain concubines and slaves for sexual and economic purposes (see Chapter 2).

Other key texts in the history of feminist theory include Nancy Chodorow's work on mothering, noting that the 'mother-daughter relationship' is central to women's experiences.[11] Mothering lies at the heart of women's universal second-class status since women give birth and suckle children, leaving them less available for other work. This assertion applies to the medieval world and raises provocative questions. For example, if the birth of a male heir enhances a queen's status, does that at the same time make the queen hierarchically less important since her body is seen as defective within medieval thought?

Chodorow argues that women's lives are apt to be more private and domestic, while men's tend to be more public and social. While that might generally be true, it depends on the definition of those words. Is it not social to be working with children? What about the countless women who labored in fields or tended animals outside? What about women pilgrims who were clearly seen in the public realm undergoing processions to shrines and socializing with their fellow devout travellers? Chodorow's influential insights, while focusing on crucial territories ripe for investigation, need to be nuanced for the medieval period. She suggests that the mother-daughter relationship is key to understanding gendered development, all the while acknowledging that certain cultures, like that in Morocco Muslim society, gravitate towards a *web* of female relationships. We could read the life of Christina of Markyate in light of vexed mother-daughter tension, but also can see a web of women interacting in Hrotsvit of Gandersheim's play, *The Martyrdom of the Holy Virgins Fides, Spes, and Karitas [Faith, Hope, and Charity]* where the mother, Sapientia [Wisdom] buries her valiant daughters before dying herself.

Another vital work in the history of feminist writings, Kate Millett's *Sexual Politics* (1970), redefined politics as "power-structured relationships, arrangements whereby one group of persons is controlled by another."[12] She understands sex as a status category with *political* implications. Just as the elder male dominates younger males, the male dominates the female. Male supremacy "lies in the acceptance of a value system which is not biological."[13] Millett reveals her sharp wit, not unlike the many sharp-tongued women of the Middle Ages, when she writes:

> [I]n patriarchy, the function of the norm is unthinkingly delegated to the male – were it not, one might as plausibly speak of 'feminine' behavior as active, and 'masculine' behavior as hyperactive or hyperaggressive.[14]

Somehow, in lacking the masculinity of lower-class men, high placed women in society cannot be said to reign supremely. While elite women may appear to be more powerful than male laborers, "a truck driver or butcher always has his 'manhood' to fall back upon."[15] It would be fruitful to see if Millett's insights bear out in medieval works that often play with upsetting conventional expectations. For example, in medieval virgin martyr legends, the pagan male governors have the power to kill Christian maidens. Yet the 'winners' are always the martyred girls who talk back in a saucy and sassy way to these powerful men. And in *Eirik the Red's Saga*, Aud the Deep-minded, one of the founding Norwegians of Iceland, leads "twenty free-born men"[16] and takes over vast territories in Iceland.

Millet asks if the rise of the cult of courtly love and chivalry helped women's roles in society. For all the praise of women in such literary works, chivalry disguises "the injustice of women's social position ... One must acknowledge that the chivalrous stance is a game the master group plays in elevating its subject to a pedestal level."[17] Women's legal and economic status remained unchanged despite this cult of womanhood. Millett also intriguingly suggests how women have more class mobility than men through marriage, a factor that does seem supported by both medieval women's lives and writings.

Women's bodies remain the focus of much feminist theory, given the negative perceptions of women's bodies since the ancient Greeks. In their 1979 classic *The Madwoman in the Attic: The Woman Writer and the Nineteenth-Century Literary Imagination*, Sandra M. Gilbert and Susan Gubar ask, "What does it mean to be a woman writer in a culture whose fundamental definitions of literary authority are ... both overtly and covertly patriarchal?"[18] While Gilbert and Gubar focus on nineteenth-century literature, much of what they say could be applied to medieval women's lives and writings. Unlike men, the female author has to justify her existence as a writer and must struggle against a male predecessor's "reading of *her*".[19] As the poet Adrienne Rich points out, "No male writer has written primarily or even largely for women ... But to a lesser or greater extent, every woman writer has written for men."[20] By transforming reality imaginatively, women writers still work to actively affect the real world.

Not only that, but "patriarchal socialization literally makes women sick, both physically and mentally." Misogyny causes disease and dis-ease,[21] which Susan Bordo goes on to explore in *Unbearable Weight* (1993), a book emerging from a period of intense scrutiny on anorexia nervosa. The concept that women's bodies must be trained to become 'docile'[22] is hugely suggestive for medieval women's bodies, both actual and imagined. While Bordo focuses on more modern manifestations of bodily disorder – such as nineteenth-century hysteria, agoraphobia (1950s), and anorexia nervosa (1980s and 1990s) – her insight that "pathology [is] embodied *protest*"[23] proves useful. The holy anorexics of the late Middle Ages have been read as resisting the misogynist interpretation of the female body. These holy women practicing self-starvation exploited cultural standards of sanctity by making their bodies docile (see Chapters 10 and 17). While this may seem disempowering and was often self-destructive, the holy anorexic gained power and esteem from both men and women.[24] In another case of embodied protest, the enslaved Irish princess Melkorka in the *Laxdaela Saga*, who refuses to speak, succeeds in "rebell[ing] against the linguistic and cultural rules of the father."[25] Her mute pathology ultimately enables her son to be offered the Irish throne.

Monique Wittig argued as early as 1981 for a materialist feminist approach.[26] She sees feminists as denigrating the material body as something to be transcended. In seeing biology as oppressive, these approaches reinforced, rather than dismantled, the Aristotelian view of man providing the active principle of form or spirit and women providing the passive matter or flesh (see Chapter 10 in this book). In the twenty-first century, material feminism has become an emerging theoretical school. The insights of this approach perceive materiality as having its own agency that can positively catalyze political and ethical alliances.[27] Perhaps as Anaïs Nin suggests, "The art of woman must be born in the womb-cells of the mind."[28]

Paula Gunn Allen reminds us that we need to keep tribal structures in mind when we read stories from Native American traditions. Otherwise, being focused on present concerns and expectations, a Euro-centric standpoint might misread a text as being 'sexist'. Allen's 'Indian-Feminist' perspective reveals that women in her culture were not oppressed, but had agency. In a parallel vein, we need to read medieval lives and texts from a *medieval* perspective. A non-medieval perspective might suggest women were merely oppressed. The more one knows and learns about medieval culture and history, the more we can see ways that women carved out for themselves spaces of dynamic freedom. Indeed, men, too, were not fully 'free' – they had to work within the confines and expectations of secular and religious authority. The more complex one is willing to be in reading about the past, the more one might see the nuances that make all lives intricate concoctions of freedom and oppression, creativity and adherence to tradition, compliance and subversion. We should cross-pollinate with medieval women, in what the Chicana writer Gloria Anzaldúa calls "an act of kneading".[29] While we may have different identities than medieval women, we can, as Donna Haraway suggests, respond to them through our mutual *affinity*.[30]

While their lives were very different, Christina of Markyate, forced to hide in a tiny closet for years to fulfill her vow as a virgin, might be seen as an early companion to Harriet Jacobs. Jacobs, born into slavery in 1813, later wrote her memoir about hiding in her grandmother's attic for seven years to escape servitude before fleeing to the North. Both women suffered physically and emotionally, finding refuge in comparably confined spaces only to be set free later on. Alice Walker revises Virginia Woolf's suggestion that all women need to write is a room of one's own and £500 a year. She writes of African-American women and the legacy of slavery. How did black women artists survive and create? Where were her own mother's stories? Indeed, her mother's stories live on in Walker herself. And her mother's garden constituted a form of art, a legacy that sustains itself.[31] Medieval women likewise kept gardens – Hildegard von Bingen's garden supplied herbs for her medicines. Hugeberc von Hildesheim created an allegorical nosegay through her writings.

We began and conclude this book by citing Virginia Woolf's famous treatise from 1929, *A Room of One's Own*. Woolf suggests that the new woman novelist need no longer limit herself

> to the respectable houses of the upper middle classes. She will go without kindness or condescension, but in the spirit of fellowship into those small, scented rooms where sit the courtesan, the harlot and the lady with the pug dog.[32]

As we have seen, medieval women entered into this "spirit of fellowship" centuries earlier, as Hrotsvit von Gandersheim did in her holy harlot plays. Simone de Beauvoir's contention that the prostitute is both a shunned yet exalted figure we see embodied in figures like St Mary of Egypt, a holy harlot whose legend was extremely popular in the Middle Ages. Woolf also suggests that, while men in novels are shown having male friends, women tend to be seen only in relation to men (fathers, husbands and lovers). Joanna Russ argues that women in Western literature mainly "exist only in relation to the protagonist (who is male)."[33] Perhaps we could apply to medieval literature something called the Bechdel test, named for the lesbian cartoonist Alison Bechdel, which explores whether or not a work (film or literary) depicts two women talking about anything other than a man. Medieval lives show frequent moments where women are concerned with the lives of other women without relying on men. While Russ points out that in Western myths, the 'Woman as Intellectual' is impossible, Hildegard, to name just one medieval woman, undermines that assertion. Indeed, as Russ herself points out, medieval literature and medieval women's lives can offer different options, such as the story of the quest, the journey of the soul, and religious experience:

> [M]odes of much medieval fiction all provide myths for dealing with the kinds of experiences we are actually having now, instead of the literary myths we have inherited, which only tell us about the kinds of experiences we think we ought to be having.[34]

Medieval women's lives and writings offer us different prototypical narratives to reflect our lives in.

Eve Kosofsky Sedgwick's magisterial opus pioneering queer theory, *Epistemology of the Closet* (1990), underscores the problem binaries such as private/public and secret/disclosure make for homosexuality. Knowledge/ignorance refers back to sexuality – as we see with Adam, Eve, and the Fall. For Marie de France, secrecy offers a private sanctuary of erotic bliss. And the towers in which jealous old husbands imprisoned their badly married wives function as closets from which they desire only to be free, not unlike the homosexual closet many individuals 'come out' of.

Judith Butler argues that all gender is performative. That is, any gender assumes "the very structure of imitation". If "*gender is a kind of imitation for which there is no original*", what does it mean for Silence to dress as a man in a thirteenth-century French romance? Is she enacting a form of drag that Butler points out gestures to the very performative nature of any gender? If, as Butler argues, the subject comes into being through performance, what happens when Silence must dress again as a woman at the conclusion of the poem? If "gender is a performance that *produces* the illusion of an inner sex or essence or psychic gender core", what lies at the core of Silence's identity?[35]

Repeatedly through history, women's access to education and the lack of such access recur as themes. Mary Astell, one of England's first feminists and herself an intellectual with public fame and successfully supported by patrons, proposes the establishment of a 'female monastery' in *A Serious Proposal to the Ladies* (1694). Not unlike Christine's vision of the City of Ladies 300 years earlier, Astell argues that such a place would be a refuge to women, where they could learn and look after the truth. "You are therefore ladies, invited to a place, where you shall suffer no other confinement, but to be kept out of the road of sin ... Happy retreat! Which will be the introducing you into such a paradise as your mother Eve forfeited." Citing a male author who contends the Middle Ages as the period when the greatest women lived, Astell promotes women's education as a way to esteem God.

> For since God has given women as well as men intelligent souls, why should they be forbidden to improve them? Since he has not denied us the faculty of thinking, why should we not (at least in gratitude to him) employ our thoughts on himself their noblest object ... Being the soul was created for the contemplation of truth as well as for the fruition of good, is it not as cruel

and unjust to exclude women from the knowledge of the one as from the enjoyment of the other?[36]

Of course, as seen with many of the medieval women in this book, nunneries were often conclaves of educational and intellectual fervor, oases of privileged contemplation.

Feminist and writer Mary Wollstonecraft in *A Vindication of the Rights of Woman* (1792) criticizes the "tyranny of man ... [W]hy should [women] be kept in ignorance under the specious name of innocence?"[37] Mother of Mary Shelley, herself author of that notorious and blood-curdling horror novel *Frankenstein,* Wollstonecraft agitates against societal conventions that lead to weak and useless women. The best education leads to virtue and independent reason.

Maria Edgeworth, who wrote in the late eighteenth through nineteenth centuries, chastises men for scorning intellectual women. Women are "excluded from academies, public libraries, &c.", yet men mock them for knowing less. "With the insulting injustice of an Egyptian task-master, you demand the work, and deny the necessary materials."[38] Born into slavery in the nineteenth century, Anna Julia Cooper argues against male criticism of female education, as though if women "nibble at any side of the apple of knowledge, there would be an end forever to their sewing on buttons and embroidering slippers."[39]

In fact, women's moral judgment can be read as fundamentally more ethical as Carol Gilligan famously argued *In a Different Voice: Psychological Theory and Women's Development* (1982). According to Gilligan, the standard male view of moral development read women as having arrested development for insisting on communal responsibility rather than individual justice. Yet Gilligan pointed out how, while men emphasized the individual, women's "morality of responsibility" lies "in its emphasis on ... connection".[40] This unifying morality lies on a higher plane as the ethics of care. Gilligan praises the myth of Demeter (goddess of harvest) and her daughter Persephone as ideal models for the "feminine attitude toward power ... The elusive mystery of women's development lies in its recognition of the continuing importance of attachment in the human life cycle."[41] Christine de Pizan likewise lauded Demeter (Ceres in Greek): "Because of this lady, humanity benefited from the transformation of the harsh and untamed world into a civilized and urban place."[42] Women's innovations have established and deepened humanity's morality and honor.

As recently as 1976, Canadian novelist Margaret Atwood could write, "In other words, there is no critical vocabulary for expressing the concept 'good/ female'."[43] The Irish poet, Eavan Boland, writes in her 'Letter to a Young Woman Poet', that *"That the past needs us.* That very past in poetry which simplified us as women and excluded us as poets now needs us to change it." By understanding and reading our historical predecessors, we can change the past. Not only that, "we need to change the past". Furthermore, "poetic authority can actually be changed, altered, radicalized by those very aspects of humanity which are excluded from it."[44]

Women poets have to know the poetic past to change the poetic future. In a parallel way, we need to understand the historical past of women to change the historical future of women. As Boland writes, "And yet my skin, my flesh, my sex – without learning any of this – stood as a subversive historian, ready to edit the text."[45] Women from the past need us.

Joan Kelly-Gadol famously asks, 'Did Women Have a Renaissance?' She points out how adding women to history problematizes the analysis of history itself. Rather than seeing prominent medieval women as *exceptional* by adhering to male role models, we should read them within their own spheres. Indeed, time periods that many assume are emancipatory[46] – such as the Renaissance – have tended not to be so for women. Indeed, Kelly-Gadol has shown that the shift from the Middle Ages to the early modern period constituted a *restriction* of women's autonomy and agency.

In the fifteenth century, Margaret Paston clearly ruled the roost. She lived just as a transition was taking place – from the medieval era to what historians call the early modern period. The medieval dynamic woman gradually became tamed into the early modern woman, whose options for agency and power eroded in some ways after the Middle Ages. Though some medieval women were considered heretics, visionaries could find acceptance in society in the Middle Ages. While some witch trials took place in the fifteenth century, such persecutions had their heyday in the Renaissance and early modern period, *not* the Middle Ages.

Women were gradually becoming identified with domestic spaces inside homes. Buildings increasingly acquired more private rooms, such as individual bedchambers or places to entertain. The consumption of goods to decorate these areas became a duty of the woman of the house. In 1580, the Italian writer Torquato Tasso wrote men should *acquire* them while women *preserve* them. "[T]he woman looks after that which has been acquired and her virtues are employed inside the house, just as the man demonstrates his outside." In 1612, an Englishman wrote that the wife's duty was "to keep the house".[47] Despite this, many female rebels and leaders of the Renaissance fought against the confinement of women to the house, including Katharina von Bora, nun and, as Martin Luther's wife, a key religious reformer; Catherine de' Medici, ruthless queen and queen regent of France; Artemisia Gentileschi, the innovative Italian painter and feminist; and Aphra Behn, the English spy and playwright.

Along with politics and economics, religion was changing. Throughout Europe, the Protestant Reformation was underway. Under Henry VIII, many irreplaceable manuscripts, buildings, stained glass, books, and artworks were savagely destroyed. Remnants of these acts of destruction can be found within English parish churches, preserving the past. Damaged glass, smashed statuary, and hacked rood screens exist as poignant visible reminders of the Middle Ages.

Adrienne Rich's 1970s manifesto 'When We Dead Awaken: Writing as Re-Vision' asserts that "The creative energy of patriarchy is fast running out; what remains is its self-generating energy for destruction. As women, we

A stained glass eye, which survived being shattered during the violence of the sixteenth-century Reformation. This lone eye, a solitary remnant, looks at visitors. We, in turn, gaze back, recognizing kindred spirits, fellow humans from a time long ago (from All Saints Church in East Barsham, England; photo by John A. Twyning, with permission and thanks)

have our work cut out for us."[48] As women historians and chroniclers of women's lives and writings, we likewise have our work cut out for us and welcome those wishing to join in this endeavor.

We began this book by suggesting that a feminist believes that women are humans. As Toril Moi in her reading of Simone de Beauvoir reminds us "women too embody humanity".[49] Medieval women lived vital lives, proving their attitudes and beliefs had validity. Medieval women were active intellectually, defended women's moral and spiritual equality, and contributed richly to the social, political, imaginative, artistic, and theological fabric of medieval life. Many fought for women's literacy, still the path to emancipation for women – and all people – today from poverty and oppression. We see in medieval women earlier reflections of ourselves today. From medieval women, we can learn, take heart, and find inspiration as we go forward as women into the twenty-first century.

Learn more

- In her art piece dedicated to women of the past, Judy Chicago's *The Dinner Party* at the Brooklyn Museum of Art displays place settings dedicated to many of the women in this book, including Hildegard and Christine de Pizan. See the exhibit here: http://www.brooklynmuseum.org/eascfa/dinner_party/home.php.
- Be sure to browse the place settings for medieval women: http://www.brooklynmuseum.org/eascfa/dinner_party/place_settings/browse.php
- Design your own place setting in honor of your favorite medieval woman.

Notes

1. Toni Morrison, 'Unspeakable Things Unspoken: The Afro-American Presence in American Literature', excerpted in Sandra M. Gilbert and Susan Gubar, *Feminist Literary Theory and Criticism: A Norton Reader* (NY: W. W. Norton, 2007), 267 [266–278].
2. Morrison, 267–268.
3. Ann DuCille, 'Blue Notes on Black Sexuality: Sex and the Texts of the Twenties and Thirties', excerpted in Gilbert and Gubar, 957 [957–962].
4. Henry Louis Gates, Jr, *The Signifying Monkey: A Theory of African-American Literary Criticism* (Oxford: Oxford University Press, 1988), 51.
5. Elizabeth Alvilda Petroff, *Medieval Women's Visionary Literature* (NY: Oxford University Press, 1986), 157.
6. All quotes from Anne Bradstreet, *Prologue*, at http://www.poetryfoundation.org/poem/172961.
7. Harriet Martineau, *Autobiography*, excerpted in Gilbert and Gubar, 108–109 [106–109].
8. James Mansfield Nichols, 'The Arabic Verses of Qasmūna Bint Ismā'īl ibn Bagdālah', *International Journal of Middle East Studies* 13 (1981), 156 [155–158].

9. Simone de Beauvoir, *The Second Sex*, excerpted in Gilbert and Gubar, 301 [300–323].
10. Sherry B. Ortner, 'Is Female to Male as Nature is to Culture?', excerpted in Gilbert and Gubar, 355 [350–367].
11. Nancy Chodorow, *Family Structure and Feminine Personality*, excerpted in Gilbert and Gubar, 368 [367–388].
12. Kate Millett, *Sexual Politics*, excerpted in Gilbert and Gubar, 337 [336–350].
13. Millett, 340.
14. Millett, 344.
15. Millett, 347.
16. Keneva Kunz, trans., *The Vinland Sagas* (London: Penguin, 2008), 26.
17. Millett, 348.
18. Sandra M. Gilbert and Susan Gubar, *The Madwoman in the Attic: The Woman Writer and the Nineteenth-Century Literary Imagination*, excerpted in Gilbert and Gubar, 449 [448–459].
19. Gilbert and Gubar, 452.
20. Adrienne Rich, 'When We Dead Awaken: Writing as Re-Vision', excerpted in Gilbert and Gubar, 192 [188–200].
21. Gilbert and Gubar, 453–455.
22. Susan Bordo, *Unbearable Weight: Feminism, Western Culture, and the Body*, excerpted in Gilbert and Gubar, 745 [744–756].
23. Bordo, 751.
24. Two key works that explore the importance of food for women in the Middle Ages and the phenomenon of 'holy anorexia', read Caroline Walker Bynum's *Holy Feast and Holy Fast: The Religious Significance of Food to Medieval Woman* (Berkeley: University of California Press, 1987) and Rudolph M. Bell, *Holy Anorexia* (Chicago: University of Chicago Press, 1985).
25. Bordo, 751.
26. Monique Wittig, 'One Is Not Born a Woman', excerpted in Gilbert and Gubar, 00 [544–551].
27. See Stacy Alaimo and Susan Hekman, eds., *Material Feminisms* (Bloomington: Indiana University Press, 2008).
28. Anaïs Nin, *The Diary*, excerpted in Gilbert and Gubar, 148 [148–149].
29. Gloria Anzaldúa, from *Borderlands/La Frontera* (1987), excerpted in Gilbert and Gubar, 250 [247–258].
30. Donna Haraway, From 'A Manifesto for Cyborgs' (1985), excerpted in Gilbert and Gubar, 591 [584–601].
31. See Alice Walker, *In Search of Our Mother's Gardens*, excerpted in Gilbert and Gubar, 212–219.
32. Virginia Woolf, from *A Room of One's Own*, excerpted in Gilbert and Gubar, 133 [128–137].
33. Joanna Russ, 'What Can a Heroine Do? or Why Women Can't Write', excerpted in Gilbert and Gubar, 202 [200–211].
34. Russ, 211.
35. All quotes from Judith Butler, 'Imitation and Gender Insubordination', excerpted in

Gilbert and Gubar, 715–716, 721 [708–722].

36. Mary Astell in *A Serious Proposal to the Ladies*, excerpted in Gilbert and Gubar, 29 [28–31].

37. Mary Wollstonecraft, *A Vindication of the Rights of Woman*, excerpted in Gilbert and Gubar, 43 [43–47].

38. Maria Edgeworth, *Letters to Literary Ladies*, excerpted in Gilbert and Gubar, 52 [48–54].

39. Anna Julia Cooper, 'The Higher Education of Women', excerpted in Gilbert and Gubar, 113 [112–118].

40. Carol Gilligan, *In a Different Voice: Psychological Theory and Women's Development,* excerpted in Gilbert and Gubar, 568 [567–571].

41. Gilligan, 570.

42. Christine de Pizan, *The Book of the City of Ladies*, translated by Earl Jeffrey Richards (NY: Persea Books, 1982), 79.

43. Margaret Atwood, '"On Being a 'Woman Writer": Paradoxes and Dilemmas', excerpted in Gilbert and Gubar, 221 [219–222].

44. Eavan Boland, 'Letter to a Young Woman Poet', excerpted in Gilbert and Gubar, 281–282 [278–287].

45. Boland, 283.

46. See Joan Kelly-Gadol, 'The Social Relation of the Sexes: Methodological Implications of Women's History', excerpted in Gilbert and Gubar, 431 [430–436].

47. Martha C. Howell, 'Gender in the Transition to Merchant Capitalism', in *The Oxford Handbook of Women and Gender in Medieval Europe*, edited by Judith M. Bennett and Ruth Mazo Karras (Oxford: Oxford University Press, 2013), 571–572 [561–576].

48. Rich, 200.

49. Toril Moi, *What is a Woman? And Other Essays* (Oxford: Oxford University Press, 1999), 83.

 **lossary**

Affective Piety: A form of intense spiritual practice in which the believer identifies emotionally with Christ's humanity and suffering.

Anchorite/Anchoress: Spiritually-minded woman who willingly allows herself to be walled into a cell to devote her life to prayer and meditation.

Anglo-Norman: The variety of French used at the English court. After the Norman Conquest in 1066, the court in England became French-speaking for roughly 300 years.

Anglo-Saxon: See Old English, the form of English spoken from about 450 until 1150 CE.

Anglo-Saxons: Descendants of Germanic peoples who invaded Britain in the fifth century, taking over and ruling the country until the eleventh century.

Annunciation: When the angel Gabriel told the Virgin Mary that she, a virgin, would bear Jesus.

Anonymous: A creator who has no name attached to her piece of written or oral verse.

Archive: A library containing original manuscripts and documents from the past.

Baptism: Christian sacrament whereby a person is accepted into the faith, comprising of the sprinkling of water and the ritual utterance of words. It is meant to mirror Christ's own immersion into the River Jordan by John the Baptist.

BCE: Before the Common Era. Formerly BC. *See also* CE.

Beguines: Laywomen living together and undertaking charitable work. Related groups include the *Umiliati* in northern Italy and followers of St Francis and St Clare.

Benedictine Rule: A Benedictine convent or monastery follows the Rule set forth by St Benedict in the sixth century. A nun or monk is dedicated to poverty, chastity, and obedience and expected to work, study, and pray. They perform the eight offices of the Work of God, with prayers taking place at intervals starting before dawn until sunset. Food is limited to one meal in winter and two in the summer when the light lasted longer. And the diet varied depending on the church year. During Lent, the days between Ash Wednesday and Easter, fasting is undertaken. *See also* Fast.

Beowulf: Most famous Old English poem written *c.* 1000 CE, featuring the hero Beowulf and his battles with monsters, including a dragon.

Bloodletting: Standard medical treatment due to the humoral theory

Book of Hours: Popular prayer book; some copies have extraordinary artwork. Such books, dedicated to the Virgin, typically included psalms, hymns, and excerpts from Scripture.

Byzantium: The Byzantine Empire was based in Constantinople (now Istanbul, Turkey). Byzantium, also known as the Eastern Roman Empire, lasted until 1453, when Ottoman Turks conquered Constantinople. The rituals in Orthodox Christianity practiced here sometimes differ from those in Western Europe.

Canon Law: Church law. It could conflict with secular laws.

Canoness: Canonesses in the early Middle Ages had many privileges nuns lacked, including the ability to retain private property and to leave a religious community at will. Later on, canonesses became more like nuns due to reform pressures.

Canonize/Canonization: The official process whereby someone is made a saint.

The Canterbury Tales: Written by Geoffrey Chaucer in the late fourteenth century, it contains many stories (both religious and funny) typical of the time period with much-loved characters.

Catholic/Catholicism: In the Middle Ages, Christians in Europe adhered to what we call Catholicism today. The Middle Ages took place before the sixteenth-century Reformation, when Western Christianity broke into two major faiths: Catholicism and Protestantism.

Catapult: Like a mechanical slingshot, such a machine would hurl stones and even flaming torches against enemies to maim and kill humans and destroy buildings and bridges. It uses force and gravity to propel heavy objects through the air to create mayhem and destruction.

CE: Common Era. Formerly AD (for *Anno Domini* or Year of Our Lord), but that favored a Christian view of history. *See also* BCE.

Celibacy: The state of being unmarried.

Chastity: Abstaining from sex.

Chivalry: From the French word *Chevalier* or knight, chivalry refers to an ideal behavior characterized by honesty, bravery, and courtesy.

Christianity: The religion that dominated Western Europe in the Middle Ages. The beliefs of today's Catholics follow those of medieval Christians, for whom the Pope was God's representative on earth. A Trinitarian religion,

Christianity holds that the Father, Son, and Holy Ghost or Spirit are aspects of this monotheistic (belief in one god) religion, with Jesus Christ as the Son of God. When I reference Christianity, I mean those beliefs dominant in the Western European Middle Ages.

Church Fathers: Holy male thinkers and theologians whose writings were considered to be authoritative.

Cistercian: The Cistercian order began in the twelfth century as part of a reform for those who wanted to live according to a stricter rule. One of the most famous Cistercians was St Bernard of Clairvaux who had dealings with Eleanor of Aquitaine, Hildegard, and Peter Abelard.

Clerk: Scholar, often religious.

College: Places of learning, often funded by nobility, including women. The College of Navarre was founded by Jeanne of Navarre. Several colleges at the University of Cambridge in England were founded by women: Queens' College by Margaret of Anjou, wife of Henry VI, and Elizabeth, wife of Edward IV; Christ's College and St John's College by Lady Margaret Beaufort, mother of Henry VII; and Clare College by Elizabeth de Burgh.

Consanguinity: Closeness of blood tie was a justification for divorce or as a prevention for marriage.

Courtly Love: *See* Fin' Amors/Fin' Amours.

Crucifixion: The form of torture used to kill Jesus Christ who was nailed to a cross. It becomes an image prevalent in medieval art and is referred to in literature.

Crusade: Conventionally it refers to an armed pilgrimage to the Holy Land from Europe. *See* First Crusade.

Cult: Saints often develop a cult, that is followers who pray to and rely on the saint's intervention in times of emotional and physical crisis.

Deaf Culture: The capital 'D' as in 'Deaf' refers to the Deaf culture and community; small 'd' as in 'deaf' refers to what is (in)audible.

Double Monastery: Not uncommon in the early Middle Ages in Germanic and Anglo-Saxon lands, a double monastery might have an abbess presiding over both male and female sections – a powerful position (*see* Hild of Whitby *and* Birgitta of Sweden).

Eucharist: In the Christian religious service called the mass, the priest utters words that transform the bread and wine into the actual body and body of Christ, according to Catholic belief. The bread that has been turned into Christ's body is called the Eucharist or the consecrated Host. The Host is the piece of bread or wafer that Christians consume in the Mass or service. Starting in the sixteenth century with the Reformation, this transformation comes under pressure by Protestants who contend the host only symbolically represents Christ's body.

Excommunication: The ritual expulsion or exclusion of someone from the Christian faith.

Fast: To reduce or restrict one's food intake. Fasting does not mean to starve, rather to limit what kinds of foods you might partake in. For example, today many Catholics eat fish rather than red meat on Fridays. During Lent, the 40 days before Easter, there were strict requirements and prohibitions, such as avoiding meat (flesh) for fish. Many spiritually inclined people would eat meagerly on what we would call a vegetarian or vegan diet. Sometimes people were punished by food restrictions. And others fasted so extremely for God, that they died (*see* Catherine of Siena in Chapter 17 and Food Habits, including those of the Holy Anorexics, in Chapter 10).

Feast Day: A feast day, often associated with a saint, is a day designated by the Church as a holy day and, as such, subject to certain rules.

Feminism: The political and social movement and scholarly approach committed to understanding and improving the lives of women and female-identified people.

Feudal/Feudalism: The political system whereby the king owns all the land, 'shares' it with his barons or lords, who – in turn – show their homage by supporting the king with knights and warfare when necessary.

Fin' Amors/Fin' Amours: Also called Courtly Love. It is a system of love, fidelity, and affection typically imagined between a (married) woman and a young man. The woman might be married to a powerful king or lord whose servant or knight was the man. While it appears as a kind of ideal in literature, many debate whether such forms of affection existed historically.

First Crusade: From 1096 to 1099, Christian European armed pilgrims made their way to present-day Middle East in order to reclaim lands for Christianity. They succeed in capturing Jerusalem, only to massacre Muslims and Jews.

Fortune: A Roman goddess who was said to spin the wheel of fortune of our lives. When we are doing well, she might spin the wheel so that we descend in our happiness; or if we suffer, she might allow us some pleasure.

Friars: Followers of St Francis, an early thirteenth-century saint who spoke on behalf of radical poverty and has been declared the patron saint of ecology for his love of nature and animals. Friars sometimes lived in friaries.

Galen: This second-century physician, who recognized that both men and women provided a 'seed' for the creation of a child, also elaborated on Hippocrates's humoral theory of the body.

Gandersheim: Almost like a queen, Abbess Gerberga II, the niece of emperor Otto I, ruled Hrotsvit's convent, one that functioned like a small country or principality ruled and populated by women.

Gender Studies: The exploration of gender identity and how gender is represented; often seen as the socially influenced aspects of gender performance.

Gentry: Gentleman or gentlewoman; the class just below the nobility.

Geoffrey Chaucer: Fourteenth-century English writer, whose tragic romance *Troilus and Criseyde* and pilgrimage poem *The Canterbury Tales* are frequently studied masterpieces.

Gothic Cathedral: Stunning architectural masterpieces, such as Notre Dame Cathedral in Paris, soar up towards heaven.

Gregorian Chant: A form of sacred music developed in monastic communities.

Guild: A guild is like a union, where workers in a common trade come together, pay dues, and support one another professionally. Paris, for example, had five guilds for women silkmakers.

Hebrew Bible: Including the Torah or Pentateuch (*Genesis, Exodus, Leviticus, Numbers,* and *Deuteronomy*). These books comprise the first part of what Christians call the Old Testament.

Heresy: Deviation from an accepted form of a religion.

Hermit: Religious person living a solitary life devoted to God.

Hours of Our Lady: Readings including hymns, psalms, and scriptural passages in honor of the Virgin Mary.

Hundred Years War: War between England and France, waged on and off from 1337 to 1453. It centered on who had the right to rule France. The king of England thought he had justification through familial connections to rule. Naturally, the French disagreed. Ultimately, with the help of Joan of Arc, the French won.

Indo-European: This family of languages includes Greek, Latin, French, Sanskrit, Hindi, Russian, Celtic, German, English, and many others.

Indulgence: Means by which sins could be more quickly made up for. It was increasingly seen as a corrupt system that favored the rich and exploited the poor, the abused, and the gullible as seen in Chaucer's story *The Pardoner's Tale*.

Infanticide: The killing of infants, often female or deformed.

Inquisition: Official judicial group of the Catholic Church charged with combatting heresy. It had power to question and prosecute suspected heretics. Later, it evolved into persecuting alleged witchcraft. Torture could be used and punishment was harsh. Once released to secular authorities, heretics who refused to repent could be burnt at the stake. Records kept by prosecutors sometimes contain opinions of common people, of high importance to historians today.

Islam: The faith founded by Mohammed in the seventh century. A monotheistic religion, it was much misunderstood by many Christians in the Middle Ages. On the Iberian peninsula in present-day Spain and Portugal, Muslim, Jews, and Christians lived in close proximity. While their political association concluded in violence, there was more familiarity and mutual influence on each other than in other parts of Europe.

Jews: Followers of Judaism. They were expelled or banned from England in 1290 under the Edict of Expulsion by King Edward I.

Judaism: The religion of the Hebrews. The Jewish Pentateuch or Torah contains much of the history and beliefs of these ancient peoples. The Christian Bible refers to these works as the Old Testament, suggesting that the New Testament supersedes or builds on them (thus offending Jews).

Judith: Jewish widow who beheads the tyrant Holofernes. Many wonderful paintings of this scene exist, including some by the seventeeth-century woman painter, Artemesia Gentileschi.

Jesus Christ: Prophet considered the Son of God by Christians.

Lai: Short romance or tale that focuses on love.

Latin: The language of the Roman Empire remained a powerful force in the Middle Ages and was the language of the Christian Church. It developed into several vernacular languages: Spanish, French, Portuguese, Romanian, and Italian. Latin ability was considered vital for scholars, theologians, and lawyers.

Lay (People): Those who have not taken religious vows and are not in religious orders.

Legal Records: Legal records can include, for example in England, Coroners' Rolls, with details of ordinary people's lives; Close Rolls, the king's private letters to subjects; Charter Rolls, public pronouncements; Patent Rolls, orders to subjects or granting a right or privilege; and Law Codes.

Leper: Leprosy, today called Hansen's disease, caused great terror in the Middle

Ages, when it was little understood. Lepers were sometimes segregated and isolated, though Christian charity demanded kindness to them, such as creating leper hospitals. Matilda of Scotland is even said to have washed and kissed the feet of lepers as a way to imitate Christ's compassion to lepers.

Magna Carta: Thirteenth-century charter limiting the English king's power.

Manuscript: Book made from vellum, or sheepskin, that had been scraped and treated so that it could absorb the ink and paint the scribe and illuminator might use.

Martyr/Martyrdom: Person who dies for her faith or a cause she believes in. The act of having been martyred.

Mass: Christian ritual during which the bread and the wine are transformed into Christ's body and blood, according to Catholic belief.

Middle English: The form of the English language spoken between 1150 and 1500. See Old English and Anglo-Saxon.

Misogyny: Anti-woman or hatred of women.

Modesty Topos: A rhetorical device used to humble oneself. Many writers in the Middle Ages would often humble themselves at some point in their writing, calling themselves a simple servant of God or a lowly creature. A women writer referred to her gender as well, calling herself weak, humble, or lowly. Some declared themselves to be 'unlettered' or unversed in Latin, even if they did, in some cases, know some Latin, the language of scholars. This device was used to gain permission from male advisors to make their works known and to signal to the reader that they are aware of the audacity of a woman writing. Some writers subvert it to daring effect (*see* Hrotsvit von Gandersheim, Hildegard von Bingen, Marie de France, Christine de Pizan *and* Teresa de Cartagena).

Monastery: In this religious architectural complex lived those who took vows, devoting their lives to God.

Moneylending: Christians were forbidden to lend money at interest (the basis of modern capitalism) due to a prohibition of usury. But some Christians got around this; the Knights Templar, for example, 'rented' money.

Monk: Male religious who lived in a monastery, obeyed strict rules, and devoted his life to God.

Muslims: Followers of Islam.

Mystic/Mysticism: A person who experiences the divine; mysticism is the act of experiencing the divine through seeing visions, hearing voices, or coming to a profound understanding of spiritual truths.

Normans: The Viking descendants who came to rule in northern France (present-day Normandy). Related to Anglo-Saxon rulers through marriage (see Emma of Normandy), the Normans invaded England in 1066. They came to speak a variety of French called Anglo-Norman that ultimately added many French words to the English language.

Norman Conquest: 1066 invasion of Norman French who took over the Anglo-Saxon kingdom.

Nuns: Female religious woman who live together in a convent or nunnery, taking vows to spend their lives focused on the spiritual praise of God and performing charitable deeds or mastering scholarship.

Old English: The form of English spoken from about 450 until 1150 CE.

Optics: The study of light and vision.

Pagan: Non-Christian, sometimes believing the system of multiple gods.

Patron: Someone who either financially or emotionally supports an artist, musician, or writer.

Patron Saint: A patron saint specializes in helping a particular cause or group of people. Saint Dymphna, for example, is a patron saint of runaways.

Penance: After acknowledging a sin or fault, a person makes up for it by undergoing penance. It might be accomplished by prayers, fasting, or even going on a pilgrimage.

Penitentials: Religious guides explaining how various sins should be punished.

Penthesilea: The queen of the Amazons who were mythical women warriors.

Periculoso: This rule appears at the end of the thirteenth century, a period when women actively sought out ways to maintain religious lives through bypassing traditional male-imposed authority, as with the Beguines. *See* Christina of Markyate.

Piety: Devout religious focus.

Pilgrim: A pilgrim typically undertook journeys to fulfill a vow, a pact with a saint who may have healed the pilgrim due to prayer. Sometimes a pilgrimage was taken to affect a cure. Visiting a holy site with healing relics, the body parts of those people considered saintly by the church, a pilgrim hoped for a miraculous healing for herself or on behalf of another. In art, a pilgrim is often identified by a hat, a walking stick, and a scrip or pouch for carrying food in.

Pilgrimage: Pilgrimages were undertaken by devout Christians in the medieval period to shrines or holy places, usually in a church or cathedral. The shrine would have a relic, or body part like a finger bone, of a dead saint.

Pilgrimage exists in many religions, including the famous Muslim hajj. Jewish pilgrims in the Middle Ages were known to buy souvenir metal badges in the Holy Land from vendors who also sold Christian badges.

Pilgrimage Shrines: Many of the miracles associated with saints had to do with healing. A person sick with an illness might undertake a holy journey or pilgrimage to a shrine – either local or far distant – to seek a cure from a particular saint. Saints would become associated with different kinds of healing cures.

Postpartum Depression: A psychological affliction women can suffer after giving birth.

Priory: A monastery where monks or nuns reside, pray, and work.

Prosopography: Rather than focusing on one individual, this type of history looks at a group of people who are related in a family or due to some other reason (a group of pilgrims going to the same shrine, or a set of farmers in an area of a country). At the same time, it is not without problems, since sources were often generated by privileged groups like men, upper classes, or educated religious. In trials, testimony of a witness speaking in the vernacular or everyday speech, such as English, French, or German, might be translated into Latin by the scribe listening to the words. Prosopography is the basis for the study of the Pastons (*see* Margaret Paston) since we can read an entire group's dynamics through their letters.

Protestant Reformation: The seeds of this movement extend back to the late medieval period. In the sixteenth century, some Christians broke away from the authority of the Papacy and Rome where the Pope lived. The most famous incident in the Protestant Reformation was provoked by Martin Luther, a German monk, when he wrote his *Ninety-Five Theses* with criticisms of the church in 1517, setting off a chain of events leading to a split among European Christians. Henry VIII joined in this break with Rome due to his desire to divorce Catherine of Aragon and marry Anne Boleyn.

Prostitute Saints: Also known as Holy Harlots. Prostitute saints constitute a subcategory of women saints, who, despite a sinful past, could partake of God's mercy and salvation in heaven. The first such example appears in Scripture with Mary Magdalene, a prostitute who becomes a follower of Jesus and is the first witness to his resurrection. Her name becomes synonymous with that of devout women who may have strayed from the straight and narrow, but whose dedication more than makes up for this. In fact, there were legends that she lived after Christ's crucifixion and ended up in France, living penitently in the wilderness. Legend says her relics survived and became housed in a church in Vézelay, becoming a hugely popular pilgrimage destination.

Provençal or Occitan: Language spoken in the region of southern France called Occitania.

Psalter: A Psalter contains the Psalms from the Bible.

Purgatory: Purgatory became increasingly developed as a concept in medieval Christian thought. It was envisioned as a space between Heaven and Hell where souls could work off their sins and eventually enter Heaven. The most famous depiction of it is in the *Purgatorio* section of the Italian poet Dante's great masterpiece, *The Divine Comedy*.

Quadrivium: *See Trivium*.

Queen Regent: The power of the queen when her husband has died and her male child is still too young to rule. In some cases the queen would function in the child's place.

Queen Regnant: A queen who rules in her own right, not on behalf of another.

Reformation: Religious upheaval in the sixteenth century. Martin Luther is often seen as the catalyst for attacks on the Catholic Church, but many Reformation beliefs and thoughts had been discussed for decades previously.

Relic: Typically a body part like a finger bone belonging to a dead saint, a relic was seen as exuding supernatural healing powers. So valuable were these, that sacred thefts of relics were not uncommon. A relic could also be something associated with a holy person, such as the Virgin's veil or the swaddling clothes in which the infant Jesus was wrapped. Notorious people would sell false relics, as the Pardoner does in Geoffrey Chaucer's late fourteenth-century masterpiece, *The Canterbury Tales*.

Reliquary: A container, often beautiful and ornate, contains relics, typically bones, of a saint.

Renaissance: A time when the ideals of Classical Antiquity became the model for emulation and admiration.

Roman Empire: Lasting over four hundred years (roughly 30 BCE–395 CE), it governed huge areas of lands and peoples in present-day Europe, north Africa, and the Middle East. It was divided into the Eastern and Western Roman Empires in 395. The Western half collapsed in 476 and the Eastern half in 1453. Rulers later in the Middle Ages revived the idea of a Holy (Christian) Roman Empire and were called the Holy Roman Emperors.

Rome: Many martyrs were killed in Roman during the early years of Christianity. Later it became the centre of the Western Christian (Catholic) Church where the Pope resides. Today, the Vatican is an independent city-state ruled by the Pope.

Saint: A person killed for his or her Christian faith. After the age of martyrs, when the Roman Empire accepted Christianity, a saint was a holy person whose life, good works, or contributions to theological teachings made him/her worthy of the designation 'saint'. While some early saints were legendary or deemed saintly by popular acclaim, in the later Middle Ages the Church designed a more organized and bureaucratic method for determining sainthood, including proof of miracles, through the formal process of canonization.

St Agnes: Legendary virgin martyr.

St Andrew: One of Christ's apostles or followers.

St Augustine: Dominant theological intellect in the Middle Ages, this Church Father (d. 430) wrote his *Confessions* and *The City of God*.

St Catherine of Alexandria: Legendary fourth-century saint, she outwitted 50 pagan philosophers and was tortured on a wheel which fell apart, injuring her enemies. In the legend, she was finally beheaded and became a bride of Christ. A twelfth-century Anglo-Norman nun, Clemence of Barking, wrote Catherine's life story. *See* University.

St Francis: Much beloved saint said to especially care for animals and children.

St Jerome: Very important Church Father – one of the key male thinkers of the Catholic Church in the Middle Ages. Fourth-century theologian, writers, and translator of the Bible into Latin. This translation was the fundamental book of Western Europe throughout the Middle Ages. While some of his writings are misogynistic in character, he also maintained strong and supportive relations with various Christian women, like the Saints Marcella, Paula, and Eustochium, with whom he corresponded. Paula and Eustochium, likewise well-versed with Biblical languages, should also be credited with this translation.

St John the Baptist: The cousin of Jesus Christ who baptized him. He was killed by King Herod at Salome's request.

St Leonard: A sixth-century hermit with a popular cult. He was seen as helpful to pregnant women and prisoners of war.

St Margaret: St Margaret's legend tells how she was swallowed by a dragon, whose belly burst when she made the sign of cross within its bowels. This freedom of the saint from inside the body of another led St. Margaret to be the patron saint of childbirth. Women in labor would call on St Margaret for help. Just as she was freed safely from within the dragon, so too women begged for the safe delivery of their soon-to-be-born infants.

St Michael: Archangel who, in the Book of Revelations, fights the devil.

St Olaf: A former Viking pirate (995–1030), he became king (1016–1029) and Christianized Norway.

St Teresa Benedicta of the Cross: Jewish convert to Christianity who was killed in Auschwitz during World War II. Born Edith Stein.

St Ursula: Legendary saint martyred in Cologne, said to have been killed while accompanied by 11,000 other virgins.

Saint's Life or Legend: Story about a saint. Typically the saint withstands torture and condemnation before dying heroically as a martyr. Also known as hagiography.

Saladin: A brilliant leader and tactician, the Muslim Saladin (late 1130s–1193) came in conflict with Christian crusaders in the late twelfth century during the Third Crusade. He ruled Egypt and Syria and managed to regain control of Palestine that had been lost almost 100 years earlier during the First Crusade. He also laid siege to Jerusalem as we see in Margaret of Beverley's story. Saladin showed mercy on numerous occasions, allowing Jews to return to Jerusalem after his successful takeover and Christian pilgrims to visit. Medieval Christian commentators acknowledged Saladin's chivalric behavior.

Santiago de Compostela: One of the main pilgrimage goals in the Middle Ages (along with Rome, Italy; the Holy Land; Cologne, Germany; and Canterbury, England), Santiago lies in western Spain. Many pilgrims would come there from as far away as Scandinavia, even Iceland. It is dedicated to St James, one of Christ's disciples, whose remains are alleged to have arrived there. A pilgrim who makes it to Santiago can be identified by the emblem of the scallop shell.

Saracen: A term to designate a Muslim or person faithful to Allah.

Scribe: Someone who writes down what is dictated or who copies a text into a manuscript.

Second Crusade: Following up the First Crusade (1096–1099), the Second Crusade lasted from 1145 to 1149 and failed in its goal to retake the Crusader state of Edessa (today in Turkey) from Muslim hands.

Secular: Non-religious.

Shrine: Housing the relics of saints, it also referred to the holy place associated with pilgrimage.

Stigmata: Wounds Christ suffered on the cross as imagined or experienced by various saints and visionaries.

Theology: The study of religious concepts, God, and the divine.

Thomas Becket: Archbishop of Canterbury whose murder instigated by Eleanor of Aquitaine's husband, Henry II, caused Becket to become a saint and Canterbury a prominent pilgrimage goal.

Topos: A traditional theme or formula in literature.

Trivium and Quadrivium: In Hrotsvit of Gandersheim's play *Pafnutius* or the *The Conversion of the Harlot Thais*, there is a simple lesson on music, ideal for an audience to learn the basics of music theory. The standard education, typically for men, included the *trivium* – grammar, rhetoric, and dialectic – and the *quadrivium* – music, arithmetic, geometry, and astronomy. A scholar could pursue canon law, theology, or medicine.

Troubadour: Singing poet. Troubadour poetry was composed and performed in southern France. Women troubadours are called *trobairitz*.

Trobairitz: Female troubadour.

Trota: She would have been known as Trocta in her native land and is often referred to as Trotula for the manuscripts she was credited with in the Middle Ages. As Trota expert Monica H. Green points out, there were many women with the name of Trota in Salerno. In fact, we know "[v]irtually nothing"[1] about her.

University: While in the early Middle Ages monasteries and convents housed educational resources, the advent of universities in the twelfth century sprang from cathedral schools where masters and students associated. Although the patron saint of students and young girls was Catherine of Alexandria, women were not allowed to enroll at university.

Vernacular: Common, everyday speech. The language spoken by everyday people. For all practical purposes, whatever language was *not* Latin and often mentioned in opposition to Latin. Texts written in Latin (St Jerome's translation of the Bible, medical and legal works, *etc.*) were identified with men, while the vernacular was associated with a non-elite audience, such as women and lower class people. However, many women did know Latin. And everyday people recited prayers in Latin. These are the three Latin prayers even illiterate people could recite: the *Paternoster* ('Our Father'), *Ave* ('Hail Mary') and *Credo* ('I believe' or Nicene Creed which sets out the major beliefs and tenets of the Christian faith). Joan of Arc tells how her mother taught her the 'Our Father', 'Hail Mary', and 'I believe'.

Virago: A man-like or heroic woman; *vir* means *male* in Latin.

Virgin Martyr: Maiden who fearlessly stands up to authority and dies for her faith, retaining her purity and defying male authority.

Virgin Mary: Mother of Jesus Christ. In Catholic belief, she is believed to be a virgin mother.

Visions: Mysterious and difficult to prove, visions are an integral element in many world religions. The visionary (the person experiencing the vision) has an experience that is beyond the normal and everyday world, generally accessing a divine and spiritual realm by seeing holy beings or hearing voices. While our scientific age may be dubious, it is important to remember that visions were accepted as possible in the medieval world. A visionary woman or mystic often needed to have male endorsement to avoid being accused of heresy or false visions. If sanctioned or approved by the Church, they lent power to the visionary (*see* Hildegard von Bingen *or* Birgitta of Sweden). If the Church was dubious, the visions could bring about the visionary's downfall (*see* Joan of Arc).

Wicca: Modern day pagan religion.

Note

1. Monica H. Green, 'Who/What is "Trotula"?' Latest update November 2, 2013. Accessed April 11, 2015. https://www.academia.edu/4558706/Monica_H._Green_WHO_WHAT_IS_TROTULA_2013_013.

⚜ibliography

Primary Works
(Modern editions of material originally written in the Middle Ages)

Anglo-Saxon Penitentials: A cultural database. http://www.anglo-saxon.net/penance/.

Atherton, Mark, trans. *Hildegard von Bingen: Selected Writings.* London: Penguin Books, 2001.

Baird, Joseph L. ed., *The Personal Correspondence of Hildegard of Bingen.* Oxford: Oxford University Press, 2006.

Baird, Joseph L. and Radd K. Ehrman. *The Letters of Hildegard of Bingen.* Volume 1. NY: Oxford University Press, 1994.

Barratt, Alexandra, ed. *The Knowing of Woman's Kind in Childing: A Middle English Version of Material Derived from the Trotula and Other Sources.* Turnhout, Belgium: Brepols, 2001.

Birgitta of Sweden. *Saint Bride and Her Book: Birgitta of Sweden's Revelations.* Trans. Julia Bolton Holloway. Cambridge MA: D. S. Brewer, 2000.

Blamires, Alcuin, ed. *Woman Defamed and Woman Defended: An Anthology of Medieval Texts.* Oxford: Clarendon Press, 1992.

Bliss, W. H., ed. *Papal Petitions to the Pope 1342–1419.* Vol. I. London: Eyre and Spottiswoode, 1896.

Blois, Peter of. *Letter 154 to Queen Eleanor, 1173.* http://www.fordham.edu/halsall/source/eleanor.asp.

Boccaccio, Giovanni. *Famous Women.* Ed. and trans. Virginia Brown. Cambridge, MA: The I Tatti Renaissance Library/Harvard University Press, 2001.

Bogin, Meg, ed. and trans. *The Women Troubadours.* NY: W. W. Norton, 1980.

Bradley, S. A. J., trans. and ed. *Anglo-Saxon Poetry.* London: Dent, 1982.

Bradstreet, Anne. *Prologue.* http://www.poetryfoundation.org/poem/172961.

Broughton, Bradford B, ed. and trans. *"Richard the Lion-Hearted" and Other Medieval English Romances.* NY: E. P. Dutton, 1966.

Campbell, Alistair, ed. and trans. *Encomium Emmae Reginae.* Cambridge: Cambridge University Press, 1949/1998.

Capellanus, Andreas. *The Art of Courtly Love.* http://www.fordham.edu/halsall/source/capellanus.asp.

Cartagena, Teresa de. *The Writings of Teresa de Cartagena: Translated with Introduction, Notes, and Interpretive Essay.* Trans. Dayle Seidenspinner-Núñez. Cambridge MA: D. S. Brewer, 1998.

Chaucer, Geoffrey. *The Riverside Chaucer.* Larry D. Benson, ed. 3rd edition. Boston MA: Houghton Mifflin, 1987.

Christine Carpenter. *Brochure from St James' Church, Shere, England.*

Christine de Pizan. *The Book of the City of Ladies.* Trans. Earl Jeffrey Richards. NY: Persea Books, 1982.

Christine de Pizan. *Ditié de Jehanne D'Arc.* Eds. Angus J. Kennedy and Kenneth Varty. Medium Ævum Monographs New Series IX. 1977. Accessed May 20, 2013. http://faculty.smu.edu/bwheeler/Joan_of_Arc/OLR/crditie.pdf

Clemence of Barking. *The Life of St Catherine.* In Jocelyn Wogan-Browne and Glyn S. Burgess, trans. *Virgin Lives and Holy Deaths: Two Exemplary Biographies for Anglo-Norman Women.* London: Everyman/Dent, 1996.

Crawford, Anne, ed. *Letters of the Queens of England, 1100–1547.* Stroud: Sutton, 1997.

Donovan, Leslie A. *Women Saints' Lives in Old English Prose.* Woodbridge: Boydell and Brewer, 1999.

Garmonsway, G. N., trans. and ed. *The Anglo-Saxon Chronicle.* London: Dent, 1990.

Green, Monica H. *The Trotula: An English Translation of the Medieval Compendium of Women's Medicine.* Philadelphia PA: University of Pennsylvania Press, 2001.

Heaney, Seamus, trans. *Beowulf: A New Verse Translation.* NY: W. W. Norton, 2000.

Heine, Heinrich. http://www.egs.edu/library/heinrich-heine/biography/.

Julian of Norwich. *Revelations of Divine Love (Short Text and Long Text).* Trans. Elizabeth Spearing. London: Penguin Books, 1998.

Kehew, Robert. *Lark in the Morning: The Verses of the Troubadours. A Bilingual Edition.* Chicago: University of Chicago Press, 2005.

Kempe, Margery. *The Book of Margery Kempe.* Ed. and trans. Lynn Staley. NY: W. W. Norton, 2001.

Komnene, Anna. *The Alexiad.* Trans. E. R. A. Sewter; Rev. Peter Frankopan. London: Penguin Books, 2009.

Kunz, Keneva, trans. *The Saga of the People of Laxardal and Bolli Bollason's Tale.* Ed. Bergljót S. Kristjánsdóttir. London: Penguin Books, 2008.

Kunz, Keneva, trans. *The Vinland Sagas.* London: Penguin, 2008.

Larrington, Carolyne. *Women and Writing in Medieval Europe: A Sourcebook.* London: Routledge, 1995.

Margaret of Beverley. http://www.umilta.net/jerusalem.html.

Marie de France. *The Lais of Marie de France.* Trans. Glyn S. Burgess and Keith Busby. Harmondsworth: Penguin, 1999.

Paden, William D. and Frances Freeman Paden. *Troubadour Poems From the South of France.* Woodbridge: Boydell and Brewer, 2007.

Pálsson, Hermann and Paul Edwards, trans. *Eyrbyggja Saga.* London: Penguin Books, 1989.

Petroff, Elizabeth Alvilda. *Medieval Women's Visionary Literature.* NY: Oxford University Press, 1986.

Radice, Betty, trans. Revised edn. M. T. Clancy. *The Letters of Abelard and Heloise.* London: Penguin Books, 2003.

Roche-Mahdi, Sarah, trans. *Silence: A Thirteenth-Century French Romance.* East Lansing, MI: Michigan State University Press, 2007.

Ross, James Bruce and Mary Martin McLaughlin, eds. *The Portable Medieval Reader.* Harmondsworth: Penguin, 1977.

Rowland, Beryl, ed. and trans. *Medieval Woman's Guide to Health: The First English Gynecological Handbook.* Kent, OH: Kent State University Press, 1981.

Saint Jerome. *Letter XXII. To Eustochium.* http://www.ccel.org/ccel/schaff/npnf206.v.XXII.html.

Shaw, George Bernard. *Saint Joan: A Chronicle Play In Six Scenes And An Epilogue* (1924). http://gutenberg.net.au/ebooks02/0200811h.html.

Sherley-Price, Leo, trans. *Bede: Ecclesiastical History of the English People.* Revised R. E. Latham. 'Introduction'. D. H. Farmer. London: Penguin Books, 1990.

Silvas, Anna. *Jutta and Hildegard: The Biographical Sources.* University Park, PA: Pennsylvania State University Press, 1998.

Straubhaar, Sandra Ballif, trans. and ed. *Old Norse Women's Poetry: The Voice of Female Skalds.* Cambridge MA: D. S. Brewer, 2011.

Talbot, C. H., trans. *The Life of Christina of Markyate: A Twelfth-Century Holy Woman.* Samuel Fanous and Henrietta Leyser, eds. Oxford: Oxford University Press, 2008.

Trask, Willard, trans. *Joan of Arc in Her Own Words.* NY: Turtle Point Press, 1996.

Twelfth Ecumenical Council: Lateran IV 1215. http://www.fordham.edu/halsall/basis/lateran4.asp.

Virgoe, Roger, ed. *Private Life in the Fifteenth Century: Illustrated Letters of the Paston Family*, NY: Weidenfeld and Nicolson, 1989.

Watt, Diane, trans. *The Paston Women: Selected Letters*. Cambridge MA: D. S. Brewer, 2004.

Wilkinson, John. *Egeria's Travels to the Holy Land*. Jerusalem: Ariel, 1981.

Wilson, Katharina, trans. *The Plays of Hrotsvit of Gandersheim*. NY: Garland Publishers, 1989.

Wolfram von Eschenbach. *Parzival*. A. T. Hutto, trans. Harmondsworth: Penguin, 1982.

Secondary Works
(Writings about the Middle Ages)

Alaimo, Stacy and Susan Hekman, eds. *Material Feminisms*. Bloomington IN: Indiana University Press, 2008.

Allen, S. J. and Emilie Amt, eds. *The Crusades: A Reader*. Toronto: University of Toronto Press, 2010.

Anzaldúa, Gloria. *Borderlands/La Frontera*. Excerpted in Gilbert and Gubar, 2007, 247–258.

Armstrong, Dorsey Ann W. Astell, and Howell Chickering, eds. *Magistra Doctissima: Essays in Honor of Bonnie Wheeler*. Kalamazoo, MI: Medieval Institute Publications, 2013.

Ashley, Kathleen. 'Cultures of Devotion'. In Bennett and Karras, 2013, 511–526.

Astell, Mary. 'A Serious Proposal to the Ladies'. Excerpted in Gilbert and Gubar, 2007, 28–31.

Atwood, Margaret. 'On Being a "Woman Writer": Paradoxes and Dilemmas'. Excerpted in Gilbert and Gubar, 2007, 219–222.

Baker, Derek, ed. *Medieval Women*. Oxford: Basil Blackford, 1978.

Barron, M. Caroline, 'The Education and Training of Girls in Fifteenth-century London'. In Dunn, 1996: 139–153, 205–224.

Baumgarten, Elisheva. *Mothers and Children: Jewish Family Life in Medieval Europe*. Princeton: Princeton University Press, 2004.

Baumgarten, Elisheva. '"A Separate People"? Some Directions for Comparative Research on Medieval Women'. *Journal of Medieval History* 34 (2008), 212–228.

Bell, Rudolph M. *Holy Anorexia*. Chicago: University of Chicago Press, 1985.

Bennett, Judith M. and Ruth Mazo Karras, eds. *The Oxford Handbook of*

Women and Gender in Medieval Europe. Oxford: Oxford University Press, 2013.

Bennett, Judith M., Elizabeth A. Clark, Jean F. O'Barr, B. Anne Vilen, and Sarah Westphal-Wihl, eds. *Sisters and Workers in the Middle Ages.* Chicago: University of Chicago Press, 1989.

Berman, Constance H. 'Gender at the Medieval Millennium'. In Bennett and Karras, 2013, 545–560.

Boland, Eavan. 'Letter to a Young Woman Poet'. Excerpted in Gilbert and Gubar, 2007, 278–287.

Bordo, Susan. *Unbearable Weight: Feminism, Western Culture, and the Body.* Excerpted in Gilbert and Gubar, 2007, 744–756.

Brown, Elizabeth A. R. 'Eleanor of Aquitaine Reconsidered: The Woman and her Seasons'. In Wheeler and Parsons, 2002, 1–54.

Bull, Marcus. *Thinking Medieval: An Introduction to the Study of the Middle Ages.* Basingstoke: Palgrave Macmillan, 2005.

Bullough, Vern L. and James Brundage. *Sexual Practices and the Medieval Church.* Buffalo, NY: Prometheus Books, 1982.

Butler, Judith. 'Imitation and Gender Insubordination'. Excerpted in Gilbert and Gubar, 2007, 708–722.

Bynum, Caroline Walker. *Holy Feast and Holy Fast: The Religious Significance of Food to Medieval Woman.* Berkeley: University of California Press, 1987.

Bynum, Caroline Walker. *Jesus as Mother: Studies in the Spirituality of the High Middle Ages.* Berkeley CA: University of California Press, 1982.

Chodorow, Nancy. 'Family Structure and Feminine Personality'. Excerpted in Gilbert and Gubar, 2007, 367–388.

Cooper, Anna Julia. 'The Higher Education of Women'. Excerpted in Gilbert and Gubar, 2007, 112–118.

Damico, Helen. 'Beowulf's Foreign Queen and the Politics of Eleventh-Century England'. In Virginia Blanton and Helene Scheck, eds. *Intertexts: Studies in Anglo-Saxon Culture Presented to Paul E. Szarmach.* Tempe, AZ: ACMRS/Brepols, 2008, 209–240.

De Beauvoir, Simone. *The Second Sex.* Excerpted in Gilbert and Gubar, 2007, 300–323.

DeVries, Kelly R. '"Because It Was Paris": Joan of Arc's Attack on Paris Reconsidered'. In Armstrong, Astell, and Chickering, 2013, 123–131.

Drell, Joanna H. 'Aristocratic Economies: Women and Family'. In Bennett and Karras, 2013, 327–342.

Dronke, Peter. *Women Writers of the Middle Ages*. Cambridge: Cambridge University Press, 1984.

DuCille, Ann. 'Blue Notes on Black Sexuality: Sex and the Texts of the Twenties and Thirties'. Excerpted in Gilbert and Gubar, 2007, 957–962.

Dunn, Diana E. S., ed. *Courts, Counties and the Capital in the Later Middle Ages*. Stroud: Sutton, 1996.

Earenfight, Theresa. *Queenship in Medieval Europe*. NY: Palgrave Macmillan, 2013.

Ebenesersdóttir, Sigríður Sunna, Ásgeir Sigurðsson, Federico Sánchez-Quinto, Carles Lalueza-Fox, Kári Stefánsson, and Agnar Helgason. 'A New Subclade of mtDNA Haplogroup C1 Found in Icelanders: Evidence of Pre-Columbian Contact?' *American Journal of Physical Anthropology* 144 (2011), 92–99.

Edgeworth, Maria. *Letters to Literary Ladies*. Excerpted in Gilbert and Gubar, 2007, 48–54.

Farmer, David Hugh. *The Oxford Dictionary of Saints*. 3rd edition. Oxford: Oxford University Press, 1992.

Ferrante, Joan M. 'Women's Role in Latin Letters from the Fourth to the Early Twelfth Century'. In McCash, 1996, 71–104.

Field, Sean L. *The Beguine, the Angel, and the Inquisitor: The Trials of Marguerite Porete and Guiard of Cressonessart*. Notre Dame: University of Notre Dame Press, 2012.

Fraioli, Deborah. 'Joan of Arc'. In Schaus, 2006, 430–433.

Gates, Henry Louis, Jr. *The Signifying Monkey: A Theory of African-American Literary Criticism*. Oxford: Oxford University Press, 1988.

Gibbons, Rachel. 'The Piety of Isabeau of Bavaria, Queen of France, 1385–1422'. In Dunn, 1996, 205–224.

Gies, Frances and Joseph. *Women in the Middle Ages: The Lives of Real Women in a Vibrant Age of Transition*. NY: HarperPerennial, 1978.

Gilbert, Dorothy. 'Juliana Berners: From the Book of St. Albans'. In *The Norton Anthology of Women's Literature: The Traditions in English*. 2nd Edition. Eds. Sandra M. Gilbert and Susan Gubar. New York: Norton, 1996, 25–27.

Gilbert, Sandra M. and Susan Gubar, eds. *Feminist Literary Theory and Criticism: A Norton Reader*. New York: W. W. Norton and Company, 2007.

Gilbert, Sandra M. and Susan Gubar. *The Madwoman in the Attic: The Woman Writer and the Nineteenth-Century Literary Imagination*. Excerpted in Gilbert and Gubar, 2007, 448–459.

Gilligan, Carol. *In a Different Voice: Psychological Theory and Women's Development.* Excerpted in Gilbert and Gubar, 2007, 567–571.

González, Cristina. 'Qasmūna Bint Ismā'īl'. In Schaus, 2006, 681.

Gouma-Peterson, Thalia, ed. *Anna Komnene and Her Times.* NY: Garland Publishing, 2000.

Green, Monica H. 'Conversing with the Minority: Relations among Christian, Jewish, and Muslim Women in the High Middle Ages'. *Journal of Medieval History* 34 (2008), 105–118.

Green, Monica H. 'Getting to the Source: The Case of Jacoba Felicie and the Impact of the *Portable Medieval Reader* on the Canon of Medieval Women's History'. *Medieval Feminist Forum* 42.1 (2006), 49–62.

Green, Monica H. *Making Women's Medicine Masculine: The Rise of Male Authority in Pre-Modern Gynaecology.* Oxford: Oxford University Press, 2008.

Green, Monica H., ed. and trans. *The Trotula: An English Translation of the Medieval Compendium of Women's Medicine.* Philadelphia PA, University of Pennsylvania Press, 2001.

Green, Monica H. 'Who/What is "Trotula"?' Latest update November 2, 2013. Accessed April 11, 2015. https://www.academia.edu/4558706/Monica_H._Green_WHO_WHAT_IS_TROTULA_2013_013.

Green, Monica H. 'Women's Medical Practice and Health Care in Medieval Europe'. *Signs* 14.2 (1989), 434–473.

Green, Monica H. and Daniel Lord Smail. 'The Trial of Floreta d'Ays (1403): Jews, Christians, and obstetrics in later medieval Marseille'. *Journal of Medieval History* 34 (2008), 184–211.

Haraway, Donna. 'A Manifesto for Cyborgs'. Excerpted in Gilbert and Gubar, 2007, 584–601.

Herlihy, David. *Opera Muliebria: Women and Work in Medieval Europe.* NY: McGraw-Hill, 1990.

Hill, Barbara. 'Actions Speak Louder Than Words: Anna Komnene's Attempted Usurpation'. In Gouma-Peterson, 2000, 45–62.

Hopenwasser, Nanda and Signe Wegener. 'Vox Matris: The Influence of St Birgitta's *Revelations* on *The Book of Margery Kempe*: St Birgitta and Margery Kempe as Wives and Mothers'. In Stevenson and Ho, 2000, 61–85.

Howell, Martha C. 'Gender in the Transition to Merchant Capitalism'. In Bennett and Karras, 2013: 561–576.

Hoyle, Victoria. 'The Bonds that Bind: Money Lending Between Anglo-

Jewish and Christian Women in the Plea Rolls of the Exchequer of the Jews, 1218–1280'. *Journal of Medieval History* 34 (2008), 119–129.

Huneycutt, Lois L. 'Alianora Regina Anglorum: Eleanor of Aquitaine and Her Anglo-Norman Predecessors as Queens of England'. In Wheeler and Parsons, 2002, 115–132.

Huneycutt, Lois L. 'Eleanor of Aquitaine'. In Schaus, 2006, 243–244.

Huneycutt, Lois L. '"Proclaiming her dignity abroad": The Literary and Artistic Network of Matilda of Scotland, Queen of England 1100–1118'. In McCash, 1996, 155–174.

Jesch, Judith. *Women in the Viking Age*. Woodbridge: Boydell Press, 1991.

Karras, Ruth Mazo. *Unmarriages: Women, Men and Sexual Unions in the Middle Ages*. Philadelphia PA: University of Philadelphia Press, 2012.

Kelly-Gadol, Joan. 'The Social Relation of the Sexes: Methodological Implications of Women's History'. Excerpted in Gilbert and Gubar, 2007, 430–436.

Kilfoyle, Sarah. Pers. comm.

Kirvan, John, ed. *Teresa of Avila. Let Nothing Disturb You: A Journey to the Center of the Soul with Teresa of Avila*. Notre Dame, IN: Ave Maria Press, 1996.

Labarge, Margaret Wade. *A Small Sound of the Trumpet: Women in Medieval Life*. Boston MA: Beacon Press, 1986.

Lees, Clare, ed. *Medieval Masculinities: Regarding Men in the Middle Ages*. Minneapolis MN: University of Minnesota Press, 1994.

Makowski, Elizabeth M. *Canon Law and Cloistered Women: Periculoso and its commentators, 1298–1545*. Washington, DC: Catholic University of America Press, 1999.

Makowski, Elizabeth M. 'When is a Beguine not a Beguine? Names, Norms, and Nuance in Canonical Literature'. In L. Böhringer, J. Kolpacoff Deane, and H. van Engen, eds. *Labels and Libels: Naming Beguines in Northern Medieval Europe*. Turnhout, Belgium: Brepols, 2014, 85–100.

Martineau, Harriet. 'Autobiography'. Excerpted in Gilbert and Gubar, 2007, 106–9.

McCash, June Hall, ed. *The Cultural Patronage of Medieval Women*. Athens, GA: University of Georgia Press, 1996.

McCracken, Peggy. 'Scandalizing Desire: Eleanor of Aquitaine and the Chroniclers'. In Wheeler and Parsons, 1996, 247–263.

McNamara, Jo Ann. 'The *Herrenfrage*: The Restructuring of the Gender System 1050–1150'. In Lees, 1994, 3–29.

Miles, Laura Saetveit. 'The Origins and Development of the Virgin Mary's Book at the Annunciation'. *Speculum* 89.3 (2014), 632–669.

Millay, S. Lea. 'The Voice of the Court Woman Poet'. In Stevenson and Ho, 2000, 91–117.

Miller, Tanya Stabler. *The Beguines of Medieval Paris: Gender, Patronage, and Spiritual Authority.* Philadelphia PA: University of Pennsylvania Press, 2014.

Millett, Kate. *Sexual Politics*. Excerpted in Gilbert and Gubar, 2007, 336–350.

Moi, Toril. *What is a Woman? And Other Essays.* Oxford: Oxford University Press, 1999

Morrison, Susan Signe. *Women Pilgrims in Late Medieval England: Private Piety as Public Performance.* London: Routledge, 2000.

Morrison, Toni. 'Unspeakable Things Unspoken: The Afro-American Presence in American Literature'. Excerpted in Gilbert and Gubar, 2007, 266–278.

Newman, Barbara. *From Virile Woman to WomanChrist: Studies in Medieval Religion and Literature.* Philadelphia PA: University of Pennsylvania Press, 1995.

Nichols, James Mansfield. 'The Arabic Verses of Qasmūna Bint Ismā'īl ibn Bagdālah'. *International Journal of Middle East Studies* 13 (1981), 155–158.

Nicholson, Helen. *The Crusades.* Westport, CT: Greenwood Press, 2004.

Nicholson, Helen. 'Women on the Third Crusade'. *Journal of Medieval History* 23.4 (1997), 335–349.

Nin, Anaïs. *The Diary.* Excerpted in Gilbert and Gubar, 2007, 148–149.

Obrist, Barbara. 'The Swedish Visionary: Saint Bridget'. In Wilson 1984, 227–251.

Orme, Nicholas. *Fleas, Flies, and Friars: Children's Poetry from the Middle Ages.* Ithaca, NY: Cornell University Press, 2011.

Ortner, Sherry B. 'Is Female to Male as Nature is to Culture?' Excerpted in Gilbert and Gubar, 2007, 350–367.

Pappano, Margaret Aziza. 'Marie de France, Aliénor d'Aquitaine, and the Alien Queen'. In Wheeler and Parsons, 2002, 337–367.

Pinzino, Jane Marie. 'Speaking of Angels: A Fifteenth-Century Bishop in Defense of Joan of Arc's Mystical Voices'. In Wheeler and Wood, 1996, 161–176.

Rich, Adrienne. 'When We Dead Awaken: Writing as Re-Vision'. Excerpted in Gilbert and Gubar, 2007, 188–200.

Russ, Joanna. 'What Can a Heroine Do? or Why Women Can't Write'. Excerpted in Gilbert and Gubar, 2007, 200–211.

Schaus, Margaret, ed. *Women and Gender in Medieval Europe: An Encyclopedia.* NY: Routledge, 2006.

Schibanoff, Susan. 'True Lies: Transvestism and Idolatry in the Trial of Joan of Arc'. In Wheeler and Wood 1996, 31–60.

Segol, Marla. 'Representing the Body in Poems by Medieval Muslim Women'. *Medieval Feminist Forum* 45 (2009), 147–169.

Shank, Michael H. 'A Female University Student in Late Medieval Kraków'. In Bennett, Clark, O'Barr, and Westphal-Wihl, 1989, 190–197.

Stevenson, Barbara and Cynthia Ho, eds. *Crossing the Bridge: Comparative Essays on Medieval European and Heian Japanese Women Writers*. NY: Palgrave Macmillan, 2000.

Sweet, Victoria. 'Hildegard of Bingen and the Greening of Medieval Medicine'. *Bulletin of the History of Medicine* 73.3 (1999), 381–403.

Tolhurst, Fiona. 'What Ever Happened to Eleanor? Reflections of Eleanor of Aquitaine in Wace's *Roman de Brut* and Lawman's *Brut*'. In Wheeler and Parsons, 2002, 319–336.

Underhill, Frances. 'Elizabeth de Burgh: Connoisseur and Patron'. In McCash, 1996, 266–287.

Walker, Alice. 'In Search of Our Mothers' Gardens'. Excerpted in Gilbert and Gubar, 2007, 212–219.

Weston, L. M. C. 'Women's Medicine, Women's Magic: The Old English Metrical Charms'. *Modern Philology* 92 (1995), 279–293.

Wheeler, Bonnie and John C. Parsons, eds. *Eleanor of Aquitaine: Lord and Lady*. NY: Palgrave Macmillan, 2002.

Wheeler, Bonnie and Charles T. Wood, eds. *Fresh Verdicts on Joan of Arc*. NY: Garland Publishers, 1996.

Wilson, Alan J. *St Margaret Queen of Scotland*. Edinburgh: John Donald Publishers, 1993.

Wilson, Katharina M., ed. *Medieval Women Writers*. Athens, GA: University of Georgia Press, 1984.

Wittig, Monique. 'One Is Not Born a Woman'. Excerpted in Gilbert and Gubar, 2007, 544–551.

Wollstonecraft, Mary. *A Vindication of the Rights of Woman*. Excerpted in Gilbert and Gubar, 2007, 43–47.

Woolf, Virginia. *A Room of One's Own*. Boston, MA: Harvest Book/Houghton Mifflin Harcourt, 1989.

Woolf, Virginia. *A Room of One's Own*. Excerpted in Gilbert and Gubar, 2007, 128–137.

Internet references

- Internet Medieval Sourcebook at Fordham University is a highly recommended scholarly source, including actual texts from the Middle Ages, as well as historical information. http://www.fordham.edu/Halsall/sbook.asp. Here are some examples:
- A basic bibliography of writings by and about women in the Middle Ages. http://www.fordham.edu/halsall/med/womenbib.asp.
- The actual testimony of the heretic Na Prous Boneta. http://www.fordham.edu/halsall/source/naprous.asp
- A letter to Eleanor of Aquitaine. http://www.fordham.edu/halsall/source/eleanor.asp.
- The Canons of the Fourth Lateran Council, 1215. http://www.fordham.edu/halsall/basis/lateran4.asp
- Information about films set in the Middle Ages. http://www.fordham.edu/Halsall/medfilms.asp

- Flip through many digitized manuscripts online. A good place to start includes university libraries and museums, such as:
    British Library: http://www.bl.uk/manuscripts/Default.aspx.
    Oxford University: http://image.ox.ac.uk/
    Bodleian Library: http://bodley30.bodley.ox.ac.uk:8180/luna/servlet/ODLodl~1~1
    You can browse at Parker Library: http://parkerweb.stanford.edu/parker/actions/page.do?forward=home
    Through this portal you can search the Getty Museum's amazing collection and turn pages of manuscripts: http://manuscripts.cmrs.ucla.edu/Manuscripts_list.php.
    Here is the St. Albans Psalter belonging to Christina of Markyate. http://www.abdn.ac.uk/stalbanspsalter/english/index.shtml

Selected Website Bibliography

A Medieval Woman's Companion. The website and blog accompanying this book. http://amedievalwomanscompanion.com/.

Epistolæ: Medieval Women's Letters. Letters to and from medieval women. http://epistolae.ccnmtl.columbia.edu/

Feminae: Medieval Women and Gender Index. This wonderful site allows you to search for non-book sources (reviews, journal articles, etc.) according to topic or author. http://inpress.lib.uiowa.edu/feminae/Default.aspx.

Labyrinth. https://blogs.commons.georgetown.edu/labyrinth/.

Medieval Feminist Forum. This site allows access to articles that have appeared in the Journal of the Study for Medieval Feminist Scholarship. http://ir.uiowa.edu/mff/.

Home page for the Society for Medieval Feminist Scholarship. http://smfsweb.org/.

Comprehensive Bibliography of Medieval Queens and Queenship. http://theresaearenfight.com/.

Anglo-Saxon Penitentials. http://www.anglo-saxon.net/penance/.

A good general site is http://www.medievalists.net/.

Educational and fun films about the Middle Ages are at YouTube.

The Evelyn Thomas Database of Medieval English Embroidery. http://ica.princeton.edu/opus-anglicanum/index.php

Index of Medieval Medical Images. http://digital.library.ucla.edu/immi/.

Find out about Brigittine nuns. http://birgittaskloster.se/en/.

For more about Hildegard: http://www.hildegard.org/.

International Joan of Arc Society. http://faculty.smu.edu/bwheeler/ijas/.

You can friend the International Marie de France Society on Facebook.

You can find out lots about Margery Kempe, including her pilgrimage routes, here: http://college.holycross.edu/projects/kempe/.

Resource for the study of women's religious communities from 400 to 1600 CE. http://www.monasticmatrix.org/.

A comprehensive discography for Hildegard: http://www.medieval.org/emfaq/composers/hildegard.html. More recordings become available all the time. Check YouTube for performances and music.

Discography for early women musicians. http://earlywomenmasters.net/cds/index.html.